The Art & Science
of Interpreting Market
Research Evidence

The Art & Science of Interpreting Market Research Evidence

D.V.L. Smith and J.H. Fletcher

John Wiley & Sons, Ltd

This publication is designed to provide accurate and authoritative information in regard to the
subject matter covered. It is sold on the understanding that the Publisher is not engaged in rendering
professional services. If professional advice or other expert assistance is required, the services of a
competent professional should be sought.

Other Wiley Editorial Offices

John Wiley & Sons Inc., 111 River Street, Hoboken, NJ 07030, USA

Jossey-Bass, 989 Market Street, San Francisco, CA 94103-1741, USA

Wiley-VCH Verlag GmbH, Boschstr. 12, D-69469 Weinheim, Germany

John Wiley & Sons Australia Ltd, 33 Park Road, Milton, Queensland 4064, Australia

John Wiley & Sons (Asia) Pte Ltd, 2 Clementi Loop #02-01, Jin Xing Distripark, Singapore 129809

John Wiley & Sons Canada Ltd, 22 Worcester Road, Etobicoke, Ontario, Canada M9W 1L1

Wiley also publishes its books in a variety of electronic formats. Some content that appears
in print may not be available in electronic books.

Library of Congress Cataloging-in-Publication Data

Smith, D. V. L. (David Van Lloyd)
    The art & science of interpreting market research evidence / DVL Smith and JH Fletcher.
        p. cm.
    Includes bibliographical references and index.
    ISBN 0-470-84424-8 (alk. paper)
     1. Marketing research. 2. Qualitative research. 3. Statistics. I. Title: Art and science of
interpreting market research evidence. II. Fletcher, J. H. III. Title.

    HF5415.2.S558 2004
    658.8′3--dc22

                                           2003067249

British Library Cataloguing in Publication Data

A catalogue record for this book is available from the British Library

ISBN 0-470-84424-8

Typeset in 10/12pt Garamond by Laserwords Private Limited, Chennai, India
Printed and bound in Great Britain by Antony Rowe Ltd, Chippenham, Wiltshire
This book is printed on acid-free paper responsibly manufactured from sustainable forestry
in which at least two trees are planted for each one used for paper production.

Contents

Foreword

It is a great pleasure to write a foreword to this book. I believe that the contents have the potential to lead a major step forward in the way in which managers in organizations use and apply evidence and fact-based knowledge to make decisions.

It is stunning that across wholly diverse industrial sectors – for example, look at market leader characteristics all the way from high technology at Dell Computers to marketing grocery and household products at Tesco stores – we are finally realizing that those who *know* more outperform the rest. Superiority in learning and sustaining that advantage through the constant search for new insights and better understanding of the drivers of customer value in the marketplace has proved to be one of the most critical corporate competencies. Yet, it is a source of competitive advantage we have underestimated so much that we have not even found a name for it.

We do know, however, that enhancing capabilities in learning faster and better than the competition to build sustained competitive advantage through superior knowledge requires far more than acquiring techniques and technology for data collection and analysis. The volume of data that the technology can produce, and the precise measurement that data collection and analysis tools can provide are important resources. However, at best they are part of the total array of clues and insights that build superior understanding of the marketplace. To believe that they are the only ways to generate and test new ways of doing things is as fatuous as pursuing the tired debate about the relative merits of quantitative and qualitative research designs. Such introspective obsessions lead us to miss the real point.

That point is the prime goal of: building understanding and insight; sensing and anticipating change; and value innovation for superior performance. Important progress towards meeting this elusive goal can be made by emphasizing the interpretation of the whole array of evidence available, regardless of type, not simply reporting data, and working with decision-makers to develop effective and sustained learning processes. The approach in this book provides a valuable framework for implementing these priorities.

There can never have been a time when the need for evidence-based knowledge as the basis for management decision-making was greater. It is timely for market research professionals to consider their future in this new scenario and the ways in which they can best add value to decision-making processes.

Professor Nigel F. Piercy

Warwick Business School
The University of Warwick

Preface

The last few years have seen the arrival of 'new' market research. Gone are the days when market research posed as a quasi-academic activity that only flirted with the business decision-making process. Today, market researchers are much more focused on improving the quality of business decision-making.

This arrival of new market research has presented the industry with an exciting challenge. This is, how best to communicate to its client base (and also to new graduates entering the industry) exactly how new market research operates. This book addresses this issue.

- It provides a comprehensive review of the frameworks that today's new market researchers use to draw together different types of, often imperfect, qualitative and quantitative data, and explains how they apply this evidence to successful information-based decision-making.

This introduction to how new market researchers now interpret data will be of interest to those fascinated as to why so many of the existing textbooks on market research bear little resemblance to how market research really operates in practice. Specifically, our account will be of particular benefit to:

- University graduates who have recently taken up posts as market research practitioners, either on the client or agency side.
- Users of market research data who need an overview of how modern market research now operates.
- Lecturers on, and students of, market research, who may wish to incorporate our practical insights into their courses.
- Individuals working in central and local government involved in evidence-based decision-making.

In sum, the book is aimed at individuals who want a simple synthesis of the way in which market research analysts are now going beyond their traditional methodological approaches, and are today operating with a more powerful set of data analysis techniques in making sense of customer evidence.

Supporting training module

To help educationalists and trainers who wish to run a module on the data analysis principles raised in this book, we have prepared a ten-unit lecture course that mirrors the content of this book. This is available in the form of a series of Microsoft PowerPoint charts. For details on how to obtain these charts visit Wiley's website: www.wileyeurope.com/go/smith. This supporting training module will:

- Help trainers in market research agencies convert the ideas in this book into a training course that could be used to introduce their new graduate trainees to the principles of 'new' market research.
- Assist lecturers on market research courses in colleges and universities to supplement their 'orthodox' teaching on market research with an up-to-date account of how many market research practitioners now operate.

In addition – working in conjunction with the supplementary points we make in the 'Notes' section – the training module will help bring alive, with concrete worked examples, many of the general principles outlined in this book.

Acknowledgements

Deciding on the final shape of a book that provides a fresh look at the data analysis craft necessitated a considerable amount of drafting. We continually had to check whether our synthesis of existing theory and commercial practice was pitched at an appropriate level for our audience: newcomers to market research. This placed considerable pressure on Christine Rooke, who typed this book, and we would like to start this acknowledgement by thanking her for her professionalism and patience in bringing this book together.

We would also like to thank Anne Smith for editing the various drafts, and for helping to make the book, what we believe, is now an accessible and user-friendly introduction to data analysis for those coming from either an arts or science background. Thanks also to Paul Costantoura for his insights on how best to engage the reader.

In preparing the book, it was helpful for the authors to be Directors at Citigate DVL Smith, part of Incepta Marketing Intelligence, the strategic market intelligence group. This meant that in writing this book we were able to draw on the expertise of various colleagues experienced in innovative data analysis. In particular, thanks are due to Andy Dexter for his ideas, and for supplying a number of specific quantitative examples.

Thanks are also due to Gavin Mulholland, who contributed some extremely useful illustrative practical examples, and to Ian Horritt for his helpful observations on various aspects of Internet surveys, and to John Connaughton for his various editorial contributions, designed to help make sure that we struck the appropriate balance between the art and science, and the theory and practice of commercial data analysis. Finally, a big thanks to Jo Smith, for helping us, throughout the whole process, to make difficult decisions about which of our data analysis ideas should go forward into print, and which should, for the time being, remain on the developmental drawing board. So in many ways, this book is a Citigate DVL Smith team initiative. Thanks to you all.

'New' market research

Summary

- Market research is moving away from its roots as a discipline that was detached from the business decision-making process, and is now more actively engaged with decision-facilitation.
- This shift has required new methodological thinking: an 'holistic' analysis approach that provides clients with a rounded view of what *all* their (qualitative and quantitative) marketing evidence is saying.
- The new approach also requires analytical frameworks that combine hard market research data with prior management knowledge and intuition.
- These new frameworks must be disciplined: intuitive thought can be powerful, but it can also be wrong. The new holistic approach to data analysis therefore needs to be based on the rigorous evaluation of prior management knowledge, as well as drawing on conventional data analysis methods.
- We introduce a ten stage guide to analysing market research data in an 'holistic' way. The ten steps are: analysing the right problem; understanding the big information picture; compensating for imperfect data; developing the analysis strategy and organizing the data; establishing the interpretation boundary; applying the knowledge filters (what we know about the survey process); reframing the data (to give us fresh insights); integrating the research evidence and telling the research story; decision-facilitation; and completing the feedback loop (evaluating the effectiveness of the research data in achieving a successful decision outcome).
- In sum, in this opening chapter we explain how the evidence available to market researchers is changing, as a prelude to outlining the critical thinking skills – the interpretation power – needed to master the new world of information.

Reducing uncertainty

The underlying principle behind market research is powerful, yet simple. Market research is about helping individuals make informed, evidence-based judgements and decisions. It is about asking intelligent questions of users, and potential users, of products and services about their opinions and experiences, listening carefully to what they say, and then interpreting the implications of this feedback. This interpretation is then used to help organizations reduce the uncertainty surrounding various decisions that need to be made.

The idea has been around for nearly a century. Thus, today, it is commonplace for businesses, and public sector organizations, to use customer feedback as one of the inputs into their marketing strategies and public policies. There is little sign of there being any downturn in the demand for market research. Who, after all, would speak against taking all the relevant soundings on any issue, interpreting these viewpoints, and taking this into account when making a decision? The issue is not about whether or not market research is useful, but a question of how research evidence should be interpreted.

Interpretation power

Information was once power. But, today, the power lies in interpreting what information *really* means. In the hands of a skilled analyst, survey data may unearth invaluable insights into what makes people 'tick'. But the same data, in the hands of a journeyman analyst, may lead to a creative idea being stifled at birth. The need, therefore, is to cultivate the talent, skill, and techniques required to make sense of customer data. It is this issue – the intelligent, holistic interpretation of market research data – that is at the heart of this book.

The drivers of new holistic market research

It is possible to identify several distinct developments that have shaped the growing demand for a more holistic approach to the analysis of market research data.

Clarifying contradictory market signals

The sheer amount of market and customer information available has increased phenomenally. There has also been a change in the type of information used to inform decisions. Increasingly, use is being made of data that are more imperfect, messy, grey, and less robust than many of the sources used in the past.

The challenge for market researchers is to develop the skills and techniques needed to weave a story from a combination of different, less than perfect, often confusing and contradictory, information sources. Researchers can no longer restrict themselves to working with single, reasonably robust, sources of customer opinion.

Providing grounded business acumen

There is also the expectation that market researchers will operate with a sound contextual awareness of the wider, strategic business picture. Market researchers are required to have a mature understanding of what the client's business is trying to achieve. This has been a driving force in encouraging market researchers to put their heads above their hitherto methodologically defined parapets.

Understanding the complete customer

Market researchers are now expected to better appreciate the 'complete' customer experience. As companies strive to build a complete picture of a customer's interactions with the organization, so too are researchers required to stretch their thinking to find ways of capturing and understanding a wider range of customer data. For example, to understand how a customer relates to a bank, it becomes important to capture that individual's experience across the various personal, business, current and savings accounts they may hold at the bank, and also at other financial institutions.

The quest for understanding and 'insight'

The word 'insight' has many different connotations. Yet whatever the exact interpretation placed on the now rather overworked 'insight' word, there is a clear message here from clients: they want more originality, innovation, clarity, and depth of thinking from their market research analysts.

Bridging the data-decision gap

Users of research data want the market research industry to be more committed and involved, than in the past, with the decision-making process, and with the initial implementation of decisions. Decision-makers, assailed with often baffling signals from massive amounts of information, need researchers to cut through this complexity. They want researchers to say what the data really means, rather than to sit back and adopt a more detached, data-centric position. The information professionals who can add this value will be at a massive premium in the future.

From detachment to engagement

In response to the above demands, we have seen the arrival of a new approach to data analysis that represents a significant change from the original conception of market research. Market research began as a discipline based on the model of psychology, sociology, anthropology, and other social sciences. Its start point was the classic notion of 'research': detached, objective, and keeping as close as possible to the agreed principles of social science-based inquiry. It was a model that worked hard to differentiate professional survey research, from canvassing and selling (under the guise of research). This tradition gave us an industry with a sound set of research practices and a well-established code of ethics.

Factoring intuition into the analysis process

This approach was right for its time and the 'detachment' model has much to commend it. However, users of market research are now looking for an approach that is better equipped to handle the 'messiness' of today's data, and one that 'engages' more with the end decision-maker. Classic, objective analysis of single-survey findings is only the start point. Today's researcher has to both make use of the best of traditional survey methods and *also* embrace more intuitive inputs into decision-making.

The arrival of 'new' market research

In describing how 'new' market research is different from the 'old' modus operandi, it is helpful to think of market research as operating on the following four fronts. First, how the quality of each piece of evidence will be assessed (robustness). Secondly, the extent to which the new incoming information will be assessed relative to relevant and related past evidence (context). Thirdly, the techniques used to evaluate the meaning and significance of each item of data (evaluation). And fourthly, the way in which the research findings are presented to the client (application).

It is possible to characterize old market research as being represented by the inner shaded area of Figure 1.1. This illustrates how old market research typically functioned on each of the above four fronts:

- *Robustness*: the emphasis, in the past, was on working with orthodox concepts, such as 'validity' (is the evidence measuring what we think we are measuring, and free from any systematic bias?), and 'reliability' (how likely is it that the data will hold good over time, and that we will be able to reproduce our results?).
- *Context*: in the past, most market researchers would get no further than checking their new incoming study against, maybe, one past related research report.
- *Evaluation*: this would inevitably focus on examining one data set and involve the application of (classic) statistical tests.
- *Application*: the study would conclude with a presentation of the research findings, possibly with some recommendations for action (but would not be *closely* related to the subsequent decision-making process).

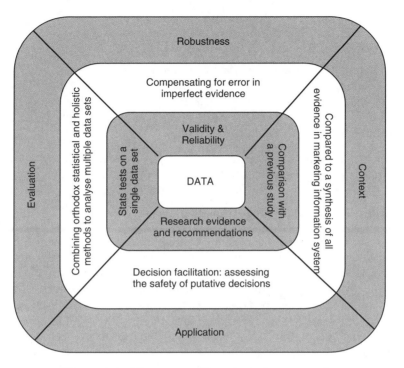

Figure 1.1 – The scope of 'new' market research.

New market research takes us into new territory. This is summarized by the activities shown in outer white panel in Figure 1.1:

- *Robustness*: the emphasis today is on 'compensating' for the imperfection in the varied data sources that market researchers now draw upon.
- *Context*: the availability of marketing information systems usually means that new market research evidence will be set in a much richer context than ever before.
- *Evaluation*: orthodox statistical analytical methods will be employed alongside frameworks aimed at factoring prior management knowledge (intuition) into the data analysis process, with this involving the analysis of multiple, not just single, data sets.
- *Application*: new market research goes beyond simply presenting research findings and making recommendations, with market researchers now much more closely involved with decision-facilitation.

The methodological challenges for new market research

There are three distinct methodological challenges in building the new holistic market research approach outlined above:

- The first focuses on finding actionable frameworks to help combine qualitative and quantitative evidence when tackling business problems.
- The second centres on how to develop frameworks to incorporate management intuition into the formal data analysis process.
- And the third involves synthesizing what we know about the overall market research 'craft' – what we know from experience does and does not work – into a form that can be made accessible to data analysts, so that this can enrich their interpretation of the data.

We briefly examine these three issues below, but we also return to these major themes throughout this book.

Integrating qualitative and quantitative data

Holistic researchers tend not to think of qualitative and quantitative research as separate disciplines. The emphasis is on finding ways to integrate the two forms of evidence. Holistic researchers recognize the power of the rigorous statistical analysis of quantitative data, but they also see merit, on occasion, in analysing quantitative data in a qualitative way. Similarly, the holistic researcher understands the benefits, where appropriate, of not only examining qualitative data in a thematic way, but also subjecting the evidence to a more quantitatively-orientated analysis.

Distinguishing the qualitative 'method' from the qualitative 'mode'

In interpreting the increasingly blurred methodological boundaries between qualitative and quantitative evidence, it is helpful to draw a distinction between the qualitative 'mode' and the qualitative 'method': that is, to explicitly delineate the idea of the qualitative *mode of analysis* from the qualitative *method of data collection*.

Most are quite comfortable with the – albeit blurred – distinction between qualitative and quantitative data collection. But what happens to that data is a different matter. We argue that the qualitative mode – an open and flexible way of *thinking* about data – should not be restricted only to the qualitative method. It should be extended to apply also to the quantitative method.

Certainly, the idea of defining 'qualitative' as a way of thinking that can be applied to *all* forms of data is consistent with dictionary definitions of the terms 'qualitative' and 'quantitative':

- *Qualitative*: involving, or relating to, distinctions based on qualities, constituents, or characteristics.
- *Quantitative*: involving, or relating to, considerations of quantities – amount or size.

In sum, the qualitative mode is a powerful concept, one that should not be restricted to the qualitative method. It can add insight to almost any piece of information. In fact, there is no reason why the qualitative mode of analysis cannot be expanded to encompass *all* forms of marketing evidence. In the matrix in Figure 1.2, we illustrate the way the qualitative mode of thinking can apply to either qualitative or quantitative data.

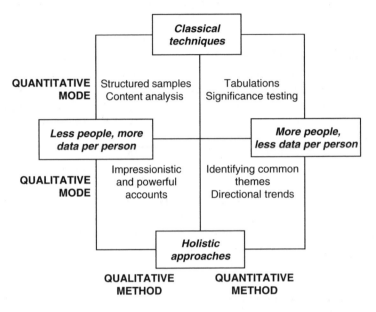

Figure 1.2 – Distinguishing the qualitative 'method' from the qualitative 'mode'.

Many will argue that, working across the qualitative/quantitative 'divide' is what they already do, and in some cases, this may be true. But the point is that the *qualitative mode* has only been sporadically articulated as a skill set in its own right, separate from the business of collecting data – the *qualitative method*. We believe that in promoting the holistic school of data analysis, the articulation of our concept of there being a qualitative mode, not just method, concentrates the mind and helps us to define what holistic data analysis is all about.

This observation challenges quantitative researchers to bring the same level of attacking interpretation to the numbers as qualitative specialists routinely deliver based on fewer, but deeper, observations. The challenge to qualitative research is to take what we define as the 'qualitative mode of thinking' out of its rather introspective methodological box.

Developing analytical frameworks to embrace prior management knowledge and intuition

In the past, it seemed that business problems were tackled via two, almost mutually exclusive, channels of thought. There would be the 'traditional' market researchers, with their scientific data, in one corner, and in the other, we would find entrepreneurial business leaders, such as Richard Branson and Anita Roddick, talking up the virtues of looking at business problems from an 'intuitive', rather than just data-led, approach. Now, it is increasingly recognized that ignoring management intuition on the grounds that it does not meet the formal criteria of 'scientific enquiry' is ill-advised.

Intuition as an 'organized' process

A key point to acknowledge is that, if we arrive at a solution using our intuition, it does not mean that we did not adhere to an organized process. If we arrive at a solution by intuition, it simply means we got there without consciously knowing how we did it. It does not mean we have not been following a sound set of principles. After all, Alan Turing broke the Enigma code by combining his brilliant, deductive mathematical logic, with his intuitive insights about how a young German soldier, asked to follow the operation manual for the Enigma machine, might actually behave in a hostile wartime environment. Another powerful analogy is the idea of modern day holistic data analysis being a kind of musical 'jamming' session. When musicians jam a jazz piece, invariably they do not just invent something completely new. They tend to start working around reasonably traditional structures, and only then begin to improvise out from this more conventional starting point.

The power of archetypal evidence

The fact that market researchers may, in the past, have been dismissive of so-called 'anecdotal' or 'intuitive-based evidence', even when it was being advanced by seasoned marketing professionals, has been largely unhelpful. A more constructive approach is to think of the powerful intuitive insights provided by senior marketing management as being potentially rich, 'archetypal' evidence. (That is, evidence that is *not* simply an isolated snapshot of one individual's 'personal' perspective on the world, but the sum of a rich body of reinforcing experiences built up over many years across various markets, and corroborated by what others also think.) This archetypal evidence, albeit informal, is indeed worthy to sit alongside formal survey evidence.

Market researchers have made progress in accepting that intuition – knowing, without knowing why – is not a mystical phenomenon that sits outside the formal decision-making process. However, the pendulum must not swing too far. It will be unhelpful if intuitive reasoning becomes exclusively associated with flair and creativity, and the evaluation of the hard customer data is relegated to being a dull and lacklustre irrelevance. This would be dangerous because, as we all know, hunch and intuition can often be plain wrong. The key to success is, of course, combining 'informed' intuition with the rigorous scrutiny of data.

Data is dumb but beliefs are blind

Arriving at what we might describe as 'informed intuition' represents a major challenge. On the one hand, we are all attracted to the power of 'intuitive thinking': we are all aware that many successful business people claim that they 'just know' what the different signals and messages are telling them to do. But beliefs, unsubstantiated and unchecked, can be 'blind'. Not all of intuitive thought will be correct. It can enrich the analysis process, but it can also point us in the wrong direction.

However, if we totally resist intuition, this can stifle our understanding. Totally literal, uninspired reportage of customer data will often be plain 'dumb'. Without that extra flair, insight, and indefinable hunch, the true power of what the data is trying to tell us may be lost.

In sum, truly informed business decision-making requires a combination of intuitive thinking skills, and a rigorous interrogation of all of our evidence. We need to embrace intuition, but only in the context of controlled analysis frameworks and with appropriate checks and balances. Responding to this challenge is one of the central preoccupations of this book.

Developing an account of how new market research 'works'

There is a gap in the methodological literature between the 'classic' (and often statistical-based accounts of how market research 'works') and the more pragmatic and flexible (yet still rather vague and abstract) approaches being advocated by the emerging holistic school of data analysis.

We do, of course, have a general appreciation of the way holistic researchers work. But this falls short of providing a practical step-by-step guide to holistic data analysis. The absence of a comprehensive organizing framework, explaining the holistic approach to data analysis, makes getting to grips with the art and science of the market research 'craft' – a mixture of classic social scientific enquiry and practitioner know-how – a particular problem for newcomers.

There are numerous excellent books, from leading academics in the field, on the theoretical grounding behind market research. There are also numerous first class contributions from practitioners on various specialist aspects of the market research process. But there is a limited number of books that – based on an overview of market research theory *and* practice – provide a transparent account of how market researchers now interpret their data in a more holistic way.

Developing an organizing framework to help us learn about holistic analysis is now vitally important. If we do not spell out exactly how market researchers, in 'real life', actually analyse data, there is the danger of an 'anything goes' approach emerging to the way research evidence is used for decision-making by the commercial and public sectors.

The challenge of developing a 'universal' framework

We strongly believe that there is tremendous value in developing a universal framework that explains how new (holistic-based) market research really works. Here, we fully accept that developing any unified account of how such a broad church as the 'market research industry' operates will be open to challenge. It is an industry with many varied niches, ranging from focus group specialists through to those who are experts in undertaking Internet surveys.

Fitness-to-purpose

In mapping out a universal framework, we must also be mindful of the dangers of implying that there is a set standard that operates across different business problem-solving scenarios. This is clearly not the case. Market research is about finding solutions to business problems that are 'fit-to-purpose'. It is a way of reducing uncertainty in business, rather than an attempt to always model itself on the 'classic' tenets of what constitutes pure scientific enquiry. So, in certain situations, the appropriate approach may be a 'classic' research study, possibly requiring an experimental design, that delivers high levels of methodological rigour. Yet, in other scenarios, the appropriate research design solution may be one that only provides broad insights and directional guidelines, with a much less rigorous methodology. Thus, in outlining our approach, the reader needs to relate what we are saying to the nature of the marketing problem under investigation.

A synthesis of key theory and best practice

There have been few attempts to synthesize what the market research industry knows about the interpretation of data into a single book that would serve as a basic introduction to the holistic interpretation of market research data for new-comers. One reason for this is that providing a synthesis of best market research theory *and* practice – the art and the science – requires making difficult decisions about which points, from the vast body of literature available, to draw upon. It is literature that incorporates statistics, psychology, sociology, anthropology, marketing, economics, geography, communications theory, and much more.

In addition, much of this literature is difficult to access for the busy market research practitioner, locked as it is in many important, but sometimes obscure, tomes. A further difficulty is that any account of everyday market research analysis also relies on a body of knowledge that exists mainly in the form of proprietary techniques and knowledge that is housed within individual market research agencies. Clearly there is a limit to the extent to which different agencies – keen to seek a commercial advantage – will put this body of knowledge in the public domain.

An overview of our 'holistic' data analysis framework

Before outlining what we have elected to label our 'holistic' approach to the analysis of market research data, a brief explanation of why we have opted to align our approach to data analysis with the word 'holistic'.

Why call it 'holistic' data analysis?

We favour the word 'holistic' because it explains the broader, richer, and fuller way in which new market researchers now successfully operate on the wider marketing information stage, offering strategic advice based on a grounded understanding of why customers say what they say. It is a term that neatly highlights the way market researchers now operate in a more integrated way, drawing together different types of desk, observation, qualitative and quantitative evidence into a combined whole, rather than just analysing solitary pieces of uncoordinated evidence. We believe that the word 'holistic' also effectively conveys the way in which researchers are now much more 'engaged' with, rather than remaining 'detached' from, the decision-making process.

Of course, the word 'holistic' is not perfect. To some, it will suggest an approach that lacks credibility and does not have any 'scientific' underpinning. It is also a word that could be seen as rather faddish. Notwithstanding this, we believe that the word 'holistic' provides a useful shorthand for conveying what client organizations now want from the market research industry. Clients are looking for an integrated, insightful understanding of what *all* their customer evidence is telling them. They want their data to have been inspected by an independent third party for its resonance with prior management thinking on the subject, and they want their data presented in an explicit, transparent, and actionable way that enhances the decision-making process. The word 'holistic' seems to convey many of these dimensions.

Our ten-stage framework

Our approach guides newcomers to market research through ten stages for better understanding the craft of holistic data analysis. Our framework lays out ideas and suggestions aimed at helping the analyst go beyond the data, to provide insightful interpretations. But our framework is not intended to be exhaustive. Our model can be no more than a set of general principles which we believe all interpretations of data, at least in part, should, as a minimum, take into account. Many of the techniques to which we refer have their origin in qualitative research, where the holistic interpretative approach comes naturally. But, at each stage of our framework, we always demonstrate how holistic data analysis principles can be applied, in a fluid way, to *both* qualitative and quantitative evidence.

- *Analysing the right problem*: we start with the all-important issue of ensuring that we understand the *real* problem that drives the analysis requirement. Get this wrong and no amount of data analysis skill will save you.
- *Understanding the big information picture*: next, we explain how holistic data analysts make use of *all* the available data on the problem. The holistic analyst knows how to combine clues, anecdotes, archetypal evidence, qualitative

evidence, survey data, conceptual marketing models, and management hunch and intuition in unravelling the overall storyline.

- *Compensating for imperfect data*: the holistic analyst knows that most customer and marketing data is 'imperfect'. They know that effective analysis means knowing how to compensate for this imperfection as part of the interpretation process. Here, we look at techniques to help the analyst establish the core robustness of, and compensate for any 'errors' in, the evidence.

- *Developing the analysis strategy and organizing the qualitative and quantitative data*: we then look at developing a clearly thought through analysis strategy, including organizing the qualitative and quantitative evidence. The emphasis here is on making the evidence accessible, thereby pushing up the chances of an insightful and creative interpretation of the true meaning of the data.

- *Establishing the interpretation boundary*: we then provide guidance on how to establish the overall 'boundary' within which a particular piece of evidence can be 'safely' interpreted. The holistic data analyst will first use the orthodox statistical and methodological principles to establish the 'constraints' within which their data should initially be interpreted. But the holistic analyst will then 'stretch' this classically derived boundary by applying various 'enabling' principles that will allow them to take the relevant prior knowledge and informed intuition into account.

- *Applying the 'knowledge filters'*: the holistic analyst will then set new data in the context of what is known about the limitations of even the most professionally designed and conducted survey research. Based on past experience of the power and robustness of different genres of consumer evidence, the skilled analyst, in unravelling 'true' behaviour and attitudes, will pass their new incoming data through various 'knowledge filters'.

- *'Reframing' the data*: we then look at how the holistic data analyst may turn the evidence on its head, and look at it from a totally fresh stance. The goal here is to throw up fresh perspectives that will provide a deeper understanding and/or add a new 'insight'. This might involve 'reframing' the evidence from, for instance, a semiotics perspective, to enhance the power of the analysis.

- *Integrating the evidence and presenting research evidence as a narrative*: next we look at ways of integrating qualitative and quantitative evidence, while also factoring prior knowledge and intuition into the analysis. This provides a platform for constructing true and powerful narratives around which to present the research story in an engaging and authoritative way.

- *Facilitating informed decision-making*: then we arrive at the key issue of establishing what our data looks like from the standpoint of those who will apply the analysis to the original problem – the end decision-makers.

- *Developing holistic data analysis*: the final part of the holistic researcher's task is to complete the loop that runs from the problem to the solution, by drawing together the general principles and lessons learnt during the analysis process. This involves looking at how effective different research designs (information packages) have been in improving the quality of the evidence-based decision process. This understanding can then be fed back into the problem-definition of the next (holistic) data analysis task, thereby helping to build a body of normative knowledge about which holistic analysis techniques 'work', and which do not.

Building on past work

This book builds on an earlier book by the same authors, entitled *Inside Information: Making Sense of Marketing Data*. In this previous work, we began the process of explaining how holistic analysis works, and laid down some frameworks to explain how today's market researchers make sense of what is often contradictory customer evidence.

This book goes one step further, by providing a far more comprehensive and detailed account of the analysis tools, concepts and principles that practising holistic market researchers use when analysing multiple data sets. In addition, we provide the reader with a number of concrete examples of how our earlier, more abstract, ideas can be applied in practice.

Scope of this book

The task we have set ourselves in this book is a very ambitious one. It requires synthesizing what we know from a *theoretical* standpoint about market research, with various *practical* approaches that are taken to the discipline. In attempting this, we realize that there will be gaps. For example, in demonstrating how to integrate different types of evidence, space has not allowed us to address the important issue of working with specialist kinds of marketing data – such as media, and continuous consumer panel, data. Neither do we tackle the complexities of data fusion. We are also aware that we have not addressed the issue of the integration of customer information with financial data.

But we believe that the overall frameworks we lay down in this book will allow others – using similar principles – to establish how best to integrate other types of marketing information into this holistic way of thinking.

Supplementary reading

We are not advocating the holistic approach as an alternative to more 'traditional' data analysis methods. We are simply suggesting that the holistic approach can often add depth and breadth to these more conventional approaches. Given this, we have tried to structure this book, so that it will guide the newcomer to market research through the principles of holistic data analysis, while at the same time – in the Notes section – referring the reader to where detailed reading of more traditional market research knowledge and techniques will pay dividends.

So, in sum, our book paints the holistic data analysis story in broad strokes. We show the reader the overall canvas on which holistic commercial market researchers operate, but we do not take any one issue into any great depth. Our aim is to explain – at a meta level – how the various holistic principles and concepts fit and 'work' together, with the supporting Notes section alerting the reader how to pursue certain issues in more detail. There is also a Glossary, which includes the key terms we have used to explain the holistic approach.

What should come first: holistic or traditional?

There is, of course, the issue of whether the principles of holistic data analysis should be read *after* a detailed review of more 'conventional' market research material, or whether our primer in holistic data analysis should be read *before* studying the more traditional analytical techniques. Here, it is difficult to be prescriptive. Much will depend upon whether the reader is coming to market research for the first time, or has already had some experience. The simple compromise would be to read our book on holistic data analysis in parallel with other more traditional market research textbooks.

In this book, we have alternated the use of the male and female pronoun on a random basis.

Not a science, but a scientific approach

2

Summary

- We explore what constitutes scientific method, and the way in which the market research discipline adapts this scientific method to address the commercial realities of undertaking research into consumers and markets.
- We look at the critical issue of exploring valid causal connections between phenomena, and focus on ways of developing robust theory based on our observations. Here, we specifically look at three different ways in which theory and observation can be related: deduction, induction and abduction (we use this term in its philosophical, rather than more ominous, everyday, sense).
- We outline the dangers of making data fit our theories, rather than developing theories based on a rigorous inspection of the data, and also our prior knowledge. This forms a platform for explaining the way in which the holistic analyst will operate in evaluating evidence.
- We explain how our approach departs from the classic hypothetico-deductive school, but nevertheless, follows a sound set of principles, while also reflecting the messiness and complexity of the commercial market research arena. Specifically, we look at the way in which the holistic researcher will blend classic statistics with that of the Bayesian approach in arriving at an interpretation of data.
- In sum, this chapter will sharpen your critical thinking skills and help you unravel the contradictions we often find in consumer evidence. It is probably best to read this more theory-based chapter before tackling the rest of, what is, a practical book. But if you find 'theory' dry, why not first dip into some of the later, more applied, chapters first. This should give you more of an appetite for getting to grips with some of the theoretical ideas that will add practical power to your analysis skills.

A scientific approach to reduce uncertainty

The issue of whether researching consumers and markets is, or can ever be considered, a science, in the same sense that chemistry or neuropsychology are sciences, is debatable. But this is largely beside the point. The fact is that market and consumer research is needed by businesses to reduce the uncertainty involved in making business decisions. It is an industry that will use the best possible, fitness-to-purpose, methods available for reducing this business uncertainty: the best framework we have for organizing this enterprise is that of science.

We shall explain how market research does, in fact, adopt rigorous scientific methods, but in ways that have to be (often ingeniously) adapted to the type of phenomenon under investigation. However, we accept that describing market research as a 'science' risks misleading audiences into thinking they are going to be served up with findings of unquestionable certainty. So perhaps we should abandon the use of the term 'science' entirely, and instead call market research methodology a 'scientific approach'.

Understanding causal connections

The best place to start comparing and contrasting market research methodology with that of the natural sciences is to look at their common subject of investigation: the world.

The naïve view of the world which people sometimes assume, is that it is rather like a room full of furniture, comprising clearly defined and discrete entities that 'sit up' for us to observe, if only we take the time to look at them. The more time you spend researching the world, however, the more a complex picture emerges. This turns out not to be a space full of objects, but a dense, interconnected web of forces and facts, blending almost seamlessly into each other and which we have to prise apart in order to study. Discovering these connections is central to the scientific approach to any subject, and taking account of the number, type, relative strength, density, and unexpectedness of these critical connections is a key challenge confronting such an approach.

The connection that is of overwhelming importance for science is the 'causal connection'. Each of us is the centre of a vast network of causal connections radiating out into the world. When we open a door, turn on the television, or shout at someone, we set in train a chain of causal events. Some of these will be short and relatively self-contained. Others, however, may extend out well beyond the limits of our control. Each of these incidents can also be seen as the culmination of a whole number of causal chains leading up to it. A scientific approach aims to analyse these causal chains, and identify the causes that contribute to the phenomena that are being studied. The way science does this is to analyse, classify and break down the phenomena it is studying. A central objective of the natural sciences is to isolate the phenomena scientists wish to find out about. The phenomena, isolated in this way, can then be studied by scientists as part of longer chains of reasoning or as sub-components in new experimental setups.

Making valid and reliable observations

Only by isolating the various causal factors which comprise the phenomena they are studying can scientists be confident of predicting and controlling the phenomena in their experiments. If unknown factors continue to play a part in the method the scientist has devised for isolating the phenomena, the method will prove either unreliable or invalid:

- *Unreliable*: as the unknown factor may, or may not, be present in subsequent attempts to reproduce the phenomenon in the laboratory, this makes the technique unreliable as a means of producing the phenomenon.
- *Invalid*: because, even if the phenomenon was always reproducible, the scientists will still not be measuring the phenomenon they think they are measuring. This will present a problem when the phenomenon comes to be used by scientists in *other* experiments, where the unknown factor will then cause unexpected and unpredictable effects.

These erroneous factors, which disrupt scientific methods, rendering them unreliable and invalid, are called *artefacts*. Of course, the complex nature of the commercial world makes these artefacts difficult to isolate and expunge from our methods of market research enquiry. This means that, although reliable and valid methods are essential to any scientific approach to obtaining knowledge, there is a paradox in using this method to arrive at an understanding of the world. If we cannot identify and/or accurately measure all the causal factors which affect a phenomenon, we must admit to a degree of uncertainty in our understanding, and subsequent predictions.

The importance of understanding how we know

So, there is a paradox in scientific method. To acquire new knowledge requires you to understand how we know. To know something is to believe that it is actually true, and to believe it for the right reasons. If you believe – but for the wrong reasons – your chance of being right again in a similar situation is very slight.

Let us illustrate the point with an example. In 1991, one of the authors, knowing nothing about racing, bet on a horse called Seagram to win the Grand National, simply because that year the race's sponsor was Seagram. As luck would have it, Seagram won the National that year. Yet the author could not claim to have any 'knowledge' about how to pick winners. This way of 'reasoning' would probably never work again: his reasons for believing Seagram would win were fanciful, and in no way connected with the complex array of causal factors that actually contributed to Seagram's victory. Had the author based his choice on the best available reasons available for picking a horse (e.g. recent form over a similar distance, or inside information from the gallops, and so on), he would have been far from certain of victory. He would be all too familiar with the complexities of weighing up all these factors and determining the precise effect on the outcome. So, we might call an awareness of the limitations of the available ways of knowing, the very hallmark of adeptness in knowledge.

Developing a theory from our observations

Implicit in all the aspects of science we have looked at so far is the notion of building theories. We can define theory as those accounts which scientists make, in words, pictures and equations, to describe a phenomenon, and the various factors or variables that have a causal effect on it. Theory faces in two directions:

- *Backwards*: in accounting for observations already made.
- *Forwards*: when it makes predictions about likely future events or observations.

The more observations a theory can account for, or the more accurate its predictions, the more powerful it is said to be. Another important function of theory is to open new avenues of investigation, or to connect findings in one area of investigation with findings in another. To generalize across a range of observations, theorists often use metaphors or pictures that can be developed to generate new hypotheses to account for observations, or make predictions in other areas besides those on which the theory was originally based.

There are three basic ways in which theory and observation can be related: deduction, induction or abduction. Understanding these three forms of reasoning is important in appreciating the way in which holistic market researchers evaluate evidence. The three ways are summarized in Figure 2.1, and discussed in further detail below.

Deduction

The method of deduction appears to produce the most certain knowledge: if all the beans in the bag are known to be white, and we take some beans from the bag, we can be certain that they will be white. But it does so only by starting off with a great deal of prior knowledge, and not moving far beyond this knowledge. With the deductive method, the ratio of prior knowledge to new knowledge, as it were, is very high.

Induction

The method of induction creates new knowledge by generalizing from individual observations. In this case, the observation made is that the beans under investigation are from the bag, and the beans are white. This leads to the *prediction* that

Deduction

Observation	All the beans from this bag are white
Observation	These beans are from this bag
Therefore (logic)	These beans will be white

Induction

Observation	These beans are from this bag
Observation	These beans are white
Therefore (hypothesis)	All the beans from this bag will be white

Abduction

Observation	All the beans from this bag are white
Observation	These beans are white
Therefore (theory)	These beans are from this bag

Figure 2.1 – Deduction, induction and abduction.

all the other beans in this bag will be white. This method provides less certain knowledge than deduction (the next bean from the bag *could* be black, blue or yellow, etc.). This is because it attempts to move us further from our base of existing knowledge. As yet, we do not know everything about the contents of the bag (as we did in the case of deductive knowledge). We are just attempting to find out more about it by making single observations. It is reasonable to assume that the more white beans we observe being produced from the bag, the more certain we can be of our conclusion that all the beans in the bag are white. By the same token, if a bean that is not white is produced from the bag, the hypothesis will be disproved, or will have to be modified.

Abduction

The method of abduction is a hybrid between deduction and induction. It shares with the deductive method the starting point of the general rule from prior knowledge, that is, that *all* the beans in this bag are white. But it then takes an isolated observation – that a particular set of beans is white – and draws from this the fairly ambitious conclusion, that the beans are from the bag of white beans. Thus, although it starts with quite a lot of prior knowledge, its conclusion does not follow with absolute certainty from this. The beans, of course, could be from an entirely different bag, or from a totally different kind of source. Abductive and inductive methods are therefore alike in that they are more ambitious than deduction in their attempt to extend existing knowledge, and so involve a degree of uncertainty: they take risks to acquire knowledge.

The critical difference between induction and abduction

Induction and abduction, however, differ in one crucial respect. The conclusion of the inductive method is exposed to the possibility of falsification every time another bean is produced from the bag. However, with abduction, it is unclear what you would need to do to *disprove* the abductive conclusion. The most you could do is cast doubt on the claim that it is the *only* conclusion by, say, showing that there were lots of other bags (or other receptacles) that had white beans in them, and which these beans could equally well have come from. So, with induction, the theory is built up from close observation (in this case, of the beans coming out of the bag). In contrast, abduction works 'top down': the theory is postulated to make a connection between two observations that have already been made. And different theories could fit the observations equally well – or none of them could fit as convincingly as the claim that there is no connection between the observations.

Informed theorizing

Concerns about our tendency to become attached to our own theories about things, to the point of making awkward data fit them, is clearly a central concern to those seeking a 'scientific' way of establishing the truth. We know we have a susceptibility to sophisticated explanations, irrespective of their truth. This is illustrated by the Watzlawick experiment, summarized in Table 2.1.

Table 2.1 – The Watzlawick experiment

- Watzlawick provides compelling experimental evidence of the power that sophisticated explanations of apparently significant patterns in random data have over us.
- In these experiments, pairs of medical experts (each kept in ignorance of the other's responses) were shown slides of healthy and sickly animal cells and asked to identify the characteristics of healthy and sickly cells by a process of trial and error.
- For each slide, the analysts had to indicate whether they thought a cell was healthy or sickly, and would then be informed by the experimenter whether they were right or wrong in their choice.
- Only one of them, however, was given accurate feedback from the experimenter; the other was given entirely random feedback.
- When they were brought together to compare their respective 'theories' of the characteristics of sickly and healthy cells, the analysts who had developed, from accurate feedback, a simple and correct view of the defining characteristics of both types of cell, were then persuaded of the truth of the sophisticated, tortuous theories of the analysts who had been given entirely random feedback.

Supporters of hypothesis-led thinking are therefore reluctant to allow the theorist an entirely free hand in adapting their theory using purely the inductive method. They want to prevent theorists simply adapting their theories to explain away new observations that appear to conflict with the original theory. This process of 'saving' the theory, they claim, results in theories that can explain everything and nothing. For example, the original model of planetary motion (first developed by the astronomer Ptolemy), kept being adapted over years to explain awkward deviations in the observed movements of the planets. It had to, very reluctantly, eventually give way to the far simpler model devised by Copernicus and Kepler.

Hypothetico-deductive method

To guard against premature and ill-informed theorizing, the hypothetico-deductive school of scientific enquiry emerged. Supporters of this school, with their very choice of methodological name, immediately signalled their beliefs. The term 'hypothetico-deductive' clearly reflects both their reliance on 'hypothesis testing' and their distrust of the inductive method. This school claims that the theory must come first – in the form of a provisional hypothesis – and then this must be tested by observations (in the way that the inductive conclusion exposes itself to falsification). If observations do not confirm the hypothesis, then the hypothesis must be rejected. Yet although such definitive tests might be possible in the case of simple, isolated systems, they are often not a viable option when investigating many of the complex social systems that market researchers investigate.

The pragmatic holistic approach

Therefore, those in the holistic school of market research data analysis would argue that insisting on the definitive test, demanded by the hypothetico-deductive school, is unrealistic in most commercial market research scenarios. They would argue that a more appropriate approach for market researchers is to start with a 'theory', which would have been developed by a combination of exploratory evidence, and prior knowledge and intuition. This theory would then be used to explain new observations as they arose. However, if an observed behaviour, or attitude, appears not to fit the market researchers' theory, we would not dispense with the whole theory: rather, we would look for ways of extending the theory to accommodate the new observations. We would look for various factors in, or related to, the observed behaviour under investigation, which might help us make sense of our data within our emerging theory or analysis framework.

So, the holistic approach is close to the abductive and inductive methods. We will keep exploring what we know and can say about the original bag from which our white beans were drawn, but not persevere with this blatant theory saving in the face of emerging evidence that challenges our original interpretation. It may lack some of the rigour of the hypothetico-deductive method, but it is robust enough to avoid bending awkward data into a pet theory. This is because it is alert to all the sources of prior knowledge that help us understand the phenomena we are investigating.

Fitness-to-context and purpose

Thus, the pragmatic approach – the basis of our holistic approach to the analysis of market research data – is a preparedness to accept inductive and abductive methods, but only if their use meets certain conditions of fitness, relative to context and purpose.

A theory can be adapted by *inductive* reasoning to incorporate observations not previously accounted for by it, provided the adapted theory continues to:

- Simplify the phenomenon it describes.
- Be useful to theorists and their peers – that is, continues to summarize the observations in a way which enables it to predict and explain other observations.
- Distinguish between 'true' patterns and random variations.

A theory can be generated *abductively* to explain observations without the possibility of further testing by observation, provided:

- A range of possible theoretical explanations has been considered.
- There is at least partial, prior, or independent support for the theory from observations other than those to which it is now being applied.
- The final theoretical explanation chosen is the best candidate available in terms of its fit with the observations and the prior, independent support that exists for it.

The above basic methodological principles underlie the two main types of interpretation which market researchers are called on to make:

- Qualitative data analysis, which proceeds by generating a conceptual framework that develops as the analyst goes through the data, is an example of *inductively* generated theory. Of the various frameworks available to help us understand the qualitative process, 'grounded theory' is a particularly accessible and concrete account. Experience tells us that grounded theory, which we summarize in Table 2.2, provides a focus for helping many qualitative practitioners think about the theoretical principles that underpin their everyday practice.
- Interpretations of quantitative, or qualitative, data which go beyond the data set to draw wider conclusions, are special cases of *abductively* generated theory.

Using statistics to isolate and measure

As explained, not all phenomena can be completely isolated physically for subsequent study by market researchers. It may only be possible to partially isolate the phenomena because the variables are too entangled with one another to identify and isolate them all. In such cases, the scientist needs to quantify, or

Table 2.2 – An overview of grounded theory

Grounded theory was proposed in the 1960s by two sociologists, Glaser and Strauss. They were reacting to the dominant hypothetico-deductive method that characterized sociology at that time and were concerned to provide a theoretical underpinning for qualitative research, based on the inductive method. Their central idea was that theories in the social sciences should be grounded in actual observations – building up one observation at a time using the inductive method. Two ideas were central to their theory: *theoretical sensitivity* and *theoretical saturation*.

Theoretical sensitivity: this involves the researcher constantly laying his or her theory open to challenge from subsequent observations: never allowing themselves to become attached to a particular theory which would then prevent them from taking seriously observations which challenged it.

> *'Potential theoretical sensitivity is lost when the sociologist commits him or her-self exclusively to one specific preconceived theory... for then he/she becomes doctrinaire and can no longer "see around" their pet theory... He/she becomes insensitive, or even defensive, towards the kind of questions that cast doubt on their theory; he/she is preoccupied with testing, modifying, and seeing everything from this one single angle'.*

Theoretical saturation: this is the idea that, as you gather qualitative observations on a subject, you start to build a dense, interlocking set of concepts. In the early stages of analysis, additional research interviews (or observations) would reveal numerous new concepts. Provided you have sampled correctly, the number of additional concepts added by successive interviews would diminish. You would move from *building* a picture to *refining* the picture of the issue you were looking at until you reached 'saturation point'. Here, subsequent interviews add no new concepts. Sampling the universe on that issue is now complete – adding a level of refinement to the more straightforward approach to sampling borrowed from quantitative methodology.

---

measure, those aspects or features of the system which present themselves for measurement. Then the goal is to use statistical techniques to isolate the variables involved and describe the relationships between them. The role of statistics in this process is threefold. To provide measures of:

- Proximity and distance between different observations, to isolate variables from one another.
- Co-variance, or correlation, between different variables to identify potential causal relationships.
- Probability that a particular measurement of distance (proximity), or of co-variance, represents a real distinction or relationship in the world, and is not just the random noise, or chaotic background activity of a highly complex system.

The two schools of statistics

There are two schools of statistics that broadly correspond to the two sides in the debate about the hypothetico-deduction and abduction schools of methodological thinking. These are the 'classical' (sometimes called 'frequentist') approach, and the Bayesian school of statistics:

- *Classical statistics*: at the heart of this approach is the notion of starting from the position of the null hypothesis. The assumption is that a theory is wrong until an observation provides support for it. It adopts a threshold approach to measuring the probability that a difference or relationship between observations reflects a genuine difference. A confidence level of 95% (or 99%) is set as the standard which a measure of difference, or relationship, has to meet to be considered statistically significant. If the observation does not meet these, the test has failed and the null hypothesis – that the theory is wrong – is affirmed. If the observation passes the test, the null hypothesis is rejected and the theory is validated.
- *Bayesian statistics*: here, by contrast, no hypothesis is ever null. There is always a probability that a hypothesis is correct – that our theory is a correct description of our data. Bayes' theorem, named after the 18th Century clergyman, Thomas Bayes, who proved it, is a logical corollary of the basic rules of probability. A straightforward expression of this formula is:

$$p(H_i \mid y) \propto p(y \mid H_i)\, p(H_i)$$

where p = probability, H_i = one of a series of hypotheses (one of which is assumed to be true), and y = the data. The formula in effect says that the probability of the hypothesis, given the data we are looking at – $p(H_i \mid y)$ the *posterior probability* – is proportional to ($\propto$) the probability that we would see this same data pattern if the hypothesis were true – $p(y \mid H_i)$, what is known as the *likelihood* or *conditional probability* of the data – multiplied by the *prior probability* of the hypothesis, $p(H_i)$, the probability that we would have attached to the hypothesis prior to seeing the data.

The theorem licenses – insists upon – the use of prior knowledge when interpreting data. The theorem makes it clear, for example, that our prior knowledge about a phenomenon is relevant to our interpretation of subsequent observations.

Rather than the theory being entirely subject to observation, as in the classical tradition, in Bayesian statistics, the theory is allowed to have an impact on the probability of the evidence. Thus, if we attached a fairly high prior probability to a theory, observations which appear to contradict it would reduce the probability of the theory being true. That is, result in a lower posterior probability. Yet it would not reduce the probability of it being correct to zero, in the way demanded by the hypothetico-deductive method.

Another important feature of the formula is the conditional probability or 'likelihood' function, i.e. $p(y|H_i)$. This enables us to consider any data or observations as evidence relative to any particular hypothesis we choose, and to make allowance for the strength or weakness of the data as evidence for that hypothesis. (Hypotheses can be suggested by the data, provided the prior probability attributed to them is kept independent of the data. That is, provided the prior probability of the hypotheses is evaluated on grounds other than those provided by the data being considered. This requires some mental discipline, but is not logically impossible.)

Thus, the Bayesian approach facilitates the development of a range of hypotheses, or theories, to explain an observation and provides the means for deciding between them. In other words, Bayesian thinking provides a formal theoretical support for the abductive method of reasoning.

We accept that Bayesian methods, although commonplace in many academic and technical research circles, are considered by most commercial market researchers to be far too inaccessible to be developed into everyday practice. However, we make no apology for giving the Bayesian approach prominence in this book. This is because the concepts that underpin Bayes provide a robust defence of the holistic school of data analysis. So, if you are nervous of Bayesian statistics, just stay with the concepts and principles behind the approach. Bayesian *thinking* will pay dividends in powering up your analysis and consumer data.

Having reviewed the theoretical underpinning for the holistic approach to the analysis of market research evidence, in the next chapter we look briefly at the theoretical underpinning for the idea of combining management 'intuition' with the formal analysis of data. Our aim is to give the analyst the confidence to work with both the data and management 'hunch'. We will provide frameworks – checks and balances – that will help the analyst differentiate between unsubstantiated whims, and insightful nuggets of wisdom, that can be constructively dovetailed into the hard consumer evidence.

3 # Data-rich intuitive analysis

Summary

- Central to the concept of holistic data analysis is the notion of factoring management prior knowledge and intuition into the formal analysis of the consumer evidence. So here, we review what we know about intuition: knowing without knowing why.
- We look at exactly what seems to characterize intuitive thought, noting the way that many commentators argue that intuition is a set of thought processes that can be cultivated and developed.
- But we also point out that intuition can be plain wrong, stressing the importance of not allowing intuition to overpower the data.
- This allows us to arrive at the conclusion that powerful analysis often involves operating in *both* data and intuitive modes.
- This chapter will give the reader the ability to spot when an argument is being advanced based on flawed logic or when it simply reflects a biased viewpoint. The aim is to give the reader the ability to differentiate between 'informed' intuition that is compatible with other sources of evidence, and wilder, speculative claims that need to be challenged.

Factoring intuition into the data analysis process

The tension between the formal analysis of data and the intuitive insights of entrepreneurs has always been a source of some concern. Anita Roddick once famously described market research as 'the view through a car's rear-view mirror': suggesting that market research only tells you where you have been, not where you are likely to be going. And many will be familiar with the claims made by senior decision-makers about the apparent shortcomings of market research. Notably, these include the view that research is often:

- Inconclusive and/or the researcher seems to lack total conviction about their results: the research seems to pose more questions than it answers, particularly when predicting future developments.

- Accompanied by a great deal of qualification: all of which appears to be at odds with the economy and clarity expected of a decision support system.

The above observations lead some decision-makers to conclude that there is little, or no, point in researching markets, and that all that is required for successful marketing is the 'entrepreneur's vision', or the marketing person's hunch, and the collective will of a well-organized business.

We agree with this, up to a point: market research data, and the conclusions made, are not sufficient, on their own, to drive correct marketing decisions. But we also know that management intuition alone – uninformed by research – is likely to lead a business astray. Examples of businesses actually succeeding by *ignoring* the findings of research are well known. Everyone has a story (the favourite one being the Sony Walkman: a 'tape recorder' that cannot record is never going to catch on said the research). Far more typical, though, but much less well publicized, are the examples where businesses made catastrophic decisions because they ignored what proved to be very sensible messages coming from the research. The Ford Edsel and the Sinclair C5 head a long, ignominious list. So critical to the goal of building a market research discipline that is more engaged with the decision-making process than before, is the task of integrating the analysis of market research evidence with the more intuitive contributions from management.

The value of rigorous data-rich thinking

The way forward for informed business decision-making is clearly to develop frameworks that allow intuition to flourish, but which still keeps ill-informed intuitive thinking under check. Thus, as indicated earlier, our view on this can best be summed up as follows: 'intuition without research is blind, and research without intuition is dumb'. Marketers need to believe in their own understanding of the market, and their wider business experience. However, they stand far more chance of making a good decision if they base this 'insight' on appropriate market research data. So, here we advocate data-*rich*, as opposed to data-*poor*, thinking: this is the basis of 'informed intuition'.

The power of informed intuition

The notion of 'intuition' – knowing without knowing why – has been around for centuries. For instance, Spinoza aligned intuitive thought with the road to truth. And everyone will be aware of the way famous entrepreneurs extol the power of that 'tingle' of intuition when making key decisions. And the stories continue to abound. For example, Musto, the sailing clothing company, now have a story to tell about how they ended up sponsoring Ellen MacArthur – Britain's around the world yachting superstar. Apparently, Musto receive over a dozen letters a week from young hopefuls seeking free clothing on the grounds that they are going to be famous in the future. Most have to be politely declined. For some reason, though, when a letter from a teenage Ellen MacArthur arrived, the owners of Musto 'somehow' decided that they would send her the clothing she wanted. They reported that there was just 'something' about her particular letter that stood out, convincing them that this was the right decision. And now Musto are reaping their rewards, with their name being associated with Ellen MacArthur every time she pulls into port to win another trophy.

What is intuition?

The Penguin Dictionary of Psychology refers to intuition as, 'immediate perception or judgment, usually with some emotional colouring, without any conscious mental steps in preparation; a popular rather than scientific term'. Other dictionary definitions tell us that intuition is 'knowledge or belief obtained neither by reason nor perception; instinctive knowledge or belief; a hunch or unjustified belief; a contemplation'. Other definitions see intuition as the 'power of the mind by which it immediately sees the truth of things without reasoning or analysis'.

A further way of beginning to understand what 'intuition' entails, is to look at the way in which different individuals describe the intuitive *process*. Here, we find references to intuition as being, 'good guesses, hunches or hypotheses, thrown up by the unconscious mind, which deserve, as a minimum, serious but not uncritical attention'. So here, intuition is seen as providing an overall initial interpretation of, or 'take' on, a situation that manifests itself not, as yet, as reasoned analysis, but as an 'inkling' or a 'general impression'. And others talk about the intuitive approach being about 'navigating ambiguity to unearth an extraordinary meaning'. Intuition is seen as 'having a floating eye – not necessarily attached to the pursuit of anything precise, but navigating left and right, collecting elements of sense, always uncertain, and proceeding often in a disordered way'.

These definitions and accounts of the intuitive process give us a flavour of what intuition is all about. Yet it is clearly helpful to go beyond this, to dissect the concept a little further. Let us start by summarizing the physiological evidence.

The physiological evidence

It is claimed that the largest part of the human brain is the neocortex, a relatively recently developed part of the brain where we do most of our so-called 'rational' thinking. Within our brain, though, there exists the 'original' visceral brain, known as the limbic system. This is the part of the brain that developed when we evolved from reptiles into mammals. Our visceral brain operates our biological bodies, but it is also responsible for generating our senses, emotions, instincts, and – yes – our intuition. Thus, the argument runs that, although we are equipped with new parts of the brain which give us our power of reason and analysis, we are still inextricably connected up to – wired into – our old biological brain. The consequences of this is that, however much we think rationally about a decision, we can only make judgements via an area of our brain that interfaces with our senses, emotions, instinct and intuition.

Put another way, according to this body of knowledge, we are physically incapable of making decisions that are based *solely* on rational thinking. Specifically, it is argued that that we construct our lives through 'somatic markers'. These somatic markers are seen as being the way we continuously order the events in our lives. For example, if we put ourselves in a dangerous position at the top of a building and we fear falling, our pulse starts to race, we break out in a sweat and our heart may pound. All of this creates a strong somatic marker that tells us that being on the top of high buildings, without taking the appropriate precautions, is dangerous. It is an emotional stimulus that shapes future (instinctive) behaviour when it comes to negotiating dangerous heights. These series of negative somatic markers act as an alarm bell. Yet positive somatic markers also exist that will physiologically associate safety and success with particular physical states.

So somatic markers are the way in which we 'intuitively' work out how to make sensible decisions in order to survive in this dangerous world. It seems that we build up a bank of somatic markers in our heads, and they then work as a kind of 'gatekeeper' for upcoming decisions: we pull down the appropriate somatic marker, as needed, to deal with particular scenarios as they arise.

Key characteristics of intuition

We now look at a number of – many overlapping – characteristics that writers seem to agree, constitute the rather elusive notion of 'intuitive thought'.

Intuition is a phenomenon that can be cultivated

The literature on intuition tends to suggest that, while some of us may be better at intuitive thought than others, we can all learn to cultivate, to a degree, this way of thinking about issues. Put simply, intuition is a dimension to our thinking, that – with the help of various conceptual tools and frameworks – we can all attempt to draw out, foster, and incorporate into our wider analytical toolkit.

Here, in edging towards a better understanding of intuition, it is helpful to examine Claxton's idea of the 'unconscious intelligence'. Claxton distinguishes unconscious intelligence from the Freudian notion of a repository of suppressed memories ('sub-conscious'). Importantly, Claxton also separates his concept of unconscious intelligence from Jung's notion of intuition being one of four basic mental functions (the other three being thinking, feeling and sensing). Jung's view is that every person has one of these four modes, which is more developed, and more used, in preference to others. So Jung saw intuition, and his other basic personality traits, as being largely unalterable. And critically, Jung held the view that the 'intuition mode' was a way of seeing *into* the unconscious, rather than being a product of it. In contrast, Claxton argues that an intuitive way of knowing can be developed and cultivated by ongoing experiences and (to a degree) actual training.

In sum, the first point we can make about intuition is that it is seen by many as a trait that is capable of being enhanced and sharpened. And the way this seems to 'work' is by recognizing the benefits to be gained from continually looping through what we already know, and also how we feel, so as to forge better 'connections' between our tacit and explicit knowledge.

Deep organized reflection

Claxton's observations about the power of cultivating intuition also link to Spinoza's notion of intuition as a kind of 'profound, unmediated understanding of the nature of things, which rises through a deep, contemplative communion with people and objects'. Spinoza argues that intuition only makes an appearance after a purposeful process of questioning and reasoning has exhausted itself. All of which suggests that (intuitive) thought processes – albeit working at a deep level – could be improved by organized reflection aimed at improving the quality of this intuitive strand in our thinking.

Intuition recognizes the power of flexible, circular, linear thinking

Another dimension to intuitive thought centres on the value – when looking at a problem in a short time frame – of constantly revisiting our initial solution to a problem. But this point goes beyond what we have just said about the value of organized reflection. The point here is to stress the value of circling back on an 'original' solution. This increases the chances that the mind will eliminate initial wrong guesses and blind alleys. The 'circling around' process, pushes up the probability of being able to more readily reject flawed thinking, and thereby arrive at a more rounded, robust solution or decision.

This reflects the way that, initially, we tend to get fixated with a particular approach, and persevere with it, even when it is not working. It seems that often we get trapped into thinking that all our efforts should follow a nice, neat, logical, linear progression. Whereas, in fact, often we should accept that the way the human brain operates most effectively – on certain problems at least – is when we circle and loop round the problem in a flexible way. We need to accept that the initial upward incursion may not be the appropriate one, and that, after a period of further, wider, broader, and new reflection, a fresh, more appropriate and correct path can then be determined.

Intuition is about picking things up by osmosis

Another characteristic of intuitive thought is the way individuals will gradually, over time, extract the patterns that are latent within a whole diversity of superficially different experiences, and forge them into a 'way of knowing'. We now know that a large part of the understanding that we acquire throughout our lives is not received via explicit knowledge. It is received more implicitly through our brains' ability to discover the underlying shapes and patterns at work, and to tune our future responses based on these learnt past experiences.

This ability to learn by osmosis is a form of basic intelligence we inherited from our animal forebears, and it is one that remains both active and valuable throughout our lives. Here, we need to remember that there will be concepts in our brains that have no word labels, and that there are some word labels that we use that have not yet been underpinned by fully thought through, grounded theoretical principles and concepts. The act of 'knowing', therefore, reflects a deep-seated, primal ability to understand. In sum, we somehow learn implicitly, over time, from the past, and we then make this learning explicit and concrete, and then we can productively harness it to the way we face new challenges.

Intuition involves both slow and gradual *and* fast and instant thinking

We live in a business environment where fast, rapid decision-making is seen as the currency of the day. It is an environment where slower, more contemplative, purposeful thought process is often not rewarded. However, some productive intuitive thought is the result of slowing down the mind, relaxing it, and shifting into a different mental mood. By changing the pace of thought, we can move into a different way of knowing. By slowing things down, observations will automatically begin to appear on the horizon. However, here, we have to draw a distinction between two types of problem solving:

- *Insight problems*: where an individual may have all of the necessary information to solve the problem, but where they may feel some kind of blockage, before eventually arriving at that new interpretation or perspective on the issue under consideration. There is much evidence of famous breakthroughs in scientific thinking that were made in this way.
- *Analytical problems*: with analytical problems, we have a kind of 'puzzle', where there is less open-ended uncertainty. Here, all the elements of the jigsaw (just like a crossword) are known, and all that needs to be done is for us to fit everything together. In this situation, clear, fast analytical thought in arriving at the optimum solution is probably all that is required.

So, in summary, sometimes intuition benefits from slow thought, but in other scenarios, immediate and speedy thought is of the essence.

The intuitive power of practical know-how, not just theoretical knowledge

As a society, we tend to value 'formal' knowledge – which can be clearly articulated in the form of an organized set of rules and procedures – over and above an individual's ability simply to 'know how to do something'. And we often make the mistake of thinking that this (formal) knowledge, once acquired, will simply transform itself automatically into 'know-how'.

We can all cite examples, particularly from the world of sport, of individuals who can do something to a high level of skill, but who lack the verbal dexterity or formal concepts to describe exactly what they have achieved. (Could Beckham articulate how he bends the ball round the wall?). This tells us that the brain is capable of acquiring 'know-how' *before* it formally understands the theoretical and knowledge rules, and procedures, for what is being executed.

In short, people's ability to articulate the rules which they think are underlying their decision(s), can sometimes be negatively related to their actual competence in execution. So it would be imprudent of the market research analyst to reject a business decision-taker's account of how something 'works' on the grounds that he/she did not first come up with the definitive mathematical proof!

The intuitive analyst tolerates ambiguity, uncertainty and imperfection

Another perspective on intuition is what we know about adopting classically rigorous, as opposed to looser, more impressionistic approaches to problem-solving. There is evidence to suggest that, in certain fields, notably when searching out completely new ideas, we can actually be hindered by adopting a more traditional, scientific-based, conservative attitude to the investigative process. It was the Wright brothers who famously said, 'Science theory held us up for years. When we threw out all science, started from experiment and experience, then we invented the airplane'. The classic approach tells us not to tolerate loose ends and ambiguity in our thought processes. The traditional methods insist on impeccable knowledge and information sources, before proceeding to the next stage of thinking. Yet we are now beginning to understand that this can actually be counter-productive.

There are various examples that show that individuals who are prepared to back hunches on the faintest of whims, and with the minimal level of supporting prior knowledge, have been successful in making key breakthroughs. It seems that individuals who cannot abide uncertainty are often unable to provide the 'good guesses' that, in uncertain situations, would take current thinking forward to the next level, and edge them towards a solution that is just around the corner.

Intuition as one of our multiplicity of intelligences

Over the last few years, there has also been growing acceptance of the idea of individuals having 'multiple intelligences'. Here, of particular note, is the work of Goleman, with his concept of 'emotional intelligence'. Goleman has argued for a rapprochement between more traditional reasoning skills and the world of feelings. In particular – and with reference to intuition – Goleman's work, in reminding us about the multiplicity of intelligence, draws our attention to the notion of 'interpersonal' intelligence (the ability to understand other people and what motivates them), and also 'intra-personal' intelligence (the ability to learn lessons about oneself that allows one to operate effectively in life).

The risk: intuition can be plain wrong

To date, a picture has been painted of the power and subtlety of intuitive thinking. However, in arriving at a way of factoring intuition into the analysis of market research evidence, we must acknowledge that not all intuitive thought will be correct. Prior management knowledge, hunch and intuition will sometimes lead us astray. So intuition can enrich the analysis process, but it can also point us in the wrong direction. So we must remember, as market researchers, that intuition can lead us away from the truth.

After all, the odds on winning the UK's National Lottery with the numbers 1, 2, 3, 4, 5 and 6 are the same as with any other combination of six numbers (one in fourteen million), but how many people will intuitively back away from selecting 1 to 6 as their set of numbers, on the grounds that it will 'never happen'? And, if you win the National Lottery on the Saturday with the numbers 1, 2, 3, 4, 5 and 6, you might as well stay with these same numbers for the next week's lottery. But who would do this? This is often referred to as the 'gambler's fallacy': that is, gamblers often change their numbers on the mistaken grounds that the same numbers will not come up twice. Specifically, the thinking here is that chance is a self-correcting process in which a deviation in one direction induces a deviation in the opposite direction to restore the equilibrium. In fact, deviations are not necessarily, or automatically, totally corrected as the chance process unfolds.

Embracing intuition, but not letting it overpower the data

So, in summary, intuition needs careful handling if we are to incorporate it into the market research process. If we totally resist intuition, then this can stifle our understanding of data. A totally literal, clinical, uninspired reportage of customer data, as said earlier, will often be plain 'dumb'. Without that extra flair, insight, and indefinable 'hunch', the true power of what the data is trying to tell us may escape us. Yet beliefs that are unsubstantiated and unchecked can be 'blind'. So, with business decision-making, clearly it is critical to combine the best of our intuitive thinking skills with the best of what we know about how to rigorously interrogate all of our sources of customer evidence. We need an approach that has its roots in more traditional data analysis, but one that also goes beyond this to look at problems by taking in a range of wider perspectives and contextual insights.

So, we need to embrace intuition, but only by ensuring that we do so in the context of controlled analysis frameworks, with the appropriate checks and balances in place. What we are saying is that intuition is not a mystical phenomenon that sits outside the formal decision-making process. However, it would be unhelpful if intuitive reasoning became associated with flair and creativity, with the evaluation of the customer data being seen as routine and pedestrian. The key to success is clearly to combine informed intuition, with the rigorous scrutiny of our data. As we have explained, if we arrive at a solution by intuition, it does not mean that we have not approached the problem in a disciplined way. So, it is helpful for market researchers to start thinking about intuition operating in a slightly more controlled environment than simply thinking of intuition as spark of genius. In sum, it is helpful to think of the way we operate in both intuitive and data modes.

Thus, if we were to think of some of the great 'intuitive' breakthroughs in science, we often find that it is not just naked, original, off-the-wall thinking, but this originality coupled with a systematic approach to problem-solving. The Wright brothers, as we have seen, threw out the existing science rule book in building the first aeroplane, but their flair was coupled with an incredibly disciplined approach to developing manned flight. They identified each of the variables that needed to be assessed, and then systematically set up experiments to test different executions of each of these critical variables. So their final success was a mixture of tight, left brain logic and lateral, free-thinking, right brain spirit, as they tested the boundaries of conventional wisdom, but in a controlled framework.

Similarly, when we hear of Richard Branson 'intuitively' deciding to pick a particular site in the West End for his first Virgin Record Store, we tend to forget that, before arriving at his final decision, he did actually count the number of people going into the different stores he was considering. So whether he was aware of it or not, Branson was undertaking observation/ethnographic research based around the concept of which store represented the best retail 'pitch'.

The power of operating in both data and intuitive modes

In the above review, we have highlighted the power, when tackling many business problems, of operating in *both* data and intuitive modes. Business problems usually benefit from tight thinking around the data. This provides the necessary clarity and rigour, and helps tease out any surrounding confusion. Often, though, there are also benefits to accompanying this formal line of data analysis with more intuitive thinking. This intuitive thinking can be abstract, incomplete, and even difficult to justify, but invariably, there will be value in accommodating both the data centric and intuitive approaches.

In sum, a combination of disciplined rigorous data analysis and a more playful and spontaneous approach to problem-solving can sometimes generate some serendipitous outcomes. It is this constant process of tightly analysing the data to help find answers and solutions, while at the same time relying on our intuition to help us re-examine the original question and possible solutions, that can pay big dividends. It is this interchange between the data and our intuitive thought processes that lies at the heart of the holistic approach to the analysis of market research data.

So, what we are advocating is bridging the void between the data and hunch with disciplined frameworks for examining issues. Business decision-making does not have to be a battle between pure subjectivity and proven statistical correlation. Today, we have the techniques to place 'intuitive' insights into the context of, for instance, the meta-analysis of consumer trends evident across different markets. And we also have the ability to run 'decision workshops' where we can formally inspect the 'validity' of woolly or prejudiced thinking masquerading as management hunch.

In the last two chapters we have reviewed some of the theoretical principles that underpin the idea of holistic data analysis. Specifically, we have looked at the way the holistic analyst will blend the deductive and inductive ways of evaluating evidence, drawing on orthodox and Bayesian statistical thinking, thereby creating an environment in which management intuition can be sympathetically, but still rigorously, assessed alongside the hard data. We now move away from the theoretical underpinning of our holistic ideas, to look at the first stage of our ten stage holistic data analysis framework: ensuring that the data analyst starts the analysis process by working on the right problem. Get this right and everything else will drop into place.

4   Analysing the right problem

Summary

- It is imperative that the data analyst starts by ensuring that he or she is not just tackling the symptoms of the problem, but the core cause. It is said that a problem that has been carefully defined from all perspectives (particularly when undertaken by a third party) is a problem that is virtually solved.
- This requires a thorough problem-definition process, including clarifying the organizational beliefs that underpinned the articulation of the brief, and establishing the exact way the data will be used at the end of the project.
- Of course, it is essential that the analyst 'puts first things first', and has a clear idea of how to prioritize the research objectives.
- The problem-definition process will also benefit from: making sure that the views of everyone in the 'decision-making unit' at the client organization has had their views taken into account; making an assessment of the likely impact of the research evidence on the end decision; and challenging any points of the research brief that do not seem to ring true.
- The process also benefits from rigorous attempts to understand the full marketing story, and from teasing out the implicit, not just explicit, knowledge that is available on the problem.
- It is critical to make sure that the analyst understands the problem from the perspective of what current related research on the topic is telling us. It is also important to look at the problem, not only from the perspective of the client, but also from the customers' viewpoint. The problem-definition phase also benefits from 'clear deep thinking' about the logic and detail of every argument being raised.

A problem defined is a problem half-solved

The precise nature of the problem being analysed should, of course, have been successfully resolved well before the arrival of the research data. Yet the reality of many data analysis scenarios is that a market research study somehow stutters into existence, without the real core issues of the investigation having been fully unearthed. So, the start point for any data analysis exercise is to ensure that the analyst is not just tackling the symptoms of a problem, but the fundamental issues.

Thus, even though a reasonable attempt may have been made at defining the original problem, there is benefit – at the start of any data analysis task – in spending further time circling around the problem to establish any fresh angles or perspectives that may have surfaced since the study was first commissioned. Here, it has to be reiterated that most intellectual problem-solving exercises – including the analysis of market research evidence – is more a circular, than linear, process. That is, the problem-definition process will benefit from continually revisiting – during the course of the data analysis – the original problem that sparked the call for new evidence.

So, let us now discuss some problem-definition issues that need to be addressed in ensuring that the true problem behind a piece of research has been identified, and on which the analyst can take appropriate action to improve the situation. Specifically, let us look at twelve issues that need to be considered to ensure the data analyst is certain of analysing the right problem.

(1) Clarify organizational beliefs

The dominant culture of the organization commissioning the research often obscures and clouds the process of accurately identifying the 'true' problem underpinning a request for market research. What can happen is that an organization's blinkered and selective view of the world can seriously blur the emergence of a clear definition of the problem being faced by the company. Thus, organizations often end up convincing themselves that their partisan view of the world is the *only* correct one, rather than accepting that there are other helpful perspectives on the problem. So, it is important for the researcher to identify, at the start of a project, what lies at the heart of an organization's true culture. Being able to spot this dominant organizational culture will put the market researcher in a strong position at the problem-definition, and subsequent data analysis, stage of any project.

(2) Start at the end

Successful data analysis requires the analyst to have a clear idea, at the start of the project, of exactly what it is their end decision-making audience expect from the study, and require of the data. Therefore, it becomes important to always ask, at the outset, the 'golden' question. This is, 'at the end of this project, what do you expect to be able to do with the evidence?'.

It is important for the data analyst, when shaping a market research study, to be clear about the way in which they elicit the expectations of decision-makers.

Specifically, it is critical for the data analyst to realize that decision-makers will articulate their expectations in three 'languages':

- *Business decisions*: there is the language of the business decisions that will be made, based on the research, e.g. with the growing availability of mobile phones, should a motoring organization close all its emergency roadside telephone boxes?
- *Research objectives*: others might articulate the problem via the research objectives that the study is expected to answer, e.g. what are motorists' expectations of a roadside breakdown service when they break down at the side of the road?
- *Survey questions*: some decision-makers may articulate the problem from the standpoint of possible survey questions that may be asked, e.g. ask motorists if they are prepared to call us on their own mobile phone if they break down?

Taking a research brief in different forms is entirely to be expected, but there is a danger that the above three (legitimate) modes of communicating a problem can become jumbled in the head of the market researcher. We can then end up with business decision outcomes being translated into inappropriate survey questions asked of respondents, and with the answers to the survey questions – rather than the business decisions and research objectives – being the focus of the final data presentation.

Thus, we could end up presenting motorists with strategic planning options as survey questions that are outside of their frame of reference. We could also end up delivering the final presentation as a series of answers to survey questions about mobile phone ownership, without any attempt to group these questions into clusters of questions that address wider research objectives, such as how 'comfortable' motorists feel about no longer having access to roadside telephone boxes.

(3) Put first things first

It is clearly important, at the problem-definition stage, to ensure that the analysis and interpretation of the data is structured in a way that reflects the true priorities of the project. So, it is critical to ensure that the study has not simply become an endless checklist of 'while you are at it' requests for information, with no attempt being made to prioritize the key issues that the organization wants to understand. Here, it is helpful for the analyst to think in terms of which pieces of evidence are going to make the greatest impact on the decision(s) that need to be made.

(4) A 360° client view of the problem

The counsel of perfection suggests that the market research analyst, at the start of a project, should make sure they are aware of *all* the different perspectives on the problem that exist amongst varying individuals within the organization commissioning the research.

We are all aware of the existence within client organizations of the so-called 'decision-making unit': the mix of individuals who are ultimately responsible for 'signing off' the (agreed) statement of a problem, agreeing the preferred market research design, and later making the end decision. This 'unit' will include not only the ultimate key decision-makers, but 'influencers' who have an opinion on the problem, and also different 'gatekeepers' who have access to pockets of information that could be relevant to the problem-definition process. So another factor that can bedevil the successful analysis of market research data is not having a 360° organizational view of the problem.

Examples of the importance of getting a rounded company-wide view will be plentiful. They will include taking into account the tensions that often exist within organizations, between the 'ivory tower' marketing department and the 'on the ground' sales force, and ensuring that the financial view of the world does not overpower, for example, the human perspective. In large measure, making sure that these types of different internal perspectives on the problem under investigation have been fully explored will be the role of the internal client market researcher. Yet it also is in the interest of the agency researcher to invest time in ensuring that all the different organizational perspectives have been fully fleshed out.

(5) Assess the impact of the research on the decision

It is also important for the data analyst, at the outset of a piece of analysis, to have a clear idea of the likely impact that their research data – as opposed to other considerations – will have on the final decision. In Figure 4.1 we provide

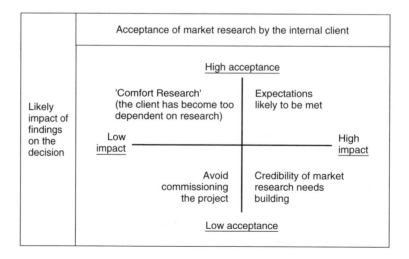

Figure 4.1 – Impact of the market research evidence on the decision.

a summary of some different scenarios, indicating the kind of expectations management that is required in each situation.

(6) Challenge the research brief

There could be merit in the data analyst, prior to the start of the analysis, challenging the client about any aspects of the original brief that seem unclear, or do not seem to ring true. Proactivity by the data analyst at this stage can pay considerable dividends. Below we outline a couple of helpful techniques for 'challenging' a research brief:

- *Clarify any queries by seeking concrete examples*: to tease out any uncertainties you may have and/or any sloppiness of thinking in the initial formulation of the problem, it can be helpful to seek, from the originator of the brief, *concrete* examples of the points, or arguments, that are being made. For example, say there was a reference to the 'salesforce's morale being lower than at any point in the history of the company'. To determine whether this is true or a flawed perception, there could be merit in asking for some concrete examples of exactly how this (alleged) low morale is manifested on a day-to-day basis. This process of 'making concrete' existing thinking and feeding it back to the originator of the problem, is an extremely powerful way of refining a research brief. It brings implicit assumptions out into the open where they can then be examined and challenged.
- *Switch from process-led to problem-led thinking*: it is often the case that the true purpose of the research will be confused by a 'hobbyist' interest in a particular methodology. Therefore, we could find research problems articulated in terms of, 'focus groups are needed to explore X'; or, 'multiple regression analysis will be required to demonstrate Y'. Clearly, the better approach is to explain the problem, and then leave the door open as to whether a particular qualitative or quantitative solution would be the most appropriate. In short, it is important to challenge process-led, rather than problem-led, thinking, in the development of the brief. This can get in the way of an appropriate delimiting of the study, and a sensible prioritization of the research objectives.

(7) Understand the complete marketing story

The data analysis process will always benefit from a full appreciation of the wider hinterland and context to the problem they are about to analyse. So it is important to ensure that no information has been concealed or hidden from the data analyst on the grounds that the *next* research must 'validate' what the organization already knows. The idea that it is sometimes inappropriate to 'release' any existing knowledge on the topic to those analysing the latest study is clearly nonsense. A professional data analyst will always benefit from having a full picture of what is already known, and should be more than capable of not letting this 'contaminate' their objective interpretation of the fresh incoming evidence.

So the experienced data analyst will always check that the context to the problem being presented has been fully, not just partially, outlined. For example, it would be an oversight just to look at research data on UK rail travellers' attitudes towards, say, a new self-serve ticketing machine, without understanding the wider context: the frustrations we know that many feel about not now being able to obtain tickets that operate across different railway companies, and so on.

(8) Tease out implicit knowledge

At the problem-definition stage, it is critically important not only to draw out management's 'explicit' knowledge, but also to tease out all the 'implicit' knowledge that exists in their heads. These tacit insights, snippets of understanding and partial pieces of knowledge, can often be invaluable to the analyst in fully understanding the problem under the spotlight.

A frustrating feature of the way most people explain a problem to a market research agency is their failure to start right at the beginning, with a full contextualization of the issue. In addition, critical observations that are ingrained in the thinking of the teller often remain implicit, and are not made explicit to the person receiving the message. This, for example, explains why most directions are unhelpful. People may tell us to make our way 181 yards down the B1467, but forget to tell us that the house we are looking for is opposite a pickled onion factory that is painted bright purple. Why? Because they have become so used to it.

Some techniques for drawing out implicit knowledge are outlined below:

- *An hypothesis flowchart*: it is helpful to develop an hypothesis about how the particular initiative under investigation may pan out in the market place, and to develop a flowchart of possible different outcomes or scenarios, and to use this decision tree/flowchart approach as a 'prompt' to tease out the client's implicit thinking on an issue.
- *Comparing and contrasting the most and least expected scenarios*: another approach is to encourage end users involved in the decision-making to map out what they consider to be the *most likely* expected outcomes: the most favourable possible scenario in which they might find themselves operating. Then it can be helpful to flip the coin and ask management to pinpoint the *most unlikely*, unexpected, unfavourable scenarios that might prevail. This simple process of setting down, and then comparing and contrasting, the most to least expected scenarios, can add considerable focus and power to the task of teasing out tacit management knowledge.
- *Laddering*: this is a way of making explicit the concepts that sit at the higher levels of our thinking, and are therefore more likely to be important to our

sense of identity. It is an idea based on George Kelly's powerful concept of, in any research study, 'mapping the personal constructs that individuals use to make sense of the world'. Thus, we may, in the beginning, on a study, for example, on attitudes towards vitamin tablets, initially identify comparatively 'small' and obvious issues, such as the price and taste. After 'laddering up', though, we may end up discussing much bigger concepts, such as the importance of high personal energy levels in achieving an individual's life goals, and so on.

- *Teasing out 'telling statistics'*: it is also helpful to tease out, from those involved in the problem-definition stage, what we have labelled 'telling statistics'. These can take (at least) four forms:
  - *The eye-opening contextual statistic*: it is helpful to prime end clients to reveal any key information that will help us to better contextualize the problem. For example, in trying to organize whether or not to offer Air Miles as an incentive in a promotion, it is helpful to know that only a comparatively small percentage of all Air Miles that have been earned are ever redeemed.
  - *The killer defining statistic*: some statistics are critical in getting to the heart of the issue being studied. For example, in a project aimed at promoting, in the UK, classic French novels in the original French, it is obviously important to know that only a tiny percentage of the British population can read French to a reasonable level.
  - *Comparative statistics*: if we learn, for example, that in London, young black men are eight times more likely than young white men to be stopped by the police and searched, this is helpful in setting up hypotheses for subsequent investigation. Here, one hypothesis is that institutional racism is prevalent in the Metropolitan Police, while the other hypothesis suggests that the stop and search rate reflects differing propensities to commit crime among black and white men.
  - *Speculative statistics*: it can also be helpful to check out speculative statistics designed to trigger creative thinking around the problem. For example, recently it was claimed that a core of organizations – that runs only into the hundreds – is responsible for sending the majority – running into billions – of 'spam' emails. This kind of statistic is just the type of data that is likely to sharpen people's thinking. Everyone will be thinking, 'can this really be true?' And this could spur further investigation.
- *Projectives*: it can sometimes be helpful *not* to ask managers to talk about their own concerns about a particular issue, but to 'project' this in some form. At its most simple, this could involve asking managers what they think concerns *other* individuals in their organization about the project, or initiative, about to be researched.
- *The Delphi technique*: the problem-definition stage of certain projects may benefit from employing the Delphi technique. This could help the data analyst to flush out informed views on the problem among individuals closely

associated with this issue. The technique involves asking different 'experts' for their perspective on a problem. The feedback of each expert is then shared with each of the panel of experts who have contributed. Each expert then examines their own judgement, or observations, in the context of what the other experts are saying. The theory runs that this will lead each expert into one of the following two positions:

— An expert could either realize that their original perspective is an outlier, and therefore, in light of the wider contextual feedback, they will adjust their initial position.

— Alternatively, an expert could argue that they have special insights, or privileged information, that means that, although they were an 'outlier', their perspective *is* one that the other experts should now reconsider.

Clearly, there are practical difficulties associated with rolling out the full Delphi technique on every study, but it is sometimes feasible to embrace some of the principles behind this Delphi thinking in an expedient way as part of the problem-definition process. One suggestion here is to distribute, to key specialists on the problem under investigation, a short summary of the range of opinions on the issue, and ask them to comment on each position. These observations could be summarized and then presented to the expert panel, with a call for any final observations.

(9) Take contextual soundings

At the problem-definition stage of a project (and also at the point where preliminary data has begun to arrive back from the study), the holistic analyst will be trying to locate the problem (and/or the early feedback) in the context of what they already know, based on their own past experience, about this genre of problem. They will be locating the incoming evidence within other 'shapes and patterns' that will be familiar to them. This could range from seeing how the new problem fits with recent *ad hoc* studies conducted on a similar topic, through to examining how the new data squares with a full market, or consumer, model that relates directly to the new data. This process could trigger the originator of the brief to sharpen their articulation of the problem.

It may also be helpful to obtain some third party feedback on the (changing) market context in which the client organization is operating. Thus, an organization may feel that it fully understands the major market in which it is operating. However, this belief could be usefully 'tested' by, for example, talking to a small pool of key opinion leaders. This need not necessarily be drawn from the same market, but from related, or near, markets. Their remit would be to challenge some of the prevailing underlying assumptions that have been made about the current situation.

There could also be merit in undertaking some small-scale informal observation and qualitative (ethnographic) research, to see whether the observations being made in the initial research brief and/or the early research findings, 'square with reality'. (For example, observations made in a research brief about the standard of service provided by a hotel chain could be usefully 'validated' by the data analyst sitting in a hotel reception for an hour, and noting the nature of the communications taking place between the reception staff and guests.)

In short, the holistic analyst finds it helpful to inspect each hypothesis cited in the brief against their own existing (albeit possibly prejudiced) prior knowledge, and any available contextual or easy-to-obtain fresh evidence, to use this as a lever to tease out from the problem originator the exact nature of the problem.

(10) Understand the problem from the customer's perspective

Another common problem in successfully undertaking a market research study is the fact that the project may not have been set up based on a full and detailed understanding of the 'customer's world'. Here, we are referring to a failure by the commissioning organization to understand all of the *fine* details of the critical issues that are important to customers. A failure to do this could mean that the analyst will accurately analyse the data in front of them, but will still never truly get to grips with what customers really think. This is because they will be analysing respondents' answers to questions that were slightly 'off-centre' in the first place.

Let us take the example of researching attitudes to the Government's policies on asylum seekers, and also on combating the threat of global terrorism. Here, civil servants and politicians – many of whom are legally trained – will no doubt immediately see a clear and sharp differentiation between the policy of offering asylum to people who have fled particular political regimes, and the altogether separate issue of introducing safeguards against terrorism. Yet it is the researcher's job to go beyond this professional appreciation of the situation, and ensure that they understand how the issue 'plays on the street'. It is the researcher who needs to take responsibility for understanding how the issue of asylum seeking and the threat of global terrorism will be perceived in the minds of ordinary men and women on the 'Clapham omnibus'. So here we know that, for many people, asylum seeking and global terrorism are issues that – egged on by mischievous reporting in the less reputable newspapers – have now become intertwined in their minds. So it is the researchers' job, at the outset of their analysis, to fully understand not just the pure logic of the situation, but the *perceptions* that have been generated in the public domain. In short, the researcher's role is to see the world through the customers', not just the client organization's, eyes.

(11) Apply clear deep thinking

Next, there is a range of thought processes to which the experienced data analyst will subject the problem under investigation *before* embarking on their analysis of the detailed data. These are summarized below:

- *Definitional checks*: it is, of course, important that every concept to be analysed is carefully defined. For example, are 'potential customers' people who have never had *any* dealings with the client organization, or customers who have had *some* dealings in the distant past, but who have lapsed in their recent custom?
- *Believability checks*: it is also helpful to subject the data being advanced in the research brief to a basic 'believability' check. (Remember the well established law: any figure that looks particularly interesting is probably wrong!) So all data needs to be initially scrutinized for potential error.
- *Clarifying ambiguity*: the next check centres on clarifying ambiguity associated with any of the concepts, principles, or arguments being presented. Say, for example, in a study on tourism there was a reference to a survey of British tourists showing that they 'preferred Sydney to New York'. Here, it would be important to establish whether this was a 'comparative' survey of tourists who had visited *both* locations, or whether the conclusion, that tourists preferred Sydney to New York, was based on two 'monadic' surveys (with a higher percentage of Sydney tourists than New York visitors rating the city more favourably on particular dimensions).
- *Flawed reasoning*: the experienced data analyst, at the outset of any data analysis, will also check out any unsubstantiated reasoning that may have crept onto the agenda during the course of the project. For example, there is sometimes confusion about the relationship between the length of prison sentences and crime reduction. Increasing the length of prison sentences may be appropriate as a punishment, but a criminal's propensity to commit a crime is not related to the length of the sentence he might receive if he is caught, but to his assessment of the probability of being caught.

(12) Concealed client agendas

Finally, it would be naïve to ignore the fact that the problem-definition phase of any market research study will, in part, be inextricably wrapped up with various political agendas, including internal organizational personality clashes. There will be individuals in organizations who will elect to deploy research for a range of Machiavellian reasons that are outside the scope of the market researcher's remit. We will all be familiar with the kinds of things that can go on within any organization.

There will be research that is steered towards proving a particular individual's prejudice, rather than seeking out objective feedback. There will also be unnecessary research that is conducted purely to aggrandize an individual's career. There will be people obsessed with various methodological techniques, who let this preoccupation get in the way of more balanced judgements about what kind of research will deliver the best organizational outcomes. And, of course, there will be situations where research will be commissioned simply to delay a difficult decision.

Beyond saying that things like this, that are outside of the data analyst's remit, will happen, and that the market researcher needs to be alert to this, it is difficult to prescribe any constructive avoidance action that might be taken in these situations. However, the simple process of identifying politically motivated agendas can, in itself, serve as a valuable contextual weapon in ensuring that the subsequent analysis and presentation of the data is not undertaken, and delivered, in a naïve way.

In the next chapter, we look at how the holistic data analyst – having carefully defined the 'real' problem – will now review all of the evidence available to them, and decide how to assemble the jigsaw of evidence that will best address the problem under investigation. In short, we look at the way the holistic data analyst will seek out the big picture by making full use of the complete range of marketing information.

Understanding the big information picture

5

Summary

- The start point for the holistic analyst is to step back from the detailed information, and to understand the wider context to the problem under investigation.
- We explain in this chapter how holistic data analysis is a process of moving along the information 'learning curve', gradually building up an understanding of how different types of customer information fit together, in order to answer the research objectives.
- The start point for the holistic analyst is to make an 'active guess' about what their initial overview of the data seems to be telling them. This initial 'purchase' on the problem, will then be validated, by working with various clues, and other anecdotal and archetypal information.
- The next point along the learning curve is to see how this initial interpretation – modified by the informal evidence – squares with the more formal qualitative research evidence.
- The process then continues by looking at what the quantitative evidence tells us about the incidence of the different types of behaviour and attitude reported in the qualitative research.
- The holistic analyst will then take their interpretation one stage further, by setting their data in the context of available customer frameworks and models on similar problems.
- At the end of our learning curve, we arrive at a point where the holistic data analyst will help apply the market research evidence to the decision that needs to be made.

Starting with the big picture and knowing how the evidence works together

Prior to looking, in close detail, at any particular piece of evidence, the holistic data analyst will always ensure they understand the full contextual information picture. Thus, the start point of the analysis process involves assessing, in broad strokes, the overall pattern of the evidence available on the topic under investigation. This reflects three fundamental features of holistic data analysis practice. These are:

- *Always start with the big contextual picture, then go to the detail*: the holistic analyst believes that understanding the full context of any problem is critical to providing a sophisticated, rather than naïve, interpretation of the detailed data. It is based on the belief that, standing back and looking at the overall pattern of the data, *before* getting involved in the minutiae of studying specific information, pays considerable dividends in improving the quality of the data analysis. It is a view based on the power of first understanding the big picture, and only then working down to the specific detail. In short, it is premised on the idea that (usually) 'context explains everything'.
- *Understand, at a conceptual level, the key principles of the way both qualitative and quantitative evidence 'works'*: the holistic analyst also subscribes to the view that professional data analysis benefits from having a strong conceptual grasp of the main methodological principles underlining the way qualitative, and also quantitative, evidence 'works'. Holistic analysis is not just about a specialist (mathematically trained) analyst studying the detailed numerical data, without any appreciation of how qualitative evidence works. Neither is it about a qualitative analyst, with an aversion to numbers, simply concentrating on the qualitative evidence, with these two independent perspectives then never being adequately brought together later. So, the holistic data analyst – to varying degrees – will understand, as a minimum, key concepts underpinning both kinds of marketing research evidence.
- *Know how the different types of customer evidence fit, and work, together*: holistic analysis is based on the belief that it is important to understand the way in which different types of customer data contributes to gradually building up the overall storyline. The holistic data analyst understands how different bits of the 'information jigsaw' can be fitted together to provide the most powerful and insightful interpretation of the available evidence.

Holistic data analysis as a learning process

It is helpful to think of holistic data analysis as a learning process. So here, we explain how the holistic data analyst will gradually progress along a learning curve, working with different types of information, eventually arriving at an informed interpretation of the evidence. (Although, the reality of many analysis assignments is, of course, that the analyst could be joining midway along the learning curve, depending on the evidence they have available to them.)

- *Active guessing and working with prejudice*: what most market researchers do, when first faced with data to interpret, is to begin by making an 'active guess' about what the data means, based on what they already know about the issue under investigation. Thus, the holistic data analyst usually starts their evaluation with some kind of 'prejudice'. They begin with a guess – supported by various existing beliefs – about what the data *may* mean.
- *Making a preliminary evaluation of the 'guess' using clues, anecdotes and archetypes*: the next stage in the learning process is for the analyst to access various clues, anecdotes, archetypes and other snippets of less informal market research evidence, in an attempt to 'validate' the initial interpretation that has been made of the data.
- *Mapping the range of behaviour and attitudes using formal research evidence*: the above preliminary evaluation would then be followed by an examination of what the more formal qualitative evidence is telling us: establishing the extent to which this substantiates, or works against, the initial interpretations based on clues and 'gut feeling'.
- *Measuring the balance and weight of opinion*: next the analyst will examine how the emerging 'storyline' holds up when we look at data that seeks to measure, rather than simply map, the range of behaviour and attitudes on the issue under investigation. So here, we are talking about seeing the degree to which the arrival of the quantitative data reinforces, or changes, the story that had been built from looking at informal and qualitative evidence.
- *Locating the evidence in the wider context of relevant market and consumer frameworks*: the holistic analyst will then locate their data in the context of available market and consumer frameworks. By locating the latest survey evidence, in the wider (normative) context of what we already know, the analyst adds power to their interpretation. It provides the reassurance of knowing that the findings are resonant with what is already known.
- *Thinking about the impact of evidence on the final decision*: the analyst will now draw together their thinking about how the research storyline will impact on the decisions that need to be made. Now is the time to prepare the path for the evidence to be successfully applied.

In the rest of this chapter, we elaborate on the above phases of the holistic learning process. We highlight the way in which a consideration of one type of evidence leads to the evaluation of the next type of evidence, and we say a little about the main methodological principles underlining the different types of evidence used at each stage in the process. Specifically, we seek to explain how the holistic analyst: will work with different weights and types of evidence; get to grips with the key methodological principles underpinning each type of data; and begin to forge together one piece of data with another in arriving at the overall storyline. (We shall illustrate each stage by using the example of a data analyst charged with the task of recommending whether or not a major car manufacturer should be the lead sponsor of a major round-the-world yachting event.)

Making active guesses and advancing 'working prejudices'

The reality of the way in which commercial market researchers operate is that our 'pet theories' or hunches, however flawed they may be, will provide the impetus to start the investigative process. What we then do is start inspecting data to see whether our initial interpretation of the evidence holds up, or whether we need to think again. As we have explained in the context of hypothetico-deductive theory, this means that commercial market researchers rarely set up a null hypothesis, to then set about attempting to falsify this proposition. What they do is make an 'active guess'.

So, the holistic researcher will usually come to the data in the context of some form of 'theory' of how the phenomenon under investigation 'works'. This may be partial, under-developed, and crude in its nature, but it does provide a start point for making sense of the data. The analyst will then, as they work the data, modify this initial working theory, bringing ever more insightful interpretations of what the data means.

Thus, holistic analysis, as we explained earlier, is a hybrid form of thinking that straddles the conventional inductive and deductive methods. It is an abductive approach that reflects the fact that, as individuals, we tend not to observe and then generalize from our observations, in pure inductive mode, to form a theory. What we tend to do is edge deductively towards a crude and partial interpretative theory, constantly modifying our initial theory, in light of the various subsequent evidence and information that becomes available to us. It is an approach that does not start from the ideal of a research investigation being free from any presuppositions about the world. This is an illusion. The commercial market researcher, in fact, does the complete opposite: they start work with what they know.

Using clues, anecdotes, archetypes and prior knowledge

The next point in the learning curve for the holistic data analyst is the process of inspecting the data, offering it up to available theories and interpretations, re-inspecting the data, and circling back to modify available theories, as fresh insights from the data are obtained. Eventually, the holistic analyst will arrive at what they consider to be a grounded and objective interpretation of the evidence. The start point for this process will be to work with various clues, anecdotes and archetypal evidence relative to the problem under investigation. The holistic data analyst will shuttle between their initial observations made on the problem and the incoming clues, anecdotes and archetypes. Throughout this process, the holistic analyst will always be prepared to re-think their initial position, as they constantly review their interpretation of the new data in relation to prior knowledge. So, we can see the holistic analysis process as being about reading the incoming data in the context of available theories, however partial or under-developed, and being flexible in examining how the incoming data might modify the initial theory. At the beginning, the holistic analyst will latch on to any clues, archetypal or anecdotal information, to give them an immediate purchase on the problem. Let us now define some of the terms to which we have just referred:

- *Clues*: commercial researchers, as part of the process of evaluating their initial 'take' on a problem, will start the analysis by calling up various (unsubstantiated) 'clues'. By 'clue', we are referring to a piece of data that was gathered for a different purpose than the one under investigation, but one that nevertheless may provide some insights on the issue we are exploring.
- *Anecdotes and archetypes*: the holistic analyst will gradually assemble 'anecdotal' evidence on the issue. This anecdotal evidence, taken from a few individuals, invariably starts coming together to provide a fairly powerful, coherent story about the topic we are investigating. Thus, by the time data reaches this form, it is more helpful to consider these so-called *anecdotes* as, in fact, providing powerful *archetypal* evidence. That is, a body of evidence that is consistent with other sources of evidence, and is now beginning to help us create some robust sense of the problem we are investigating.
- *Prior knowledge*: this is what we already know about the problem under investigation, outside of the new incoming evidence. Whereas the 'orthodox' statistician seeks to eliminate prior knowledge from the analysis process, the Bayesian school of statistical thought – to which holistic researchers subscribe – takes the view that *ignoring* prior knowledge is very *un*reasonable. Holistic researchers attach considerable importance to comparing the incoming information against what they already know. Seeing where the new piece of data fits with their own prior internal beliefs is seen as a common-sense approach.

Strangely, there has been a marked ambivalence in the attitude of many market researchers to accepting the power of prior knowledge as part of the interpretation process. The practice has, of course, been at work in many on-going, continuous quantitative measurement products for years, under the acceptable guise of applying 'normative data' to the interpretation process. However, in *ad hoc* research, our academic inheritance has inhibited its use, or certainly its explicit use. This is because the hypothetico-deductive method only allowed prior knowledge to be a neutral start point. The final word always had to go to the data. In the classic research tradition, prior knowledge was certainly not meant to act back on the data.

Today, the need to provide clients with *insight* from our, now massive, yet often imperfect, data sources has made us realize the value of utilizing prior knowledge in making sense of data. What seems to have happened in the past is that the management intuition 'probability' was relegated to play second fiddle to the survey data; but this is all now changing. The market research world is now accepting that it is important to genuinely challenge the explicit findings of survey research, by offering this up to the richness of the implicit knowledge of clients' understanding of market trends, and their close day-to-day dealings with customers.

A yachting sponsorship example

We are now going to take a worked example – that we continue at various points throughout this chapter – that explains how market researchers gradually build up the 'jigsaw' of information that will eventually be brought to bear on the end decision. Let us say, a leading European car manufacturer is considering sponsoring a major, single-handed, round-the-world yacht race. Here, the initial active guess may be that, given the fact that the car manufacturer produces engines for boats, there could be some positive synergies at work with such a sponsorship. This initial 'take' could be tested by various clues picked up on by the way the yachting press seem to talk positively about the car manufacturer's prowess in marine engineering. The anecdotal and, building on this, archetypal evidence that would be collected here might include accounts from senior management at the car company, showing that if such a sponsorship was in place, then they could use this as the basis for a major company promotion at key venues around the world yachting circuit. So, this preliminary assessment of internal company and market feedback seems to suggest that sponsoring this event could be a positive move for the company.

Mapping the range of behaviour and attitudes from qualitative research

The next phase of the journey along the holistic data analysis learning curve takes us beyond the archetypal evidence, to reviewing the more (formal) qualitative evidence. Here, we can think of qualitative research as being a methodology for identifying the *range* of behaviour and attitudes that exist on a particular topic. The key characteristic of this phase is that it will access evidence collected as part of a reasonably formally structured, commissioned research exercise, unlike clues, anecdotes and archetypes, some of which might have been collected in a more serendipitous way. The qualitative evidence might include the following:

- *Group interview options*: group-based research techniques, embracing focus groups (group discussions), and also mini-groups, friendship groups, conflict groups, reconvened groups, sensitivity groups, and other group formats.
- *Individual interview options*: the qualitative research could also include the different forms of individual interview. These will range from the hour-long depth interview, through to shorter mini-depths. It could include

semi-structured interviews, tele-depth interviews, paired interviews, accompanied shopping interviews, and a range of other types of one-on-one interview.

- *Other options*: here we could also include, as part of the process of mapping the range of attitudes and behaviour, 'non-participant' and 'participant' observations, and any available desk research and secondary analysis on a particular topic.

The rational and interpretative schools

Before demonstrating how the holistic data analyst will interpret qualitative evidence, we first need to explain the fact that there are two very broad 'schools' of qualitative research.

The rational school

There is what we might label the 'rational' school of qualitative research that is more in the positivist tradition. This research will not be taken to any particular 'psychological depth'. It is based on the premise that there are many issues on which – with sensitive probing – people both *can*, and *will tell*. By this we mean that there are numerous issues on which people are quite prepared, and able, to communicate their attitudes. This school of qualitative research will use various sympathetic probing techniques to build up a picture of people's behaviour and attitudes.

With this school, the emphasis will be on fairly 'conventional' group discussions and 'standard' depth interviews. Typically, the moderator/researcher will employ a reasonably well-structured guideline, and there will probably be an expectation among clients that the moderator will adhere reasonably closely to this guideline. With this type of qualitative research, there will be comparatively little use of various *enabling* techniques designed to help 'open up' the respondent.

The interpretative school

In contrast, the interpretative school of qualitative research seeks to explore, in some depth, how people think and act in the context of their day-to-day lives. This school draws heavily on the disciplines of psychology, anthropology and the best traditions of ethnographic research. The aim here is to go into the territory where individuals are *reluctant to*, or *cannot*, tell. Here, we have to remember that we are not talking about active suppression by people of their feelings. We refer simply to the sheer inaccessibility of certain motives, behaviours and values to many individuals. It has to be accepted that many respondents do not have these psychoanalytical skills to get close to their views, and will therefore need facilitation. Thus, the emphasis here is on understanding the respondent's emotional agenda in the appropriate social and cultural milieu. With this school, there will be quite extensive use of various enabling techniques, based on particular psychological schools of thought.

The pragmatic holistic school

Most holistic data analysts will feel comfortable in working with evidence drawn from both the 'rational' and 'interpretative' qualitative schools. They will analyse both types of evidence applying the principles of grounded theory. That is, the incoming qualitative evidence will be constantly evaluated in the context of our prior knowledge. It is this ability – to scrutinize prior knowledge and, where appropriate, apply it to the interpretation process – that lies at the heart of the holistic analysis process.

The yachting sponsorship example

Our analyst may now have had the benefit of feedback from depth interviews and focus groups that will help with the validation of the initial 'working prejudices', and anecdotal evidence about whether yachting sponsorship would 'work'. This feedback could have been conducted according to the principles of the 'rational' school or the 'interpretive' school. Either way, given what we have already explained about grounded theory, this evidence will provide a robust basis for validating amongst different research audiences (internal management, the yachting community, the purchasers of the company's cars, and so on), just what people feel about aligning the car manufacturer with the yachting event. Specifically, if the balance of opinion in the depth interviews and focus groups, albeit based on small samples, tells us that there are quite strong affinities between the profile of the kinds of people who buy the client's cars and the world of yachting, then we would go to the next quantification phase, not expecting any substantial turnaround of this particular position. So far then, all the evidence seems to be coming nicely together to suggest a 'go' decision.

Beginning to measure the emerging understanding

Once the holistic data analyst has built up a grounded qualitative understanding of the problem, the next part of the journey along the holistic learning curve is to begin to measure, rather than just understand, people's range of attitudes and behaviour. Entering into the measurement process takes us into explaining just how many people are aligned to different types of behaviour, opinions and attitudes. This will include examining the full range of quantitative surveys, ranging from *ad hoc* studies to omnibus surveys, through to continuous tracking surveys. In addition, there is a whole range of marketing and financial data that might be accessed by marketing professionals. When it comes to interpreting this quantitative data, the holistic data analyst can draw on six main bodies of knowledge:

- *Logic and reason*: certain quantitative data will take the form of a census, or full audit, of the particular population, and therefore will not require any interpretation of sampling theory. Therefore, in these situations one of the primary tools of making sense of quantitative data is simply applying logic and (deductive and inductive) reasoning to the data set.

- *Sampling theory*: much market research evidence will, of course, be based on samples, and this requires an understanding of the properties of the 'theoretical sampling distribution'. That is, within what margin of error, and at what level of confidence, can we interpret particular statistics drawn from different sizes of sample surveys.

- *Orthodox statistical tests*: there are, of course, a variety of statistical techniques to help us evaluate numerical data. These range from simple methods of assessing measures of variation, through to other tests designed to assess the relationship between two sets of numbers, and assess the likelihood of differences between various statistics being significant, or simply due to sampling error.

- *Bayesian statistics and thinking*: as we have explained, there is also a body of Bayesian statistics that allows us to factor prior knowledge into the data interpretation process.

- *Empirical knowledge*: statistical theory is premised on the idea of the 'ideal' sample having been drawn but, in reality, this is rarely possible. So, market researchers have built up a body of empirical knowledge about the implications of there being certain imperfections in the research and sampling process. This body of past experience, therefore, allows us to interpret samples that are not based on an ideal set of assumptions.

- *Practical norms*: market researchers can also draw on knowledge that has built up over time about the accuracy of surveys in predicting marketplace behaviour. For example, how robust are survey-based indicators of likelihood to purchase when compared to what happens when a product is launched?

The holistic data analyst will feel comfortable drawing on all of the above bodies of knowledge, in making sense of quantitative data, and will also feel at ease in looking at the inter-relationship between qualitative evidence and the quantitative data, possibly building this into an overall 'model' of how a group of customers (or a market) may behave.

The yachting sponsorship example

Let us say that the data collected on the yachting sponsorship issue included a study of 1000 motorists, with questions being asked about how the image of the car manufacturer 'fits' with the image of yachting. Here, given the strong directional indication from the qualitative research, we would be expecting the quantitative evidence to support the overall theme that has been emerging through the analysis process. Solid quantitative evidence could provide confirmation, which could be important in convincing key decision-makers at the car company – who need hard concrete evidence before committing funds – to find in favour of investing in the sponsorship. The quantitative analysis also opens up opportunities for looking, within the overall storyline, for any particular varia- tions among key sub-groups, such as young people being particularly enthusiastic about the sponsorship, and so on.

Locating the evidence in market and consumer frameworks

As explained in the introductory chapter of this book, one way in which new market research differs from what went before is the access we now have to such a vast array of marketing information within which to contextualize our incoming survey. Yet this point extends not just to the way market research information can now be located in the context of marketing knowledge management systems located within a company, but also to the burgeoning explosion in the mar- keting literature of various bodies of learning – models and frameworks – that help us better understand the context of the issue we are investigating. These frameworks – conceptual models – can range from general descriptive schemas, through to more predictive models that will help us understand the relationship between survey findings and the success record of these types of surveys in predicting actual market share.

This contextualization is helpful in understanding our own markets by allowing us to look up various yardsticks, norms and milestones that others may have achieved. These frameworks are also helpful in giving a horizontal glimpse of how this particular problem plays in related industry sectors. It is also helpful in helping researchers focus on relating the evidence to the decisions that need to be made. Specifically, these models – which give us an understanding of the overall shape and patterns at work in markets and organizations – also help researchers ask questions of an organization, in identifying the nature and extent of limits to possible action.

Should the car manufacturer sponsor yachting?

Going back to our yachting example, we now need to take into account the fact that there is a considerable body of knowledge in the public domain about the effectiveness of different types of sports sponsorship in promoting various categories of company. So, locating our yachting evidence in this wider body of knowledge will be invaluable. For instance, this would tell us how sponsorships usually build over time, indicating that a company would do well to stay with the sponsorship over a number of years, rather than dip in and out of different activities, and so on. This body of knowledge about sponsorship would, among lots more, also alert the company to the risks of sponsoring an individual (whose boat might sink) as opposed to an event (which must have a winner).

Application to the decision process

Throughout the analysis process, the holistic data analyst will have one eye on how the end decision-taker is likely to see the data. They realize that the entire purpose of their interpretative efforts is to improve the quality of the information-based judgements that senior management will be taking on a particular project. Specifically, the holistic analyst will be prepared to assess the 'safety' of putative decisions to be based on what the customer evidence is saying. Moreover, the holistic analyst may, to conclude the assignment, also take responsibility for ensuring that there are no errors in the actual implementation of the research evidence.

Concluding the yachting sponsorship example

It may be helpful to examine the sponsorship decision – is it yes or no – by adapting an analytical framework developed by economists: 'cost–benefit analysis'. Thus, it could be helpful to list all of the *costs* associated with sponsoring the event (ranging from specific identifiable costs through to less clearly definable costs). Similarly, with the *benefits*, we could begin to identify the concrete, measurable, tangible benefits, such as lines of media coverage, through to softer, intangible benefits that could result from sponsoring yachting, such as building goodwill amongst the yachting community. In sum, this cost–benefit framework could serve as a useful decision-facilitation framework to help focus senior management's evaluation of the customer evidence in relation to the 'go–no go' decision.

So we have been across the following stepping stones to arrive at our final assessment: searching for clues; qualitative, then quantitative, research; and then setting the data in the context of available theories and models.

A diagrammatic representation of the holistic data analysis learning curve

As we have explained, by way of a teaching aid, we have presented the holistic analysis process as being akin to the analyst gradually moving along a learning curve. We show this diagrammatically in Figure 5.1. We can see how the process begins with clues, anecdotes and archetypes, and works through different analytical processes, eventually arriving at the application of the evidence to the decision process. Although, for the sake of exposition, we describe this process in a sequential way, in practice, the holistic researcher may, of course, be called in at various points along this learning curve to address a particular problem. In sum Figure 5.1 provides a helpful conceptualization of the holistic data analysis process.

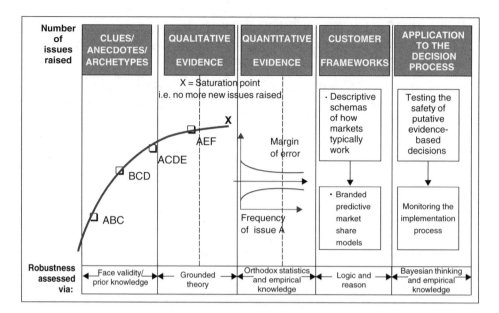

Figure 5.1 – The holistic data analysis learning curve (ABCD, etc. refers to the issues and concepts that are emerging from the investigative process).

In the next chapter, we look at the way in which the holistic data analyst, having identified the jigsaw of evidence available to them on the topic under investigation, will now start assessing, in closer detail, the robustness of each piece of evidence, with a view to compensating for any imperfections at the interpretation stage.

Compensating for imperfect data

6

Summary

- Today's data analyst needs the skills, and confidence, to work with consumer evidence that falls short of the ideal. Experienced analysts know how to harness 'imperfect' evidence to the task of reducing some of the uncertainty associated with decision-making. In short, the holistic analyst needs to know when they must reject data, and when it can be taken forward because – taken in the context of other information – it can still help our understanding of the problem.
- The first port of call for the holistic data analyst in deciding how to 'compensate' for any shortcomings with their data, is to fully understand the context in which the study was conducted, and how this might have impacted the results.
- There are also a range of issues the analyst will need to understand about the representativeness – of both qualitative and quantitative studies – and the level to which what was achieved needs to be compensated for. There is also the issue of the impact on the findings of the choice of data collection method – depending on whether a face-to-face, telephone, self-administered, or online methodology has been chosen. And there is also the issue of the quality of the interview itself: just how good were the interviewers? Were the questions framed and structured in an appropriate way? And were the questions unbiased?
- Next, there is the issue of just how well the study was executed. We may have a near-perfect research design, but one that was conducted to a poor quality standard. Finally, there is the issue of the context in which the study tabulation (results) have been presented.

The compensation principle

Today, there is often an unavoidable gap between the quality of the raw data and the kind of market research evidence to which we aspire. These days, much research will offend against the classic canons of what makes for sound evidence. Studies have to be completed very quickly to enable marketers to respond to changing conditions, and, as a result, quality is inevitably often compromised. Samples now are often less than perfect and the sub-samples less than respectable. Whereas in the past, 'suspect' evidence may have been rejected, today, most data is often taken forward to be part of the overall holistic picture.

New evaluation criteria for a new information era

In the past, this task of assessing the robustness of the incoming research data would have revolved around applying more 'classic' methodological concepts, such as assessing the validity and the reliability of the information. These traditional concepts, of course, remain important to the holistic market research analyst. However, in this new marketing information era, new evaluation criteria are required. These days, what the data analyst will tend to do is to identify potential 'errors' (sub-optimum approaches in the research process), assess whether these shortfalls are critical to the integrity of the data, and then establish how best to 'compensate' for these errors at the analysis and interpretation stage. This is an important difference between the 'classic' way of evaluating the robustness of incoming data and more holistic-based methods.

So, increasingly, the emphasis is on making intelligent judgements about how to compensate for the shortfall. Whereas in the past, imperfect evidence may have been rejected, today we are more minded to take such data forward because we are now learning how to build this into a bigger, overall (holistic) picture. By interpreting a 'suspect' piece of marketing information in the context of several other similar, or related, readings, these days we would carry this less than robust item of evidence forward.

Setting *ad hoc* data in its marketing context

Market researchers have much more immediate access than ever before to a wealth of contextualizing data, available through the Internet and company intranets. In the past, when such contextualizing data were much harder to identify and access, it was prudent to discard all evidence that failed to meet the strict quality criteria of the 'hypothetico-deductive' model of enquiry and the strictures of classical statistics. In this current, information-richer climate, though, data now tends to be rejected only after establishing it as a complete outlier that we cannot corroborate (or triangulate) in any way whatsoever.

Given the mass of contextualizing data available to us – the emphasis is on evaluating data with a view to compensating for any imperfection. In the past, the data analyst's assessment of the quality of available incoming data may have led to the rejection of certain unsubstantiated evidence. Now, with more and more incoming evidence falling into the 'imperfect' category, we have to find ways of compensating, at the interpretation stage, for the kinds of shortfalls that typically characterize different types of marketing data.

The key compensation points

To help in the process of establishing where, and to what degree, 'compensation' is required when interpreting a piece of marketing research evidence, we provide in Figure 6.1 a summary of the key 'compensation points' in the market research process, covering the issues of robustness, execution, and the interpretation of meaning.

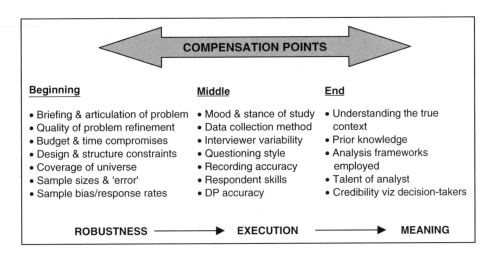

Figure 6.1 – Key compensation points in the market research process.

In this chapter, we shall not be addressing each individual item from Figure 6.1. Instead, we will be looking at eight broad areas – that largely embrace each of the above points – where it is important for the analyst to ask the right methodological questions. In summary, the eight key methodological questions any data analyst should ask are:

(1) Could the context in which the research was conducted have affected responses?
(2) Was the research design fit-to-purpose?
(3) Was the sample representative of the target audience?
(4) Was the most appropriate data collection method used?
(5) How natural was the dialogue with the respondent?
(6) Were the questions asked neutral and unbiased?
(7) Was the study professionally executed?

(8) Have the study tabulations/results been presented (or put into the public domain) from a neutral standpoint, or in a way that might seek to advance a particular position?

(1) Could the context in which the research was conducted have affected responses?

Below, we look at various contextual issues which are important to understand when evaluating the robustness of any piece of marketing research evidence. If the data analyst feels they have a *full* understanding of the nature, and likely impact, of each of these contexts, then the chances are that the data – with a minimum of 'compensatory' interpretation – can be usefully included in the overall analysis.

What was going on 'around' the study?

The first context to explore is, of course, the broader environmental, or marketing, context in which the data was collected. Making general statements about what the analyst should look for is difficult. So let us simply illustrate the overall point with an example from the world of financial research.

Let us assume that we have just learnt that a survey has shown that two-thirds of UK small businesses are in favour of the United Kingdom joining the Single European Currency. Here, we would need to be alert to the fact that a host of bigger picture, 'macro contexts', will have a bearing on the *claimed* level of endorsement from small businesses. These would include: whether the survey was conducted in the context of a recent favourable, or adverse, report on the economic prospects for the wider European Economic Union; whether the survey was taken at a high or low point in the fortunes of other economic trading groups to which the UK is aligned, such as the USA; and a host of other macro contexts, such as whether the euro/sterling exchange rate was plummeting, or in the ascendancy, at the time of the study, and so forth.

How the study was introduced?

The way a research study was 'pitched' could also affect the subsequent results. One issue here is whether or not the survey was conducted on an anonymous or an attributable basis. Some clients assume they can collect the same quality of information when respondents are not provided with an explanation of who will be receiving the results, compared to when the study is attributed to a particular organization. This is it not the case. Most people wish to be helpful in market research, but inevitably they withhold information if they do not know to whom they are supplying it. This is particularly true in business-to-business research, where business respondents are very reluctant to supply information into a vacuum, but may be prepared to do so to a named organization.

The name of the sponsor of the research may also have an impact on the results. For example, with our Single European Currency example, the alignment of a study with a specific political party known to support a particular position on Europe, could, of course, bias the results. Here, respondents may 'exaggerate' their view to 'make a point' to the sponsoring organization.

The wrong agenda

Many surveys fail because they are conducted on totally the wrong agenda. Instead of working in the respondents' world, they go no further than the familiar and possibly atypical world of the researcher. This builds on the point we made earlier about the importance of ensuring, at the problem-definition stage of a project, that we identify the constructs that are driving *customers*' attitudes.

So, when evaluating the quality of the interview-generated consumer data, it is important to identify any mismatch between the way the instigators of the research have elected to shape a problem, and the way in which the respondents actually taking part in the survey are really thinking about the issue. Mismatches between the very real world of the respondent, and the often blinkered world of the person who commissioned the study, can be critical, and will need compensating for at the analysis stage.

The way the questions were framed

Some survey questions fail because the respondent cannot relate to the frame of reference within which the question was originally placed. So, for example, it may be relevant to the police to ask a series of questions of householders about whether their police officers, to help them shape their crime prevention strategy, should focus on car crime *or* house burglary. Yet for an individual who has recently had *both* their car stolen and their house broken into, questions about where the police should place its strategic focus fall largely outside of the respondents' frame of reference. Respondents do not live in the world of how best to effectively deploy scarce police resources. They live in a world of wanting the crime that affects them stopped.

Salience of the line of questioning

Related to, but different from, the above point, there may be questions that are important to the researcher, but that seem to be of little salience to the respondent. For instance, a researcher may seek to elicit precise measurements, that are critical to a research study, from a respondent who has no way of judging why this level of precision is so critical. For example, to a researcher interested in the way small shifts in alcohol consumption may be related to liver disease, a question about how many 'units of alcohol' are consumed each day seems salient. Yet an individual who thinks the study is about leisure, recreation and social drinking patterns may consider that they are being helpful by giving general answers, rounded not to the closest unit, but to the nearest bottle!

The way the questions were positioned

We all know that the way in which questions are actually worded will have a marked effect on the responses given. Later in this chapter, we provide a checklist of the key issues to look out for. However, the positioning of questions, in relation to others in a questionnaire, will also affect responses. So there are a number of contextual issues to look out for here. For instance, the point at which a concept is released in an interview will clearly affect the answers to subsequent questions. For example, if you introduce the idea that mobile phones can now take photographs *before* establishing how satisfied customers are with their existing mobile phones, then this clearly distorts the current satisfaction rating.

(2) Was the research design fit-to-purpose?

Any market research design is invariably the result of a *trade-off* between the 'ideal' way the study should have been constructed, and what is 'practicable'. Here, it is helpful to think of survey design as being a trade-off between the following five key variables:

- What level of precision is required on the survey?
- What depth of understanding is needed?
- What are the practical (and ethical) constraints in undertaking such a survey?
- What timing constraints exist?
- Within what budget must the study be conducted?

Virtually every survey will be a trade-off between these five factors. Thus, every survey design will be less than 'optimum', in that it will depart, to a greater or lesser extent, from the ideal way of researching the problem at hand. So, a key question for the analyst is, to what extent, given the nature of the problem, is the overall structure – the fundamental nature of the survey design chosen to address this problem – fit-to-purpose? In other words, is the data we are about to analyse from a study that comes close to the optimum design? If yes, then fine. If not, how do we now make the necessary compensatory adjustments so we can still make use of this data?

Thus, we could be working with a research design that comes close to the 'ideal' as a way of tackling the problem at hand. Alternatively, we may have a research design that was just slightly 'off-centre', thereby allowing the analyst, at the interpretative stage, to compensate for this shortfall. But we could have a problem to research design 'fit' that reveals a fatal flaw, such that no amount of interpretative 'compensation' will overcome these fundamental weaknesses.

Taking a gamble

For example, let us say we are analysing six group discussions conducted among a cross-section of the UK population, to establish attitudes towards the UK National Lottery. Here, the fact that we have limited representation of the different age, gender and sub-groups, is a concern, but one we could accommodate (by applying the compensation principle) if our research objective was simply to provide some topline feedback on how easy it is to fill out the entry forms. However, let us say our objective was, on behalf of Her Majesty's Government, to address the question of whether the UK National Lottery was corroding the values and morals of our society by providing a segue into heavy gambling. In this case, we would then have to be more circumspect in suggesting that we can compensate for the shortfalls of this small qualitative survey, when addressing this 'big' research objective.

(3) Was the sample representative of the target audience?

In commercial research, the question of whether there has been any drift between those we set out to interview, and those we actually spoke to, is one of the fundamental issues that can affect the quality of our survey information. Thus, it is important to evaluate whether the analyst needs to compensate for any discrepancies between the representativeness we should have achieved on a study, and what actually happened in practice. This is not about sampling 'error' (the error margin) within which we should interpret a particular statistic. This is about whether the study has been conducted with the appropriate audience. So here – in the context of making key 'compensation' decisions – we are addressing the critical issue of 'sample bias'. When we refer to 'sample bias', this is derived from two sources:

- *People who should have been included in the survey but were not*: the first source of sample bias is where the 'sampling frame', that is the list of people from which the sample is being drawn for the study, does not contain everybody who is relevant to the study. For instance, with the most rigorous type of sampling available to market researchers, probability sampling, let us say using the UK's Electoral Register, we will find that this is deficient in listing *all* eighteen-year-olds. This could, of course, be a major problem on a study where the views of young people on, for example, rap music, were critical! Similar discrepancies can occur in quota sampling – another method of sampling used by market researchers – where the research could start off on the wrong foot by using quotas that do not reflect the wider universe, and therefore exclude, at the outset, certain categories of people from the survey (more on this later).

• *Non-response by those who have been included in a survey*: the second type of sampling bias centres on those who were correctly identified for inclusion in a study, but who declined to take part. This type of non-response bias is a major source of distortion on many surveys. Many data users will think that, simply because they have a large number of responses to a survey, they have robust evidence. Yet this large number of responders to a survey could be a highly 'self-selected' sample, one that is not reflective of the overall universe.

Compensating for non-response

In some cases, a small 'drift' between the ideal and the actual respondent profile can be accommodated at the interpretation stage as part of the 'compensation process'. However, other more serious 'drift' – sample bias – may render a study fatally flawed. To help analysts make these kind of judgements, there are some rules to guide us. This relates primarily to *probability*-based sampling; but we can extrapolate out from these guidelines to make judgements about interpreting data drawn from other types of sample. Here, the methodological research conducted by market research agencies over the years tells us that if we want to make an assumption that those who *have* taken part in our survey have similar attitudes and behaviour as those who *have not* taken part, then we should secure responses from at least 65% of our (ideal) target audience. Any shortfall that takes us below this percentage will need to be 'compensated' for at the interpretation stage of the project. (We shall pick up on the issue again in Chapter 10.) In Table 6.1 we discuss representativeness in qualitative research.

(4) Was the most appropriate data collection method used?

We now look at the different data collection methods that are deployed on market research studies, with a view to deciding on the level of 'compensation' the data analyst will need to apply at the interpretation stage. As we all know, the medium chosen for any interview will affect the quality of information provided by the respondent. This is a massive methodological topic, and in the space available, all we can do is provide – via some illustrative examples – some of the issues of which the data analyst must be aware when analysing data collected by

Table 6.1 – The 'representativeness' of qualitative research

The assessment of sampling 'bias' in qualitative research is slightly more fluid than is the case for quantitative survey research. However, there are still certain sampling 'principles' that will help the analyst decide to what extent they can legitimately 'compensate' for any departure from the 'ideal' representative sampling picture. Below, we look at three possible criteria that can be employed to assess the representativeness of a *qualitative* sample.

- *A spread of usage contexts*: we must ensure the qualitative sample covers the relevant usage contexts, or settings, in which the phenomenon under investigation nestles. For example, in researching Internet usage, it is important to understand how the Internet is used both in the work and home setting. Clearly, both these contexts should be reflected in our sampling of respondents for qualitative research.
- *A full distribution of consumer profiles*: our qualitative study should also provide a spread of the different consumer profiles associated with each of the relevant usage contexts. For example, if it is important to include 'heavy' and 'light' users of a particular product, then this should be reflected in the qualitative sample.
- *Reflecting the determining variables*: we should also obtain an adequate representation, in our qualitative sample, of the key determining variables that are critical to shaping attitudes and behaviour on the issue under investigation. For example, if it is known that English-speaking people, who are fluent in another European language, have dramatically different views on the UK entering the Single European Currency from those who do not, then this *dimension* should be factored into the sampling approach chosen for the qualitative research.

each of the main types of interview method. We have also provided some key references in the Notes section.

Face-to-face interviews

Personal (one-to-one) interviewing is an important way of collecting data in the UK, and in some countries they form the only viable, and socially acceptable, data collection method. The face-to-face method is a 'powerful' method of collecting data, given the control it provides the interviewer in being able to interpret the respondent's body language, and to respond to their verbal responses. It is also a method that facilitates the use of various visual aids that can assist the interviewing process.

However, the costs associated with face-to-face interviewing for commercial research, and the expertise that market researchers have now developed in making telephone interviewing so effective, means that, in the UK, only a comparatively modest proportion of market research will be conducted face-to-face. In addition, although the presence of an interviewer can provide a considerable amount of control, we also have to take into account what we know about 'interviewer variability'. That is, two different interviewers asking exactly the *same* question of the *same* respondent can produce different answers. This is because the interaction between the interviewer and the respondent could affect the responses being given (see Table 6.2).

Table 6.2 – Interviewer variability

- We know that on sensitive topics, such as, attitudes towards racial discrimination or sexual abuse, the race and gender of the interviewer asking the questions, could influence the answers given to survey questions by the respondent. And we also know that, even with apparently simple factual questions, there could be an 'interviewer effect'. For example, we know that if a woman is asked how many children she has given birth to, there could, even here, be a different answer, depending on who asked the question. (In certain cultures, adopted children will automatically be included by the interviewer, but in other cultures they will be excluded, and so on.)
- The general point to make here about interviewer variability, is that with the bulk of commercial research, the issue under investigation does *not* require the 'matching' of particular interviewers to certain respondents. The issue with most market research centres less on the personality of the interviewer, and more on the variability with the way in which a survey is actually executed in practice.
- This variability in execution includes issues, such as: the overall capability and competence of the interviewer; the quality of the interviewer briefing; the precision taken in developing the questionnaire; and the comprehensiveness of the inter-viewers' instructions, and so on. Without professionalism and precision in each of these areas, different interviewers could each be asking questions, and coding the answers, in a different way.

Telephone surveys

The telephone is now used for a very high proportion of the market research interviews conducted in the UK. Market researchers have become skilled in developing an interview, in a conversational format, that can be administered without the need to see the respondent. However, there remain certain inevitable limitations, such as possible comprehension difficulties, linked to the fact that respondents cannot be physically shown possible response statements, concepts, or other visual material. So, with telephone interviewing, there is the possible risk of respondents being pushed too far in terms of what they can comprehend and understand. Thus, judgement will be needed by the analyst, about whether the respondents were properly engaged during the interview, or whether they had been pushed into simply giving superficial responses while on some kind of vague 'autopilot'.

One further issue, given what we have said above about interviewer variability, is that, paradoxically, the anonymity of the telephone method may, in certain situations, produce more robust results than the face-to-face interview. For example, there is research to suggest that, rather surprisingly, information about, for example, the number of criminal convictions someone has, is more likely to be reported accurately over the telephone than on a face-to-face basis. It seems that the anonymity of the telephone leads to more truthful reporting than when an interviewer asks the same question of a respondent on a face-to-face basis.

Self-administered surveys

These account for a comparatively small proportion of the market research interviews undertaken in the UK. Self-administered questionnaires, however, can produce extremely robust information, provided they have acceptable response rates. (Here, we need to bear in mind that self-administered questionnaires could be returned by post, or – for example, in the case of employee research conducted at an office – via some other method.) Self-administered questionnaires are effective when they are not used as a 'second-best', low-cost option, but because it is the most appropriate method for the particular situation. (For instance, self-administered questionnaires are ideal for recording food consumption throughout the day as part of a dietary study.)

Where the postal method is limited – over and above the response rate issue – is in the lack of control it affords the researcher. For instance, respondents can read the last question before the first question, thereby denying the researcher an element of 'control' in the release of concepts. This, for example, is particularly problematic when asking questions about awareness – where we need to know 'spontaneous' awareness, and only then segue into a series of 'prompted' awareness questions. So, clearly, 'compensation' decisions will be required in establishing whether the data can be usefully interpreted.

Internet surveys

The Internet is increasingly becoming an extremely important interview tool that has attracted considerable attention. It is a robust way of collecting data, providing the focus of the research is on individuals who are on the Internet (rather than using Internet users to be 'representative' of the entire population). For instance, if we were to stay with our illustration of whether or not Britain should enter the Single European Currency, an Internet survey on this topic would be questionable. Such a study could be biased towards more progressive, technologically-minded individuals who, it could be argued, are more likely to be pro, than anti, European in their outlook. However, increasingly, market researchers are becoming experienced in applying what is called 'propensity

weighting' to adjust an Internet sample to be reflective of the wider population. We discuss this issue in Chapter 10. In Table 6.3 we review the issue of
researching via electronic communications.

Table 6.3 – The psychology of electronic communications

- The use of the Internet for market research raises some interesting issues about
  electronic communication. For example, we know that the Internet has much of the
  informality of the telephone, but it also embraces some of the 'distance' and formality
  of letter writing. So, it is a medium that offers an opportunity to be instantaneous in
  one's response, while also offering the user the opportunity to be reflective. All of
  this is linked into lots of opportunities for frivolity and fun on the Internet. We also
  know that with the Internet comes the opportunity for widespread social interaction,
  but this is coupled with high levels of anonymity, privacy and the opportunity to
  'disguise' oneself. On balance, the evidence seems to suggest that when people
  are in 'Internet-mode', they are less inhibited than in 'real life'. On the Internet
  there is a lower sensitivity to the social and personal constraints on our *normal*
  behaviour.
- The above observations reflect what we know about the psychology of 'Reversal
  Theory'. This tells us that people could alternate between different psychological
  mood states at different times during the day.
- The researcher needs to be mindful that they may find themselves accessing the
  'playful' respondent, but on other occasions the more 'dutiful' respondent. Thus, it
  seems to be the case that Internet surveys, with their non-linear, multi-media feel, are
  more likely to encourage people to switch more quickly than they would do normally
  between these different mood states. The result being that this makes it difficult for
  the survey researcher to know the exact status of the information – attitudes – they
  have captured from someone over the Internet.
- The Internet is clearly here to stay as an interview medium, so the challenge for
  the holistic researcher, when they interpret consumer evidence delivered over the
  Internet, is to be alert to the possibility of bias. If the Internet is going to be the
  way that the next generation communicates, shares opinions, and expresses their
  feelings, then the next generation of 'new' market researchers need to understand
  this, be part of it, and know how to 'compensate', when using the Internet to conduct
  interviews, for any imperfections or shortfalls.

(5) How natural was the dialogue with the respondent?

Shortly, we shall be looking at the extent to which the analyst will need to
compensate for any shortfalls in the way in which the questions in the survey
were worded, but here we step back to look at another critically important
issue, namely, the way in which the dialogue between the respondent and the
researcher has been constructed.

The data analyst needs to establish, at the data interpretation stage, just how
much they need to compensate for the fact that the dialogue (which may have
taken place face-to-face, over the telephone, or via the Internet) did, or did not,

capture how respondents truly feel about a particular issue. Was the interview natural and flowing, or a tortuous and stilted exercise that produced flawed and distorted responses? If there are problems, how do we adjust for this at the interpretation stage?

This is a critically important issue, because many of the problems with market research data centres on its failure to set up a dialogue between the interviewer and the respondent, that does true justice to the respondent's knowledge, feelings, and attitude on the topic. A key issue of concern to the data analyst here is whether or not the interview successfully struck the right balance between 'depth' and 'shallowness'.

For some surveys, or for different parts of a certain survey, it will be legitimate to pursue issues at a comparatively 'shallow' level. For instance, a researcher may deliberately want to tap views in a fairly shallow way, getting individuals' top line attitudes towards particular issues, such as who should be deported from the 'Big Brother' compound. This will be all that is required of the survey in relation to the problem.

In other cases, though, much more depth of understanding will be required to generate powerful and actionable insights. For example, depth is required when looking at attitudes towards the use of genetic tests in setting individual's insurance premiums. So, clearly, a survey that necessitates depth, but that only delivers shallowness, will present a challenge for the data analyst. If we offer a

Table 6.4 – Observation effects

- It is important to be mindful that the viewing of focus groups and depth interviews could affect the respondents' responses. This is not to suggest that the observation of research by clients and end users is to be discouraged. Clearly, it is an extremely constructive way in which end users of data can, at first hand, experience what customers are saying.
- However, the methodological evidence shows that respondents may behave slightly differently when they are being viewed. At the level of common sense, it would be naïve to expect people who are being viewed to behave exactly the same as they would if they were not being viewed. The critical issue, though, is the degree to which this 'research effect' dramatically takes us away from the 'truth'.
- The short answer here is that much will depend upon the topic under investigation. So, if we have small businessmen, who feel very hostile about the way they have been treated by their bank managers, being viewed by bank managers, then we might expect the worst in terms of small business people playing to the gallery to make their point (and another thing...!). Similarly, if we ask people to talk about advertising in front of the people who designed the advertising, we might expect certain, but not all, individuals to play the role of the 'art critic', rather than respond, as we want them to, as 'ordinary' consumers. There will be other scenarios where these viewing effects are less pronounced. Thus, the critical issue is understanding that this phenomenon exists, and in knowing how to make the appropriate 'compensatory' adjustments at the interpretation stage.

rather trivial, shallow line of questioning when depth is required, then clearly, we could be totally misled by our survey feedback.

Thus, striking the right balance between *shallowness* and *depth* in an interview is important. If this is not achieved, we could end up setting up a dialogue with the respondent that is unlikely to truly get to grips with their true attitudes. We shall be a long way away from establishing the 'true story'. Again, the key issue for the data analyst, is 'can any shortfall be laid off – compensated for – at the interpretation stage?' For some surveys, this will be possible, but for others, it could be extremely risky to use such superficial responses, even if skilfully interpreted, to unearth attitudes to a complex issue. For a review of the issue of observation effects, when qualitative research is being viewed, see Table 6.4.

(6) Were the questions asked neutral and unbiased?

There is a rich body of knowledge that alerts us to the way inappropriate question wording could lead to major inaccuracies in the reporting of factual information. In Table 6.5 we provide an overview of some of the 'errors' that may have been introduced into particular question wording that will need some compensation at

Table 6.5 – An overview of how the phrasing of questions may contaminate the quality of survey data

- *Shrouded in ambiguity*: the answers to some survey questions will be questionable because of the ambiguous way in which they were actually worded, e.g. a question asked in a survey on paint: 'When did you last decorate your living room?' Answer: 'Last Christmas!'. Or, 'Do you agree or disagree with the following? 'It should be easier for members of the public to get onto the Council?'. (To 'get onto' means to complain to, and also 'to become a member of'.)
- *Baffling complexity*: answers to questions may often produce questionable evidence because of the inherent complexity of what is being asked of respondents. For example, 'On average, what percentage of your annual income do you spend on petrol (excluding petrol used for your lawnmower, but including any petrol used for pleasure boating)?'.
- *Defies human memory*: there will be other questions where an answer is received, but it is of questionable value, given the feats of memory involved, e.g. 'How many cups of tea have you drunk in the last month?'
- *Makes false assumptions*: some questions will make inappropriate assumptions, e.g. 'Are your two most major current telecommunication suppliers British?' (One may be, one may not be.)
- *Implies standards*: some questions suggest an accepted code of behaviour, e.g. 'How often do you clean your teeth in a typical day?'.
- *Introduces subtle bias*: not all 'leading' questions are blatant, e.g. 'Do you like your job?' will produce exaggeratedly positive responses. It should be, 'Do you like or dislike your job?'.

Table 6.5 – (*continued*)

- *Closes down the respondent's range of response options*: the question, 'What do you think about the local news coverage on TV?' which then gives the following options: want 'more local news', 'less local news', or 'about the same as now', forces the respondent to talk about the concept of 'amount of local news', rather than allowing them to comment on the 'quality of the local news'. So this has steered the respondent in a particular direction.
- *Introduces confusing mind games*: some questions will produce answers from respondents, but ones that we may not feel confident about using, because there is a high probability that the respondent has been confused when giving a reply, e.g. 'Do you agree or disagree with the following: employers should not be compelled to employ the long-term unemployed?'
- *Cast in unreality*: asking respondents hypothetical questions may generate results of questionable value, e.g. 'Would you tell me how much longer you plan to keep your current photocopier?' Or, 'If you won the National Lottery would you consider buying a Ferrari?'
- *Puts respondents in a conflicting dual role*: questions that ask respondents, for example, to 'Imagine you are the Chief Executive of your Local Authority', and then ask them what improvements they would introduce, can provide a useful supplement to questions that simply cast respondents as rate payers. Care, though, must be taken when asking respondents to switch in and out of roles in a survey. This is because we know that when cast in the role of, for example, the Chief Executive, respondents will tend to raise issues of community interest (health, education, and transport). Whereas, when asked for their opinion as a rate payer, their views are more likely to centre around entertainment, recreation and more hedonistic pursuits. So, switching the respondent in and out of different roles can create some very difficult-to-interpret feedback about what the priorities for a community should really be.
- *Uses emotive wording*: this can range from the outrageous, 'Do you think that the menace of drug taking requires tougher legislation?', through to the slightly more subtle, 'What do you think of the military?'. (The term 'military' clearly carries a certain amount of 'baggage'.) In both scenarios, loose emotive wording can get in the way of obtaining balanced feedback from respondents.
- *Leads the respondent towards an outcome*: and finally, some questions are, of course, clearly overtly biased: 'Most people think that National Service is a good way of making young people more disciplined, do you agree with this?'. Here, the analyst will probably be minded to reject the responses to such a question, rather than attempt any form of compensation.

the analysis stage. Specifically, we list 12 areas that need to be carefully reviewed prior to interpreting the responses to a survey question.

Particular care must be taken by the researcher when assessing attitudes. This is a wide-ranging topic, but it is helpful – as a minimum – for the data analyst to have an appreciation of some of the key principles about how attitudes 'stretch', and might be appropriately 'grouped'. In other words, the data analyst will need to be knowledgeable about the use of attitude scales in market research. Without this knowledge, there is a danger of naïvely interpreting survey responses. In Table 6.6 we provide a review of some of the principles behind the development of attitude scales.

Table 6.6 – Types of attitude scale

- *Nominal scale*: such scales are ordered, but there is no suggestion of any relationship from one point on the scale to the other. Let us take the example of establishing the importance of distance, relative to other factors, in the choice of a supermarket. So a nominal scale could be:

  Example:

  Which of the following describes your reasons for usually shopping at Supermarket X?
  - The price of the goods
  - The quality of the products
  - The distance from my home to the supermarket

- *Ordinal scale*: such scales have ordered concepts, but will not have points on the scale that are equidistant.

  Example:
  - I would always go to the supermarket nearest to my home, rather than one that had the cheapest prices
  - I might consider travelling to a supermarket that was not the closest, but only if the prices were particularly low
  - I am prepared to travel some distance to get a really good deal at a supermarket

- *Equal interval scale*: this is a scale that attempts to position one point reasonably equidistant from the other.

  Example:

  I want you to tell me how much you agree or disagree with the following statement: 'Distance from my home is the most important factor in the choice of supermarket'. Do you. . .
  - Strongly agree
  - Slightly agree
  - Agree
  - Neither agree nor disagree
  - Disagree
  - Slightly disagree, or
  - Strongly disagree?

- *A ratio scale*: here, the idea is to develop a scale where it is possible to mathematically draw comparisons between different points on the scale.

  Example:

  Please tell me, for each of the following types of goods, the furthest distance in miles you would be prepared to travel to a supermarket to purchase these types of products. . .
  - Grocery items
  - Clothing
  - Household goods

(7) Was the study professionally executed?

Surveys are a rough and tumble, less than perfect affair. During the course of most surveys, many pragmatic compromises – trade-offs – will have to be struck to complete the survey on time, and within budget. Once again, this issue centres on the degree to which these executional shortfalls in quality can be compensated for at the interpretative stage, as opposed to flaws that suggest the evidence should be rejected. The full list of quality control checks that the analyst may wish to deploy is long. In Table 6.7 we provide a list of ten key telltale signs that may alert the data analyst to the fact that there may be a question mark over the robustness of the data they are studying.

Table 6.7 – Ten telltale indicators of a 'low quality' survey

- *A big number stands out in the overall pattern*: remember the rule: 'any figure that looks particularly interesting is probably wrong'. So always go back and check.
- *The rows do not add up to the total sample*: if the cross tabulations, e.g. gender, age, socio-economic group, etc., do not add up to the total sample, this could indicate sloppiness in the overall filtering regime employed in the survey. This will need checking.
- *The columns never add up to 100%*: it is always worth establishing why a column of figures does not add to the declared base presented of 100%.
- *'Lost' respondents*: each of the following is a distinct and different outcome to a survey question: 'not asked'; 'don't know'; 'none'; 'refused'; 'other answer' and 'not answered'. A failure to keep track of the difference between each of the above is an indicator of loose professionalism – from data collection through to data tabulation – in the execution of a survey.
- *Unexpectedly high 'don't knows'*: if the proportion of a sample answering 'don't know' to a question is in excess of 20%, there is a prima facie case to suggest that the question has not 'worked'. Clearly, in a test of general knowledge, high levels of 'don't know' responses might be expected in response to difficult questions, but on survey questions aimed at assessing an individual's behaviour, or their attitude towards events with which they are familiar, the above 20% rule is a useful guide as to where there *may* be problems.
- *Too many 'other' responses*: as a general rule, if the proportion of respondents having their answers to an open-ended question coded as 'other' (i.e. an unspecified answer) exceeds 10%, then there is a case for examining whether there was a flaw in the original question and/or a less than rigorous approach taken to the development of the coding frame.
- *Percentages used on small bases*: the general convention is for percentages only to be used on bases of 30 respondents, or more. (This follows from the central limit theorem, namely that with samples of 30 or more, it is safe to assume that the sample approximates the normal distribution, and therefore the principle of confidence limits can be applied. Below 30, 'small', rather than 'large', number statistics apply.) So, beware survey practitioners who break this convention.

(continued overleaf)

Table 6.7 – (*continued*)

- *Inconsistent logic*: the experienced researcher will also immediately be able to spot fundamental flaws in the 'logic' of a survey. For example, in a study where we know that 50% of the total sample have a car, we need to check that at least 50% of the sample are 17 years of age or over, given that this is the minimum age for an individual to hold a valid driving licence. We know there will be some people driving illegally, but we do not expect any wholesale inconsistencies, with the proportion of drivers being far less than the number of people over 17. If there are, this will need checking.
- *Unexplainable sub-group variations*: the experienced analyst will also be alert to where the pattern of results for a particular sub-group (or sub-set) within the data does not fit with how variations on the total theme *typically* 'work'. We elaborate on this in Chapter 7. But, in most surveys, the sub-group analysis simply refines the overall story. It is true that, occasionally, there will be a completely different story playing itself out within certain sub-groups. However, given the fact that this is comparatively rare, the experienced analyst will immediately be able to see any 'strange' variations in the data set that will then need double-checking to establish whether or not this is a 'legitimate' variation.
- *Unusual patterns*: the experienced analyst will also know, from 'prior knowledge' of how surveys 'work', how answers tend to play out. Let us take the example of questions on how satisfied people are with their mobile phones. Here, experience tells us that one manufacturer's mobile phone is not that dissimilar from another. So one would expect levels of customer satisfaction with different brands of phone to fall within a reasonable range. If this is not the case, there is reason to investigate why this unexpected survey result has appeared. This experience also comes from knowing about the internal 'workings' of typical distributions of opinions obtained in surveys. This would include, for example, knowing what variation it is reasonable to expect in the pattern of responses from one *interviewer*, in relation to the next, and also what variation is reasonable to expect from, say, customers of one retail outlet to another. So, in sum, the experienced analyst will be alert to 'patterns' that do not, in broad general terms, conform to some of the 'general principles' on how survey responses are typically distributed.

(8) Have the study tabulations/results been presented from a neutral standpoint?

It is clearly important for the data analyst, in making sense of the information in front of them, to be aware of the different angles from which the data they are about to analyse has been presented. These perspectives could include the following.

Presented to 'promote' a particular position

There will be scenarios where research will have been commissioned by a particular lobby group, and will, to varying degrees, be presented in a way to 'accentuate' a particular position. This is not to suggest that the research evidence, *per se*, will be manipulated, but it certainly could be presented in a selective or partial way. An example of this might be research evidence collected by the cigarette lobby and presented in a way to give a certain legitimacy to the cigarette industry. So clearly, the analyst needs to be alert for the possible selective presentation of research findings.

Presented in soundbites

In a world where there is increasing pressure to communicate one's message in minimalist 'soundbite' form, there is the danger of the research being misunderstood. The stripping away of explanations of the context in which the data was originally collected, can reduce our understanding of what the message is really about. Paradoxically, by cutting out so much context, it makes it more, not less, difficult for the reader to understand exactly what the research is saying. So the data analyst needs to be alert to the need to search out key contextual information to fully understand the evidence that is being presented.

Presented in a naïve way

Another shortcoming that the data analyst must be alert to centres on data that is presented in a naïve way. For example, it could be a piece of analysis that has failed to get behind some of the key drivers of behaviour and attitude, and provides only a superficial explanation of the data. For instance, a report may suggest that people in a particular region like a product more than people in another region, failing to realize that this is not, in fact, a regional difference, but simply a feature of marked gender differences between each of these regions.

Relevance to the present

A further issue centres on evidence being presented as relevant to the present that may not be topical and generalizable. This is not necessarily a simple linear matter of progressively rejecting information as it falls more and more out of date on the time criteria. Clearly, some information is very time critical in this simple way, but other information may contain key concepts and principles that have a strategic value that will hold good over time.

So the critical question centres on the extent to which the information is still relevant to our strategic understanding. For example, a study conducted in New York, on attitudes towards airline security pre-September 11th, will clearly now have been totally overtaken by events. However, a study conducted, at a similar time, on New Yorkers' attitudes towards, for example, using the subway, as opposed to private transport, may have only been marginally affected by events.

Table 6.8 – An illustrative example of the compensation principle

Data	Issue	Compensation
• Face-to-face survey of small and medium sized enterprises (SMEs) who are part of a federation of small businesses	• Possibility of over-representation of SMEs who belong to a particular political party	• Identify, possibly from Internet sources, attitudinal survey data for all SMEs and compare, on key attitude dimensions, the SME federation sample with wider-based attitudes
• Internet survey of small businesses	• Under-representation of less technologically orientated businesses	• Classify issues where more leading-edge technology skills could be an influence, as opposed to other more common generic issues where technological leadership is less of an issue
• TV programme with invited audience of pro and anti European small businesses	• Self-selecting sample organized by media to reflect the 'extreme' positions of attitude	• Identify issues where there is resonance across the pro and anti groups, while also attempting to locate data for the 'silent majority'
• Low budget telephone sample of small businesses	• No records kept of exact response/strike rate, possibly leading to significant sample bias	• Profile telephone sample against data on the entire small business population, identify gaps and develop hypotheses about implications of any under-representation of key groups, e.g. small businesses that undertake international research and where the owner/managers travel extensively in Europe, and, as such, may not have been included in the telephone research study, but could be pro European, etc.

Therefore, the former evidence would probably have to be rejected, but the latter, with some adjustment (compensation), could still be used at the analysis and interpretation stage. A simple example of compensation is provided in Table 6.8.

Having understood the character and imperfections of our data, and made the appropriate compensatory decisions, the next step for the holistic data analyst is to develop the analysis strategy, as a prelude to organizing their qualitative and quantitative evidence. We look at this next stage of our analysis framework over the next three chapters.

7 Developing the analysis strategy

Summary

- The next stage of our model – developing the analysis strategy and organizing the qualitative and quantitative data – is the subject of the next three chapters of this book.
- We realize that the holistic analyst will often be dealing with the above activities simultaneously. But for sake of exposition, it is helpful to allocate a chapter to organizing the analysis strategy, and to follow this with separate chapters on organizing the qualitative, and then the quantitative, data.
- We start by outlining the importance of the data analyst developing a detailed analysis strategy that specifically demonstrates how the business decisions to be made will be addressed by the particular analytical approach chosen.
- We explain the holistic approach to data analysis as being akin to the principle of the Hermeneutic Circle. This is a powerful concept in understanding the way in which holistic market researchers, in making sense of evidence, will study the detailed evidence in relation to the whole, and the whole evidence in relation to the detail.
- In sum, we explain the power of first trying to understand the picture for the total sample, and only then looking at variations by sub-group, given the fact that most sub-group analysis of market research data only 'refines' the main story, rather than 'suppressing' other substantial variations of this central storyline.

Developing an effective analysis strategy

We start this chapter by running over general good practice principles to adopt when preparing to analyse any data set. There are, of course, points of difference in handling qualitative and quantitative evidence, but it is possible to lay down some universal holistic data analysis principles (see Table 7.1).

The Hermeneutic Circle: studying the whole in relation to its parts, and vice versa

The notion of the 'Hermeneutic Circle' is a powerful concept in understanding the way in which the holistic market researcher makes sense of their evidence. Hermeneutics was originally concerned with deciphering the meaning of ancient manuscripts. The approach considers the way in which meaning is derived, and an interpretation reached, based on a process of studying parts in relation to the whole, and the whole in relation to its parts. It is a process that can be seen as an analytic flow, moving back and forth between the abstract and the concrete.

The Hermeneutic Circle process starts with the interpreter's initial grasp of the whole text, the detailed reading of which, in turn, can lead towards a revision of the original overview. This dialogue between reader and text then proceeds through various iterations in a circular process, eventually arriving at the final 'valid' interpretation.

The big picture grounded in small detail

The 'validity', referred to above, is a reflection of the way the researcher ties together the small details of what was being reported with the abstract ideas, conceptualizations and models that, over the years, have sought to explain the phenomenon under investigation, such as, what we know about consumer behaviour. So here, validity is about the way our big picture and small detail understanding is grounded each in the other. It is, in effect, an iterative process of 'abductive' and 'inductive' reasoning.

Of course, contained within the concept of the Hermeneutic Circle, are all the tensions of whether the researcher, when adopting such a process, could be accused of closing down their conclusions too early, as opposed to keeping the interpretative process open, as they go through another iteration of data inspection, evaluating the detailed evidence in relation to the whole.

This takes us onto the issue of the analytical techniques and processes that the professional holistic data analyst will introduce into their evaluation of qualitative and quantitative evidence, in order to ensure that sufficient checks and balances have been introduced into the process of seeking out new insights, while at the same time, staying true and close to the data.

Understanding what makes the decision-makers tick

Another key general principle of effective analysis is to start the process with a precise understanding of the exact expectations of the end decision-makers. Specifically, it is worth reviewing what kinds of data are likely to be of particular interest to different individuals within the 'decision-making unit'. Ask yourself:

Table 7.1 – Some essential differences between the way a qualitative and quantitative analyst will work

- The principle of the Hermeneutic Circle will inform the way the holistic analyst will approach both qualitative and quantitative data. With both kinds of evidence, there is a commitment to shuttling between the big picture and the detail. The goal is to see how the understanding of the whole changes our appreciation of the detail, and how our mastery of the detail refines our understanding of the whole. However, as the qualitative researcher will invariably have personally collected (some of) the data they are analysing, not surprisingly, there are points of difference in the way in which a qualitative and quantitative researcher will work.
- Thus, when it comes to constructing the big picture – identifying the total sample storyline – the quantitative researcher has the advantage of being able to quickly access the statistics for the total sample. In contrast, the qualitative researcher's initial thinking may be dominated by their direct data collection experiences, and it may take time to see how this initial 'take' squares with other colleagues working on the same qualitative assignment.
- Switching to mastering the detail, as part of the Hermeneutic process, the qualitative researcher is, here, at an advantage. Given their closeness to respondents at the data collection stage, they will be able to 'compare and contrast' one respondent against another, to tease out fine detail. In contrast, the quantitative researcher will be forced back to using various statistical measures to understand some of the finer, possibly critically important, determinants of variations in attitude.

do they have any particular angles of interest?; is there a high expectation of the data producing some kind of unique insight?; what are the particular types of evidence the decision-makers will most want to see? You should also identify data that is likely to leave the end decision-maker confused or uninterested, even though it may be true. This line of thinking is important in ensuring that your final analysis and 'storyline' is concrete and focused, rather than naïve and abstract, and is appropriate to the target audience. So, on completion of this task, you will know what data is absolutely critical to answering a specific marketing issue, as opposed to information that is, at best, 'nice to know'. In addition, you will be well placed to start thinking about strategies for handling the questions that different types of decision-maker could be asking about various types of evidence.

Linking the business goals to the data analysis objectives

As part of the problem-definition process, you will already have clarified the business outcomes, research objectives, and established, in general terms, how these relate to various survey questions. Now is the time to take this thinking one step further and to identify your *precise* analysis objectives. For example, you will need to be clear that, to effectively answer a key business objective, you must address various research objectives, which in turn will mean putting the analysis focus on a particular combination of survey questions.

From this review, it is possible to start building up an understanding of how the data from different questions are likely to come together to begin to build an 'answer' – storyline – that will address the key decision outcomes. At this stage, the analyst will also benefit from reflecting on how they will begin to advance their arguments – tell the story – from a *combination* of statistically significant data, and evidence that may not be statistically significant, but that is, nonetheless, logically sound and supported by prior knowledge.

Know the details of your data set

Having already familiarized yourself with what kinds of data address different research and business objectives, you must now move beyond this to master the detail of your evidence. So, it becomes important to spend some time gaining an understanding of your data set(s), in close detail. You will need to know, for example, what types of sub-group analysis are available for each line of questioning. You will need to clarify the bases for various statistics (always bearing in mind the need to watch out for changing base filters in the survey). You must also be aware of the 'basics': which way the percentages operate (row or column), and so on. And make sure you are totally clear about the difference between the 'none', 'not answered' and 'don't know' categories. As discussed earlier, you must also be absolutely certain about the exact context that lies behind a question, in addition, of course, to being clear about how the wording of the question may have impacted on the responses given.

First apply common sense

Having clarified the end client's decision outcomes, prepared your analysis objectives, and familiarized yourself with the details of the data set, the next step is to begin to place some *initial* interpretation on the data. Here, it is always worth starting with the 'believability test'. Thus, when first inspecting your data, ask yourself the following key questions: did you expect this finding?; do you believe it intuitively?; would you feel confident explaining it?; what other data supports this argument?; and, what are the key sources of disbelief? (the research design employed, the respondents' ability to articulate their views, sampling difficulties, questionnaire design, data processing errors, and so on).

It is also important to remember that focusing purely on the data – without understanding the real world – can send the analyst down a totally inappropriate path. So keep giving your initial interpretation of the data a 'reality check'. Factoring in what you already know about this particular issue – taking into account your own prior experience of this genre of problem – will be invaluable in moving you up the holistic analysis learning curve. Working with what you already know, as a jumping-off point for getting into the data, is entirely legitimate: it will *not* contaminate the objectivity of your overall analysis.

So, in sum, it is entirely legitimate, when first getting to grips with the data, to start applying a simple 'common sense' approach to the interpretation of the data.

Beginning to identify and understand the main patterns and relationships

Before beginning the process of analysing the data in close detail – remembering the Hermeneutic Circle principle – it is worthwhile, while in a preliminary overview analysis mode, to look for any broad patterns and relationships that are emerging from the data. Here, it is helpful to look at how, for example, any attitudinal differences may, or may not, correspond with behavioural differences. Now is the time to also examine whether there are similarities where you would have expected to find differences, and so on. All of this will be helpful in beginning to compare and contrast how different competing putative storylines in the data may be building up a picture in your own mind about what this data is saying. You may wish to begin to follow up on any aspects of the data that you feel are unlikely to be accurate, by searching out any corroboratory evidence. At this point, you will also be able to make an initial assessment of whether or not your data is going to be able to meet the initial research objective (possibly by setting in train calls for extra, more detailed analysis to plug any gaps).

Establishing what the total sample story is telling you

Having understood the overall relationships at work within the data set, it is now time to start laying down the fundamental story that is being told by the data. As a general rule, the 'story' behind most survey data can be told round the total sample (assuming it is representative). So, when beginning to analyse any data set, it is helpful to quickly move to a position where you have established the storyline for the *total* sample. That is, at this stage, do not worry about analysing variations within the different analysis sub-groups. Simply concentrate on studying your total sample data in relation to your overall analysis objectives. Then, see if you can tell yourself (in five minutes) the *overall* storyline for the total sample that is emerging about the problem under investigation.

A helpful tip here, for a survey research study, is to write on the questionnaire the results for the 'total sample' (without worrying at this point about any sub-group variation). Then, working with a photocopy of the questionnaire (showing the total sample), 'cut and paste' (group together) the questions that seem to answer the various analysis objectives. In this way, you are beginning to create a 'story' that could form the running order of your final presentation or report. This is clearly preferable to the rather naïve approach of simply reporting the answers to all of the questions, in the order of the questionnaire.

Refine the main storyline with the sub-group analysis

Having understood the overall total sample storyline, it is now time to begin to understand what is happening in the sub-groups. Most sub-group analysis tends only to *refine* the overall storyline. Rarely are the sub-groups suppressing a totally different storyline that needs telling for different sub-groups. Most sub-group analysis simply adds a variation to the overall theme. Rarely does this overall analysis lead to the necessity of telling a series of multiple sub-plot stories

- There is a statistical technique called Chaid (Chi-squared Automatic Interaction Detector).
- This technique is helpful in ensuring the analyst does not fail to detect the key determinants of attitude or behaviour by not properly structuring the sub-group analysis. Thus, it could be that an analysis of the total sample by a *separate* cross-break for age, and a *separate* analysis break for gender, may fail to unearth differences of, say, *age within gender,* that are critical to telling the true story.
- The Chaid technique, by systematically examining the 'distance' between every possible combination of sub-group, will alert the analyst to where they are missing key insights
- Chaid takes a given dependent variable (the one you want to be able to predict), and a set of independent variables (the ones you want to use to predict the dependent variable), and develops a flow chart according to how strongly different independent variables seem to explain differences in the dependent variable.
- For example, if we wish to examine the variations in the number of fiction books read each year by the total population by age and gender sub-group differences, the final outcome of the Chaid analysis might look as follows:

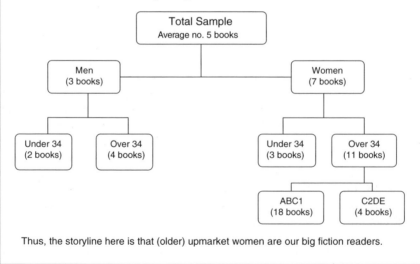

Thus, the storyline here is that (older) upmarket women are our big fiction readers.

Figure 7.1 – The Chaid technique for analysing sub-groups.

that are at complete odds with the total sample. (This can, of course, happen, but not in the majority of scenarios.)

Here, with quantitative data, a useful rule of thumb is to quickly establish what differences will be needed between, for example, two key sub-samples, for there to be any statistically significant variation, and then to scan the data only looking at data that is distanced by the requisite percentage points, or more. So, if you had two key sub-samples of 200 each, you would go looking for differences of *at least* 10% points, or more. (In the Notes section we identify a source for checking the significance of the difference between two sample statistics. And in Figure 7.1, we summarize a technique for analysing sub-groups.)

Holistic data analysis as successive waves of analysis at varying levels

So, to conclude this chapter on the general principles of holistic data analysis, a picture is emerging of the holistic analyst being involved in successive waves of analysis. The first wave will concentrate on establishing the fundamental patterns and shapes emerging from examining the total sample in fairly broad strokes. The next wave of analysis will put the spotlight on the detail. Specifically,

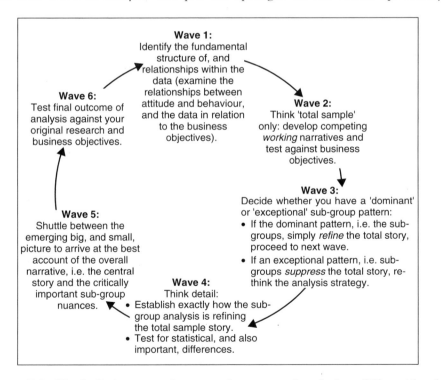

Figure 7.2 – The holistic approach: successive waves of analysis at different levels.

the emphasis here will be looking at whether the analysis of the sub-groups follows the *dominant* pattern of simply refining the overall storyline, or whether we have an *exceptional* case, whereby the analysis of the sub-groups reveals contradictory sub-plots that are being concealed (or suppressed) by our focus on the total sample. (If it is the latter, then we will have to take a different approach to telling the research story.) In Figure 7.2 we provide an illustration of the different iterations in the holistic data analysis (Hermeneutic) process.

Having reviewed the general principles of data analysis, in the next chapter we look at ways of organizing qualitative data.

Organizing the qualitative data

8

Summary

- We start by reviewing the various frameworks of thinking that will inform the way in which qualitative researchers, from different schools of the discipline, will broach the task of analysing qualitative data.
- We then look at some qualitative analytical techniques for understanding the big picture, while also providing opportunities to drill down to analyse the close detail.
- We then briefly review the options for physically handling and organizing different types of qualitative material: the transcripts, tapes, notes, etc.
- Following this, we look at ways of presenting verbatim comments, and at ways of using various graphical devices when summarizing and communicating qualitative evidence.

Three levels to organizing qualitative data

There are three levels to the task of organizing the qualitative research prior to analysis. First, there is the issue of deciding on the overall *framework of thinking* that will be employed. Secondly, there is the question of the *analytical method* that will be used. And thirdly, there is the specific approach to be taken when actually *handling,* sorting, and making sense of the various types of qualitative material – interview notes, tapes, transcripts, and so on. We examine each of these areas below.

Frameworks of thinking

Not surprisingly, the two broad approaches to qualitative data collection that we discussed earlier – given that qualitative data collection and analysis are so intertwined – also form the basis of the frameworks of thinking that inform the analytical process. To recap, we outline these two frameworks below:

- **Rational:** this approach to qualitative research is close to the scientific (or positive) model, and is a style that will use comparatively few projective or enabling techniques. The emphasis is on interpreting the responses to fairly direct qualitative questioning with sensitivity and insight, but without recourse to any particular psychological model that will drive the analysis process.
- **Interpretivist:** this school may elect to draw on specific psychological and/or analytical models in making sense of the evidence, including the following approaches:
  - *Freudian models*: some may broach their analysis applying the Freudian paradigm. The 'pure' use of this psychoanalytic theory is comparatively rare these days in market research; but the techniques derived from this analytical paradigm, notably 'projection', are still widely used. Another Freudian framework, around which some researchers from the interpretivist school may elect to structure their thinking and analytical approach, is the notion of Transaction Analysis (TA). This has its origins in Freud's division of the personality into superego, ego and id. In TA, personality is seen as containing the three ego states: parent, adult and child. (The 'parent' contains instructions, moral codes, and should's and ought's; the 'adult' ego state evaluates and acts on information; and the 'child' is the home for playfulness and creativity.)
  - *Neurolinguistic programming*: other qualitative analysts may elect to focus their analysis framework around the concept of neurolinguistic programming (NLP). This can be helpful on studies where the researcher needs to understand how people absorb and process communications and information. NLP is a framework that helps us to understand that people see things from the following different positions:
    * In the first position, people see things from their *own* point of view.
    * The second position involves seeing the world from the point of view of the *other person* in the transaction.
    * The third position means stepping outside the situation and seeing issues from the point of view of a *third party*.
    NLP reminds us that people receive information in various sensory channels: the visual, the auditory, the kinaesthetic (perception of movement of effort) and the digital (mathematical or reasoned thinking). The idea being that people use all of these modes, but may have a preferred mode.
  - *Ethnographic approach*: this takes its cue from observing how people behave in more natural settings, rather than placing the emphasis on collecting information in a research setting. So, the commercial ethnographic analyst will place considerable importance on fully understanding the marketing context in which an individual is playing out their behaviour (and expressing their attitudes). The ethnographic school of data analysis has a long tradition in social research, and is now popular again with commercial market researchers. Although the commercial application of

ethnography will fall some way short of the total immersion, over long periods of time, demanded by social research.

For most *holistic* data analysts, the dominant framework of thinking adopted for the analysis of qualitative evidence will be a fairly eclectic and pragmatic one. It will be one that will be sensitive to each of the various analytical schools of thinking discussed above. Thus, it will reflect the rational school, through its rigorous interpretation of the hard consumer data. However, it will also show awareness of the value of subjecting particular types of evidence to various 'interpretivist' treatments. In sum, on any specific problem, the holistic data analyst will elect to choose the most appropriate framework for thinking, rather than being a devotee of any one specific framework for thinking.

Analytical approaches used by the holistic school

The main analytical process in understanding qualitative research, as explained earlier, is one of going back and forth between the overall picture under investigation, and the details of the data. It is the idea of developing a rolling hypothesis that is constantly being checked against the available data, concepts, and principles. Thus, the holistic analyst, in looking at qualitative evidence, will start the analysis process by immersing themselves in the data, noting, as they do so, any big 'thoughts'. They will then circle through the data again, picking up any small clues that help verify the first 'big' idea, while also beginning the process of identifying the next 'big' thought.

We now explain this analytical process in more detail, dividing this task into two categories:

- Looking at ways to help the analyst get to grips with the 'big picture'.
- Examining techniques to help the analyst study the 'detailed' qualitative evidence.

Mapping the big picture

The best analysis strategy is to first identify the evidence that has the biggest impact on the key issues and decisions to be taken. So we start by looking at some techniques to help the analyst of qualitative data quickly get to grips with the 'big picture'. This is the process of identifying the overall storyline, and beginning to compare and contrast themes emerging from different sub-groups. The analyst is beginning to select information for its relevance, making decisions about which information is going to be central to the final presentation of the data, as opposed to evidence that will play a less prominent part in advancing different arguments.

It is at this stage of the process that the analyst will be looking for inter-relationships, shapes and patterns, or alternatively discontinuities, in their qualitative evidence. At this point, the analyst will also be searching out metaphors that may help throw light on the analysis and/or be locating the data in the wider context of available models that explain some of the dynamics, relationships, and generalizations at work.

To achieve this goal of understanding the big inter-relationships and patterns at work within the data, it is often helpful to prepare some form of 'cognitive' map or some other kind of 'visual display'. This technique, of which there will be numerous variants, is designed to graphically map the inter-relationship between attitudes, behaviour and different individual characteristics and/or look at the inter-relationship between the different elements within the analysis. The above approach could start by constructing such maps for individual respondent case studies, and could then build up to become a composite account of how groups of respondents seem to be responding.

An example: small businesses' attitudes towards entering the Single European Currency

For an illustration of the 'cognitive mapping' technique, we have taken the example of a qualitative study, aimed at assessing small and medium sized businesses' attitudes towards the UK entering the Single European Currency.

In Figure 8.1 we have itemized the key features of 'one' managing director's attitude towards the UK entering the Single European Currency, and then mapped out how some of the major attitudinal themes link together. The cognitive mapping technique is a useful way of plotting the story for an individual. It can then be developed to provide an account of 'clusters' of individuals with similar attitudes.

There will be various ways of actually constructing a cognitive map. In our approach, comments in bold *squares* are 'factual' observations; comments in *circles* summarize respondents' expressed attitudes; observations from the analyst appear in *octagonal boxes* in italic typeface; and the *thickness of arrows and dotted lines* can be used to link together different emerging themes and ideas, and to convey their comparative intensity.

Here, we can see the way that this particular managing director is essentially pro-European, but carries a number of anxieties about a decision that could have a major impact on his business, and the way he is perceived by working colleagues in Europe.

Analysing the detail

At the same time as understanding the big picture – following the principle of the Hermeneutic Circle – the analyst will also be examining the significance of different detailed findings. There is a wide range of techniques for exploring the detail in qualitative evidence. Some qualitative researchers will simply 'absorb' the detail by close study of the respondent's comments. Others will use specific

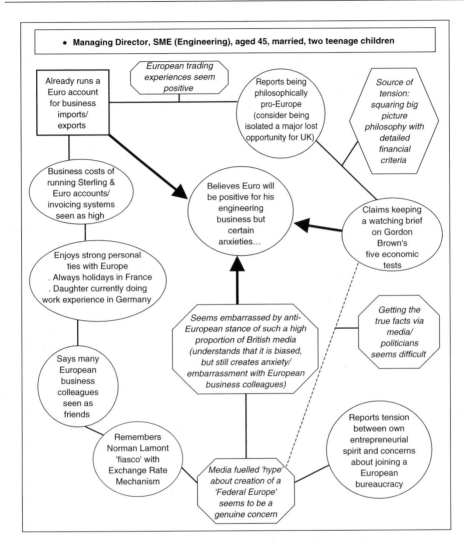

Figure 8.1 – A diagrammatic summary of the attitude of the managing director of a small engineering business towards the UK entering the Single European Currency.

techniques, including various counting techniques and content analysis. We outline these approaches below:

- *Content analysis*
    - Based on prior knowledge, and a preliminary overview of the themes coming through in the transcripts – *en route* towards preparing a cognitive map or some other summary – the analyst will draw up a framework of the issues and concepts that may emerge in this project.

— The analyst will then attempt to identify, from the transcripts (and/or by listening to the tapes), words, phrases, and other content, that provides support (or not, as the case may be) for the different pre-prepared ideas and concepts in the analysis framework.
— As this process continues, the analyst will adapt the initial framework to accommodate new concepts, ideas, and principles that emerge through successive waves of detailed analysis.

In Figure 8.2 we provide an example of how a content analysis may be constructed to look at the issues associated with the use of genetic testing information by insurance companies when deciding what insurance premium to charge people who represent different health risks.

• *Counting*: some qualitative researchers favour counting mentions of a particular piece of behaviour for different sub-groups, or a frequently expressed attitude, in order to highlight a particular point. For example, in a study on attitudes towards healthcare over the Internet, it can be helpful to actually count particular observations made by different age and gender sub-groups, given that we know use of the Internet for online healthcare varies considerably among these categories.

   Thus, to pursue the Internet healthcare example, it would be helpful to analyse the replies in the following groups: young working women; women with young children; men in full-time work; and retired men. For each group, specific references to the following ways in which the Internet can be used for healthcare would be recorded:
   — Looking on the Internet for *general* information on healthcare.
   — Searching the Internet for *specific* information about a particular illness.
   — Identifying information on how to *prevent* a specific illness.
   — Seeking out information on a specific illness, with a view to providing a *cure*.
   — Using the Internet to *purchase* prescription drugs.
   In short, specific groups can be identified and precise attitudes and types of behaviour pinpointed, with the incidence of these being 'counted' across the transcripts, with this information appearing (possibly in a matrix grid) in the final presentation.

Here, we need to note that many qualitative researchers are often reluctant to actually count the various references to different activities mentioned by varying categories of respondents. Instead, many qualitative researchers favour making general references along the lines of, 'the majority of respondents took a particular view', or by noting a 'greater prevalence of a particular view among a certain sub-group', and so on. Ultimately, the decision about whether or not to 'count', and cite this in the final presentation, will depend upon the project. On the one hand, obsessive counting seems unnecessary, when a broad indication of

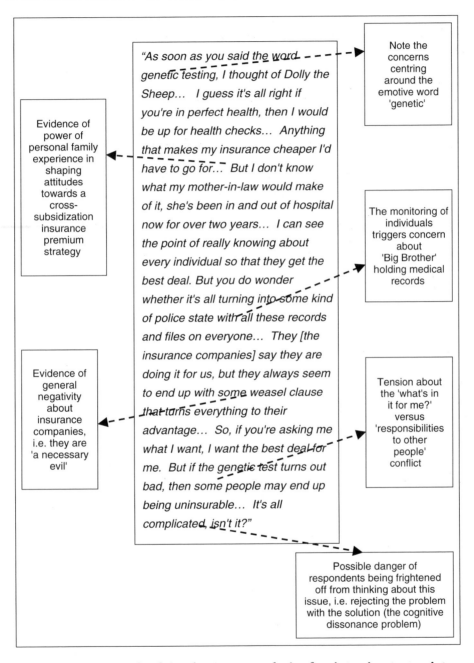

Figure 8.2 – Example of simple content analysis of an interview transcript.

the majority of opinion would have been quite sufficient. Yet in other scenarios, loose, impressionistically gained statements about the quantity of support for a particular viewpoint, may be counter-productive. For example, in an interview about the effectiveness of using a celebrity to sponsor a particular product, it may be helpful to count exactly how many times the celebrity's name was mentioned by the respondent during the course of an hour-long interview.

Processing the qualitative raw material

We have established that the holistic data analyst – following the principles of the Hermeneutic Circle – will constantly be switching between sorting the detail of a point and generating schemes and conceptual frameworks that explain what, in overall terms, is happening. The holistic data analyst will constantly be attempting to understand the detail, fit this into the whole, and then modify the whole to accommodate the details. This process will continue until they feel they have arrived at a grounded 'resolution' of what the data is saying.

However, the exact way in which different qualitative researchers will *physically* process the various forms of qualitative evidence in the above way will vary dramatically. The precise way in which the materials are handled will be personal from researcher to researcher. The actual handling process is, after all, only a tool. Different analysts will use procedures that work best for them on a fitness-to-purpose basis. Thus, for example, those analysts who are good at simultaneously absorbing the big picture *and* the detail, will place less reliance on detailed methods for annotating group discussion transcripts to capture the detail. Whereas those who are stronger on seeing the whole, but may struggle to remember the detail, may require more elaborate annotating systems for capturing detailed 'quotes' to be used at the reporting and presentation stage. So it is clearly inappropriate to lay down tight prescriptions about what constitutes good qualitative 'materials handling practice'. It is helpful, though, to look at the kind of material that is in the qualitative researcher's toolkit, and briefly review some of the handling options. (See also Table 8.1.)

The raw material of qualitative research

The various types of *qualitative* research raw material used could include the following:

- Audio recording of groups/depth interviews.
- Video recording of groups/depth interviews.
- Transcripts of the above.
- Notes made *during* the focus groups/depth interviews.
- *Post*-group/depth interview notes.
- Comments and observations made by clients (and/or research colleagues) attending a group.

Table 8.1 – Recent evidence on techniques used to analyse qualitative evidence

A study conducted by Dolan & Ayland sought to examine the effectiveness of three types of qualitative analysis. They referred to these as: holistic and interpretative; cut and paste; and computer-assisted qualitative data software:

- The holistic approach involved the researcher reading the entire transcript, writing interpretative thoughts in the margin, and annotating the script en route. Here, the emphasis was on the research: identifying patterns and relationships, beliefs and assertions; studying how language, terminology and descriptions were used; and looking for areas of consistency, commonality and convergence. There was no specific prior coding, or cutting and pasting, of material with the holistic interpretative approach. (It is an approach associated with Glaser & Strauss's idea of grounded theory, described earlier.)
- The cut and paste approach involved the researcher starting with a framework of codes, and then allocating segments of text to codes within this framework. The approach involves breaking (cutting) the transcripts or tapes down into segments, and allocating these comments to codes or themes.
- The computer-assisted qualitative data analysis software approach is similar in principle to the cut and paste approach described above, but with text retrieval software programs, such as Discourse Analysis, being used to identify themes (what is being said about a particular theme by different kinds of respondents, and in what way).
- The study concluded by highlighting the power of the holistic interpretative approach because, unlike the other methods, to quote the authors, 'it identified additional important findings that were missed by both the cut and paste and computer software methods'.
- The computer software approach was recognized as offering the discipline of precise coding, and the subsequent linking of codes, but was seen as, 'no substitute for the thoughtful prior human encoding and intelligent analysis'. The research also identified a role for the cut and paste approach, but only on the pragmatic grounds that 'sometimes a fast turnaround was needed and that this may be appropriate on more structured qualitative projects, where there was not much variability between different types of respondents'.
- So, in sum, the holistic approach was seen as offering the important benefit of ensuring that each interview is considered as a whole, rather than as a set of discrete responses. In contrast, the cut and paste and software methods, which first involved coding the data, were seen to effectively discourage the analyst from thinking in terms of the whole of the interview, and instead, concentrated the analyst, in a micro way, on attaching codes to particular segments of data.

The handling options

Notwithstanding the above caveat, about the way qualitative material is handled being personal to the researcher, it is helpful to provide a short checklist of some of the options open for handling the qualitative material:

- Some analysts may opt for a process of total immersion and reflection on the topic, supported by listening (repeatedly) to group discussion or depth interview tapes (usually – but not always – making notes as they do so).

- Some will prepare, after each depth interview and group discussion, a set of notes on the main issues that arose, and use these notes as the basis of the analysis. This would include possibly preparing summaries of individual interviews or groups of interviews in the form of variants of the cognitive map, outlined above.
- The use of detailed typed transcripts of group discussions/depth interviews is also extremely popular. Analysts will then make use of various marginal, and other annotational, mechanisms to record significant 'big picture' and 'micro-points' emerging on each page. Again, here some will make use of various summary techniques, such as cognitive maps, to record the overall storyline, while also possibly using various counting mechanisms to look at the detail.
- Some researchers – working individually, in pairs or in teams – may 'brain dump' from memory their observations and recollections of their participation in the qualitative research process.
- Others will literally cut and paste sections of the transcripts, sorting and arranging them under headings that relate to the key research objectives spelt out in the research brief/proposal.
- Some will place the emphasis on quantification, and will, from the out-set, construct data grids or matrixes along the lines explained above in terms of content analysis and counting, to assemble concrete facts under different headings.
- Some may use statistical software to help with their analysis (although this is currently not widespread among commercial qualitative market researchers in the UK).

Presenting qualitative evidence

The way qualitative material is displayed is, of course, an integral part of the analysis process itself. It is the way the analyst starts to explain the data to themselves. Yet these various display mechanisms – matrixes, cognitive maps, and various tabular accounts – also, of course, form the basis for the way the data will be presented to the end decision-maker. However, invariably the matrixes used during the *working* process of understanding the qualitative data maybe too elaborate for the purposes of the final presentation of the storyline. So, in this last section on the organizing of qualitative data, we focus on the subject of how to adapt working matrixes to display evidence in an impactful way to support the qualitative-based storyline. We start with the role of verbatim comments.

The 'rules' on the use of verbatim comments

There are some general rules about the presentation of verbatim comments (often called 'quotes') in commercial research. In most market research studies, the way language is used is clearly important. But this usually falls short of needing to conduct an etymological and/or syntactical analysis of the way words have appeared, and been used. Commercial market researchers clearly need to take into account the way in which individuals will discuss brands, taking care to examine the language that is deployed. Yet this is different from, for example, a social research project conducted among people with a language-based learning disability. Clearly there is a need here to pay very close attention in the reporting of verbatim comments. For instance, with this example, a long pause in an answer being provided, or a sentence that was started and then withdrawn and replaced with an alternative opening, could be important. This should therefore be recorded on the transcript and be explained, with the appropriate labelling device, within the verbatim comment itself.

Thus, for most commercial research, it is generally accepted that the analyst will judicially edit the verbatim comments, to avoid unnecessary repetition and deviation, while also changing any words that have obviously been used in error by respondents. It is also common practice to link together different short extracts taken from a longer verbatim comment. Here, where there has been a gap in what the respondent has said, it is the convention to explain this by the use of (three) connecting dots. In commercial research, however, other linguistic conventions, for example, to indicate that there had been a particularly long pause in an opening reply, or to signal a sentence that was unfinished, and so on, are not generally used, at least at the final presentation stage.

This procedure, after all, is close to the precedent that is followed in Hansard's editing of the comments made in the Houses of Commons and Lords by MPs and Peers of the Realm. Thus, somewhere in Westminster, there is an editor charged with eradicating the solecisms of our less than articulate representatives, while still communicating the essence of the point being made, and also defending the principle of freedom of speech!

Differing ways to deploy verbatim comments

Verbatim comments can be used in (at least) two different modes during presentations (or reports):

- *To instantly communicate the extent of a viewpoint*: to demonstrate the quantitative extent of the support for a particular line of argument, the analyst may want to list a large number of fairly bland repetitive, and not particularly revealing or distinctive, individual quotations. The central point being made here is that the analyst did not have any difficulty in locating lots of evidence to support a fundamental point. For example, the analyst may want to demonstrate that, although this was a qualitative study of only 30 respondents, over 25 of them raised substantial problems in understanding how to, let us say, operate a particular digital camera. So, here, the analyst may list eight or so similar comments, that send out the signal that 'there are lots more where these came from'.

- *Getting over the intensity, or depth of feeling, on the issue involved*: an alternative approach to the use of verbatim comments is to apply them more sparingly to demonstrate the intensity of feeling that is felt by respondents on a particular issue. So, there could be a scenario whereby only a minority (numerically) were dissatisfied with, for example, their new mobile phone. Those who were dissatisfied, though, had experienced a number of deeply frustrating and irritating experiences. The data analyst will want to demonstrate these by choosing carefully selected 'quotes' that colourfully communicate the passion behind much of this user angst.

The display of qualitative data

Some of the techniques outlined above for analysing qualitative data, as indicated, could be used in the final presentation of data. However, it is usually helpful for the holistic data analyst to go one stage beyond this, and develop representations that attempt to conceptualize key issues, thereby better telling the overall storyline, while still conveying the colour of respondents' raw feelings, with the use of verbatim comments.

In Figure 8.3 we return to our example of an insurance company assessing attitudes towards the idea of using genetic tests and other past medical data as a basis for setting insurance premiums. The challenge here is to convey – by way of a one-page summary – how individuals feel about the price of their life and health insurance being based on the *personal* risk they pose to the insurance company, or whether individuals should be expected to be involved in some form of *risk pooling* (or cross-subsidization) of risks, given that a policy of rewarding those without any health risks could result in a two-tier society, with some people being uninsurable.

In the next chapter we look at ways of organizing quantitative data.

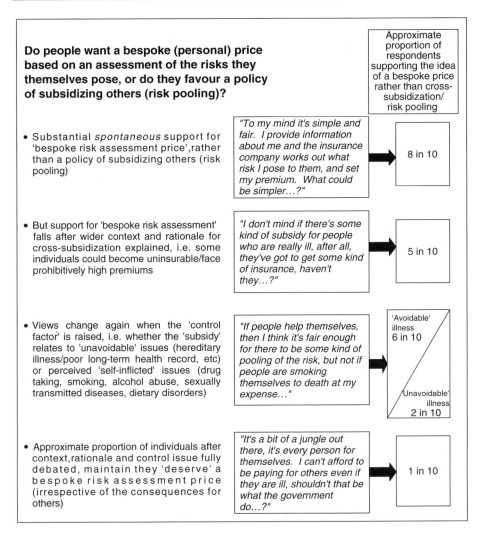

Figure 8.3 – A representation to show how attitudes towards the idea of using medical histories (including genetic testing information) in the setting of insurance premiums change as the implications of the respondent's initial position are explained.

Organizing the quantitative data

9

Summary

- We start by looking at various techniques for making quantitative data easier to absorb and understand. Specifically, we provide a ten-stage guide to some key data reduction principles.
- We then provide an example of how many of these data reduction techniques work in practice, starting with a mass of fairly incomprehensible data, and working through a series of simple data reduction principles, to arrive at an informed understanding of the original data.
- We follow this with an overview of the hierarchy of data analysis options that are available when examining a data set. Specifically, we take a data set, and start by demonstrating how simple techniques, such as the application of cross tabulations and the use of various measures of location and variation, enhance our understanding. We then move up our hierarchy, looking at how our understanding may be further aided by introducing various other analysis techniques, such as trade-off (conjoint) analysis and the application of segmentation analysis.
- We conclude the chapter with some general principles for the analysis of quantitative data.

Data reduction

In making sense of quantitative data, it is important to reduce the material to a form whereby it becomes easier to make intelligent judgements about its meaning. This process of organizing quantitative data prior to analysis, by reducing a mass of computer tabulations down to more manageable proportions, is often called data reduction.

Here, a useful general tip is to work on the basis that the final table (or graphical display) that you are constructing, should be instantly self-explanatory. Somebody who knows absolutely nothing about the background to the study or the survey, should be able to look at the table and, given the way you have laid out the data and described its different components, be able to arrive at – in seconds – a sensible interpretation of what this information is telling them.

Below, we provide a summary of ten key data reduction techniques, although, in practice, many of these stages will be undertaken concurrently.

- *Cutting the sheer data mass*: at the heart of data reduction is the goal of reducing the absolute amount of numbers on the page.
  - This could include *rounding* percentages to the nearest decimal place (unless the whole study pivots on the first decimal place, which is very rare in most market research studies).
  - It could also include cutting the data mass by *grouping* various rows or columns that are not, in themselves, differentiating between the different categories, and re-presenting this as a combined group. For example, if there is no difference between North East and North West London, then this could be grouped as North London to save one column of data. Here, careful attention needs to be paid to adding together percentages from different-sized bases; this will, of course, involve re-percentaging, rather than simply adding percentages together. Similarly, care needs to be taken when combining percentages from questions where respondents have been invited to give multiple answers. Clearly, in making statements about the percentage of *respondents* who mentioned item (a) *and* item (b), we need to be sure we have de-duplicated the data, i.e. one respondent may have mentioned both items (a) and (b).
  - We could also use various averages or other *summarizing* measures instead of the full distribution. Here, a word of caution – often it is the distribution that tells the story in market research, rather than the bland column average. So, it is important not to go a bridge too far in presenting purely measures of location (mean, median and mode), rather than giving the reader a feel for the pattern of the overall data.
- *Selective use of data*: a further port of call with data reduction will be to make decisions about 'dumping' unnecessary data that does not support the main arguments on which you are focusing as part of your analysis strategy. This can take the form of:
  - omitting some data completely, and/or
  - making decisions to present certain detailed evidence in some supplementary form, possibly in an annex or appendix.

  It is difficult to provide general prescriptions on which data to select and which to reject, beyond outlining the value of working through the general principles of professional data analysis outlined in Chapter 7. These pivot around knowing how each piece of data fits into your overall analysis strategy: how it works to support the emerging storyline.
- *Reordering and restructuring columns and rows*: an alternative to actually combining rows and columns of data is to consider ways of reordering columns and rows from the way they may have initially appeared on the

computer printout. At all times, try to restructure the data to best tell the reader the (emerging) storyline. The options here include:

— Reordering the columns and/or rows of data shown in the original computer printout in a more logical and/or impactful way. As a general rule, the dominant subject, for example the brand, should be the row, and the sub-group variation, e.g. region, should be the column.

— It may also be appropriate to reorder columns and/or rows to present the story in terms of numerical highs to lows (or vice versa).

— There could also be merit in reordering columns and/or rows into a sequence that better fits the topic under investigation, and the emerging storyline. For example, the original computer printout may list complaints about a hotel in a fairly random order. Yet there could be merit in grouping these complaints into broad categories, such as problems with the hotel reception, difficulties with car parking, and so on, from high to low or low to high.

- *Adding clarity via improved labelling*: the aim here is to instantly tell the reader what the table is saying. Using simple words to summarize complicated data all helps add clarity. These small interventions will all add to the ease with which the end data user can make sense of the information. There are a number of options here, including:

— Re-labelling the overall title of a table, so that it is impactful and totally self-explanatory, is a useful starting point. (For example, not 'A forecast of the likely number of cars on UK roads', but 'How many more cars?')

— Re-labelling the (working) titles of individual columns and rows (and also any sub-totals) more in line with the emerging storyline can also be effective.

— It is also important to ensure that all the bases for percentages are carefully and precisely described

— And it is critical to make sure that there is total clarity in terms of labelling the following three scenarios: (a) 'don't know' – i.e. this being a positive response to a question; (b) 'not answered' – i.e. the person did not give an answer to the question, but did not categorically say they did not know the answer to the question; and (c) where the question was not asked at all, because these respondents were filtered out. (Remember, there are also the 'none', 'other', 'refused', and some further problem responses to sort out too.)

- *Re-percentaging to highlight a point*: it is also helpful to examine the data and make decisions about whether a particular point can be better made by re-percentaging the data on an *alternative* base:

— For example, a study conducted among the entire adult population on their attitudes towards the National Health Service may benefit by removing from the analysis all individuals who have had no direct experience of the National Health Service over the last ten years, so as to

sharpen up the salience and impact of some of the positive and negative points that are being raised
— There is a tendency for some data to be presented by reflex, with the percentage sign (incorrectly) on the column, rather than (correctly) on the row. This can be another source of 'noise' and confusion for the reader. So it is important that the percentage sign (%) tells precisely which way the percentages actually run: whether this is column or row.

- *Taking out unnecessary noise*: the computer printout may contain technically precise data which, in practice, paradoxically could introduce some noise: comprehension difficulties. Included here are:
  — Column and row percentages being 'rounded' by the computer – sometimes to be more or less than exactly 100%.
  — The bases for the different sub-groups may not add to the total sample because some respondents, from which the sub-group was derived, did not answer the question.

All of this creates unnecessary noise for the reader of the table, and decisions need to be taken on how to address this. One approach is appropriate editing (that is, making small adjustments to take out the noise and irregular-ities – perhaps with a footnote somewhere in the presentation, or report, to explain the principles adopted). The other option is to make it clear to the reader what has happened by providing precise definitions. Either approach is acceptable. What is less acceptable is letting this noise from the original computer tabulations stay, in the vague and lazy hope that it will not affect the reader's comprehension of the data.

- *Imaginative use of design devices that aid comprehension*: in crafting a well-constructed table, the analyst should be mindful of various design devices that can be deployed, in a consistent regime, to improve clarity. These can include:
  — The use of 'white space' to separate columns and rows.
  — The use of bold and dotted lines to separate out, for example, the total sample from sub-groups.
  — The use of different types of typeface, ranging from bold to italics. For example, using bold type to always indicate a summary of the question that was asked of respondents, and italics being used for 'not answered' or 'don't know'.
  — The use of tinted and coloured panels to differentiate parts of the table.

- *Devices to signal key data*: the analyst can use icons and symbols in order to draw attention to particularly critical data. For example, circles, squares, arrows and the shading of inset panels, can be used in parts of the table to draw attention to particularly important information. It is also possible to introduce short verbal summaries of particularly complicated data to reduce the data mass.

- *Clarifying special cases*: there will be certain data scenarios that need particular attention. For example, care needs to be executed in a workplace survey, where the data could be presented as a proportion of all *employees* at business establishments, and also on a base of total *establishments*. Similarly, there could be scenarios where *weighted* bases are being used. Here, it is important to indicate to the reader, at some point in the table, both the unweighted and weighted bases.

- *The table/graphical display composite*: increasingly, with the availability of more sophisticated computer graphics packages, there is the option for the data analyst to use devices for the presentation of tabular data that are a hybrid between the table and graphics. In the next section – where we provide a worked example of data reduction in practice – we provide some illustrations of such graphics. We also return to the issue of the presentation of data in Chapter 13, when we look at the question of telling the research story.

A worked data reduction example

Below, we provide a worked example of some, but by no means all, of the different data reduction devices available to the data analyst. Our example is data on ownership of different entertainment equipment. We start by looking at how the original data might be presented. We then follow a series of data reduction principles, eventually arriving at a format that tells the essential story, but with substantially less data.

The starting point: a mass of incomprehensible data

We start in Table 9.1 with a mass of unordered, jumbled and confusing data. We need to begin to make some sense of what we are seeing and, to do so, we need to reduce the data.

Introducing order

- First, as shown in Table 9.2 we begin to organize the data into some logical sequence.
- In this case, we have ranked the ownership of products from highest to lowest overall.
- We have added headings and labels so that we can quickly determine what we are looking at.
- Any data that is not adding to the 'story' is removed, and 'none' and 'don't know' responses have also been taken away.

Combining the cross-breaks

- Once we have the data in some form of logical sequence, we might consider reducing the data further by combining some of the cross-breaks.

Table 9.1 – An incomprehensible mass of data

	Total 1000 100%	M 500 100%	F 500 100%	AB 200 100%	C1 300 100%	C2 300 100%	DE 200 100%	18–24 285 100%	25–29 145 100%	30–34 150 100%	35–39 112 100%	40–44 174 100%	45–50 120 100%	50+ 14 100%	S 482 100%	N 518 100%
CD Player	48%	49%	47%	22%	40%	48%	84%	34%	40%	50%	50%	60%	60%	70%	48%	48%
Stand-alone Radio	87%	80%	94%	79%	89%	88%	90%	70%	88%	93%	93%	95%	97%	100%	87%	87%
Video Recorder	72%	66%	78%	60%	69%	78%	82%	90%	88%	68%	60%	62%	45%	44%	79%	65%
Nintendo G.B.	22%	32%	12%	30%	34%	28%	12%	40%	30%	20%	15%	10%	4%	–	24%	20%
DVD Player	35%	35%	35%	40%	38%	32%	28%	40%	36%	37%	32%	31%	30%	30%	36%	34%
TV	99%	98%	100%	100%	98%	100%	100%	98%	100%	100%	100%	100%	100%	98%	99%	99%
Portable TV	42%	50%	36%	46%	38%	44%	40%	56%	44%	32%	35%	33%	37%	58%	44%	40%
Walkman	18%	17%	19%	27%	20%	14%	10%	40%	32%	12%	6%	–	–	–	18%	18%
MP3 Player	12%	16%	8%	24%	12%	8%	4%	20%	20%	15%	–	2%	–	–	14%	10%
Playstation	35%	42%	28%	38%	36%	34%	30%	68%	54%	35%	18%	6%	–	1%	42%	28%
Playstation 2	12%	20%	4%	26%	10%	9%	3%	12%	24%	18%	–	–	–	–	14%	10%
Xbox	7%	14%	–	12%	7%	5%	3%	18%	9%	5%	2%	–	–	–	8%	6%
Game Cube	7%	8%	6%	14%	8%	4%	2%	6%	18%	8%	–	–	–	–	8%	6%
None	2%	4%	–	2%	2%	–	2%	–	2%	2%	4%	4%	–	4%	2%	2%
Don't Know	4%	–	8%	2%	–	–	2%	4%	4%	4%	–	4%	6%	5%	–	4%

Table 9.2 – Introducing order

Product	Total	Gender		Socio-economic Group				Age							Region	
		Male	Female	AB	C1	C2	DE	18–24	25–29	30–34	35–39	40–44	45–50	50+	South	North
	1000	500	500	200	300	300	200	285	145	150	112	174	120	14	482	518
	100%	100%	100%	100%	100%	100%	100%	100%	100%	100%	100%	100%	100%	100%	100%	100%
High																
TV	99%	98%	100%	100%	98%	100%	100%	98%	100%	100%	100%	100%	100%	98%	99%	99%
Stand-alone Radio	87%	80%	94%	79%	89%	88%	90%	70%	88%	93%	93%	95%	97%	100%	87%	87%
Video Recorder	72%	66%	78%	60%	69%	78%	82%	90%	88%	68%	60%	62%	45%	44%	79%	65%
Medium																
CD Player	48%	49%	47%	22%	40%	48%	84%	34%	40%	50%	50%	60%	60%	70%	48%	48%
Portable TV	42%	50%	36%	46%	38%	44%	40%	56%	44%	32%	35%	33%	37%	58%	44%	40%
DVD Player	35%	35%	35%	40%	38%	32%	28%	40%	36%	37%	32%	31%	30%	30%	36%	34%
Playstation	35%	42%	28%	38%	36%	34%	30%	68%	54%	35%	18%	6%	–	1%	42%	28%
Nintendo G.B.	22%	32%	12%	30%	34%	28%	12%	40%	30%	20%	15%	10%	4%	–	24%	20%
Walkman	18%	17%	19%	27%	20%	14%	10%	40%	32%	12%	6%	–	–	–	18%	18%
Low																
MP3 Player	12%	16%	8%	24%	12%	8%	4%	20%	20%	15%	–	2%	–	–	14%	10%
Playstation 2	12%	20%	4%	26%	10%	9%	3%	12%	24%	18%	–	–	–	–	14%	10%
Xbox	7%	14%	–	12%	7%	5%	3%	18%	9%	5%	2%	–	–	–	8%	6%
Game Cube	7%	8%	6%	14%	8%	4%	2%	6%	18%	8%	–	–	–	–	8%	6%

Table 9.3 – Combining columns

Product	Total	Gender		SEG		Age				Region	
		Male	Female	ABC1	C2DE	18–24	25–34	35–44	45+	South	North
	1000	500	500	500	500	285	295	286	134	482	518
	100%	100%	100%	100%	100%	100%	100%	100%	100%	100%	100%
High											
TV	99%	98%	100%	99%	100%	98%	100%	100%	99%	99%	99%
Stand-alone Radio	87%	80%	94%	85%	89%	70%	91%	94%	99%	87%	87%
Video Recorder	72%	66%	78%	65%	80%	90%	78%	61%	45%	79%	65%
Medium											
CD Player	48%	49%	47%	33%	62%	34%	45%	56%	61%	48%	48%
Portable TV	42%	50%	36%	41%	42%	56%	38%	34%	39%	44%	40%
DVD Player	35%	35%	35%	39%	30%	40%	37%	31%	30%	36%	34%
Playstation	35%	42%	28%	37%	32%	68%	44%	11%	–	42%	28%
Nintendo G.B.	22%	32%	12%	32%	12%	40%	25%	12%	3%	24%	20%
Walkman	18%	17%	19%	23%	12%	40%	22%	2%	–	18%	18%
Low											
MP3 Player	12%	16%	8%	17%	6%	20%	17%	–	–	14%	10%
Playstation 2	12%	20%	4%	16%	7%	12%	21%	–	–	14%	10%
Xbox	7%	14%	–	9%	4%	18%	7%	–	–	8%	6%
Game Cube	7%	8%	6%	10%	3%	6%	13%	–	–	8%	6%

- Now instead of having four socio-economic groups (SEG) and seven age bands, we have just two for SEG and four for Age (Table 9.3).

Finding the story

- Now that we have our data in an easily understandable format, we can begin to 'tell the story': some stories are better told in words (see Table 9.4).
- We have therefore ascertained the main points from the North/South columns (i.e. that ownership is consistently higher in the South apart from radios, CDs and Walkmans), stated them clearly, and removed the two columns of data.
- We have also added various design enhancements for ease of comprehension, including removing % signs.

Developing a hybrid table/chart presentation

- We now use a simple bar chart/text box hybrid in order to summarize the data still further:

Table 9.4 – Finding the story with further design enhancement

Product	Total	Gender		SEG		Age			
		Male : **Female**		**ABC1** : **C2DE**		**18–24** : **25–34**		**35–44** : **45+**	
Base for %	1000	500 : 500		500 : 500		285 : 295		286 : 134	
	100	100 : 100		100 : 100		100 : 100		100 : 100	
High:	%	% : %		% : %		% : %		% : %	
TV	99	98 : 100		99 : 100		98 : 100		100 : 98	
Stand-alone Radio	87	80 : 94		85 : 89		70 : 91		94 : 99	
Video Recorder	72	66 : 78		65 : 80		90 : 78		61 : 45	
Medium:									
CD Player	48	49 : 47		33 : 62		34 : 45		56 : 61	
Portable TV	42	50 : 36		41 : 42		56 : 38		34 : 39	
DVD Player	35	35 : 35		39 : 42		40 : 37		31 : 30	
Playstation	35	42 : 28		37 : 32		68 : 44		11 : –	
Nintendo G.B.	22	32 : 12		32 : 12		40 : 25		12 : 3	
Walkman	18	17 : 19		23 : 12		40 : 22		2 : –	
Low:									
MP3 Player	12	16 : 8		17 : 6		20 : 17		– : –	
Playstation 2	12	20 : 4		16 : 7		12 : 21		– : –	
Xbox	7	14 : –		9 : 4		18 : 7		– : –	
Game Cube	7	8 : 6		10 : 3		6 : 13		– : –	

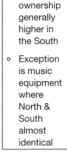

o Product ownership generally higher in the South

o Exception is music equipment where North & South almost identical

- Product ownership has been reworked into meaningful sub-groups:
  * Visual
  * Audio
  * Gaming
- All gender differences have been represented graphically.
- Any useful variations in either SEG or Age have been clearly stated in the text boxes.
- We have now summarized all relevant and useful data from an incomprehensible mass of numbers and percentages, into easily digestible chunks of useful information (see Figure 9.1).

Understanding the hierarchy of data analysis options

In the rest of this chapter, we take a data set – on banking products and services used by different businesses – and review the analysis options open to the researcher by working through a hierarchy of techniques available to help us gradually reduce the data, make sense of its meaning, and identify the storyline. (The inexperienced quantitative analyst should read this next section in conjunction with the references cited in the Notes for this chapter. These explain in further detail many of the concepts we touch on in this overview.)

In Figure 9.2, we provide a summary of our ten levels of analysis. Thus, it can be seen that at step one, we start with the raw data, and proceed

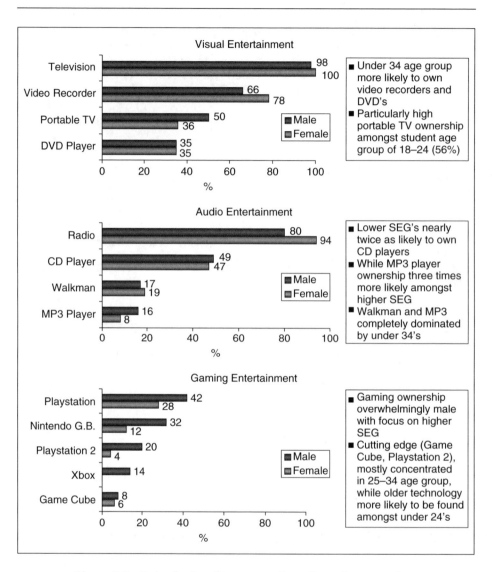

Figure 9.1 – Introducing diagrammatic and word summaries.

through various data reduction and cross-tabulation techniques, leading on to the application of various measures of location and variation, together with measures of significance. We then continue the process – still working with the same banking provider's data set – looking at how the application of various correlation and visual mapping, trade-off, and factor and cluster techniques, will aid our understanding of the data set.

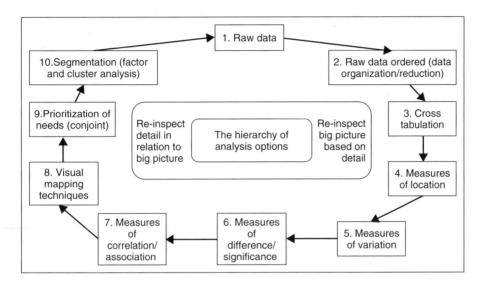

Figure 9.2 – A summary of our overview of ten levels of data analysis.

Step one: assembling and understanding the structure and pattern of raw data

Table 9.5 shows the types of products used by a sample of businesses. In Table 9.6 we show the response given by the business sample to certain attitudinal questions on business strategy.

Step two: ordering the raw data

In Table 9.7 we have ordered the tables on banking services used. For the importance ratings, we have elected to streamline, by ordering attitudes on the basis of the total percentage that finds each service 'at all important' (see Table 9.8).

From this reordering, we discern a general 'inward focus' amongst businesses: consolidating and making the most of what they have, before considering 'outward looking' strategies.

Step three: introducing cross tabulation to examine sub-group variations

In Table 9.9 we look at the ordered data by the turnover of the business. This immediately tells us that the general usage of products increases with size (and implied complexity) of business. Thus, the combination of ordering vertically by general prevalence, and ordering horizontally via the turnover cross tabulation, generates a clear storyline along the 'diagonal' of the table.

In addition, a cross tabulation of the data by sector reveals a slightly different, less clear-cut subplot (see Table 9.10).

Table 9.5 – Products used by businesses

	TOTAL
Base	1,100
Q: *Which of these banking services does your business use?*	(%)
Telephone banking	7
Deposits of cash and cheques	93
Euro accounts	5
BACS credits and debits	73
CHAPS payments	30
Payroll	25
Electronic and PC banking	25
Overdrafts and short-term finance	77
Term loans exceeding three months	52
Asset finance and leasing	15
Factoring/invoice discounting	3
Currency accounts	14
International payments	22
Foreign exchange	19
Deposit and short-term investment accounts	42
Treasury services	15
Investment banking services	5
Vehicle management services	1

Step four: measures of location

We now examine three key elements of the attitudinal data. We see that the normal measures of location (mean, mode and median) provide us with an option to summarize the data differently for the final presentation context. We have assumed the following scale values: very important = 4; quite important = 3; not particularly important = 2; not at all important = 1 (see Table 9.11).

Step five: measures of variation

We now need to comment on the variation in our data set. In cases A and B in Table 9.11, the normal measures of variation work well, i.e. the standard deviation (average distance of the population or sample values from the mean) and variance (the average squared distance of all measurements from the mean). In case C, though, caution must be exercised in using any measure of location, because the distribution of responses does not approximate the normal distribution. Diagnostic statistics, such as standard deviation and variance, supplement our intuition formally: clearly we can be confident in the location measures on statement B, moderately so for statement A, but must treat these measures with great caution for statement C (see Table 9.12).

Table 9.6 – Importance ratings

		TOTAL
Base		1,100
Q: *How important are each of these to your business strategy?*		(%)
• Diversify into new sectors or markets	Very important	23
	Quite important	33
	Not particularly important	25
	Not at all important	19
• Grow the business amongst existing customers	Very important	32
	Quite important	36
	Not particularly important	24
	Not at all important	8
• Check that your customers are satisfied	Very important	30
	Quite important	64
	Not particularly important	4
	Not at all important	2
• Improve internal cost efficiencies	Very important	36
	Quite important	27
	Not particularly important	20
	Not at all important	17
• Invest in marketing and promoting the business	Very important	16
	Quite important	34
	Not particularly important	27
	Not at all important	23
• Avoid risk	Very important	46
	Quite important	36
	Not particularly important	15
	Not at all important	3
• Use the latest technology	Very important	21
	Quite important	35
	Not particularly important	31
	Not at all important	13
• Focus on international markets	Very important	37
	Quite important	13
	Not particularly important	15
	Not at all important	35

Step six: measures of significance and difference

We now extend our analysis to apply the standard 95% confidence interval procedure to the difference between two percentages. A rule of thumb will usually suffice. We revisit the sector data to find that there are significant differences across sectors (see Table 9.13). These are summarized in Table 9.14.

Table 9.7 – Services ordered from high to low

	TOTAL
Base	1,100
Q: *Which of these banking services does your business use?*	(%)
Deposits of cash and cheques	93
Overdrafts and short-term finance	77
BACS credits and debits	73
Term loans exceeding three months	52
Deposit and short-term investment accounts	42
CHAPS payments	30
Payroll	25
Electronic and PC banking	25
International payments	22
Foreign exchange	19
Treasury services	15
Asset finance and leasing	15
Currency accounts	14
Telephone banking	7
Euro accounts	5
Investment banking services	5
Factoring/invoice discounting	3
Vehicle management services	1

Table 9.8 – Importance ratings ordered

	TOTAL
Base	1,100
% considering each important to business strategy	(%)
Check that your customers are satisfied	94
Avoid risk	82
Grow the business amongst existing customers	68
Improve internal cost efficiencies	63
Use the latest technology	56
Diversify into new sectors or markets	56
Focus on international markets	50
Invest in marketing and promoting the business	50

Step seven: measures of correlation/association

As we have seen from the cross tabulation of product usage according to business turnover, there is evidently a relationship between the size of business and product use. This is a type of correlation (a technique that tells us about the relationship between two different sets of data). Thus, we see that as

Table 9.9 – Cross tabulation by turnover

Banking services used	Total	Turnover (£)						
		Less than 0.5 m	0.5–1 m	1–2 m	2–5 m	5–10 m	10–50 m	50 m +
	(%)	(%)	(%)	(%)	(%)	(%)	(%)	(%)
Deposits of cash and cheques	93	92	93	93	92	94	93	93
Overdrafts and short-term finance	77	76	80	78	84	81	77	90
BACS credits and debits	73	65	77	84	80	89	80	90
Term loans exceeding three months	52	56	54	53	48	42	55	52
Deposit and short-term investment accounts	42	37	42	47	53	61	61	76
CHAPS payments	30	20	30	38	44	56	71	93
Payroll	25	13	32	39	37	40	38	55
Electronic and PC banking	25	13	29	34	44	48	54	76
International payments	22	9	20	36	40	65	64	76
Foreign exchange	19	9	18	29	30	45	57	79
Treasury services	15	6	13	19	29	39	51	69
Asset finance and leasing	15	13	15	19	20	19	20	24
Currency accounts	14	5	11	20	21	42	43	69
Telephone banking	7	7	8	9	5	8	19	27
Euro accounts	5	1	4	7	11	22	14	55
Investment banking services	5	5	4	5	4	7	12	10
Factoring/invoice discounting	3	1	4	4	7	1	4	3
Vehicle management services	1	0	1	0	3	8	6	3

turnover increases, so does (a) the likelihood of using certain products, and (b) the *total* number of products used. A simple table of this type is often sufficient to establish the direction of correlation, e.g. for total average number of services used (Table 9.15).

We can be reasonably confident that this is a *causative* relationship – in other words, as business size increases, it *leads* to a greater complexity of service requirements. However, other types of correlation are not necessarily causative, but simply express, for example, a relationship between different attitudes (see Table 9.16). Back to the attitude data.

The picture becomes clearer (see Table 9.17) when we order the data as in Table 9.8.

It now appears as if the attitudes do cluster into two major groups according to how they correlate with each other. If the correlations are sufficiently strong, the analysis can be reduced further using factor analysis, which we explain shortly.

Step eight: visual mapping

Our analysis (along with all other variables) can be usefully displayed as a visual map using techniques such as multiple correspondence analysis. Here, we also explore the relationship with turnover and sector. Figure 9.3 shows a typical visual map of a data set.

Table 9.10 – Cross tabulation by sector

	Total	Business sector			
		Manufacturing	Retail	Service	Wholesale/dist
Base	1,100	250	300	250	300
Banking services used	(%)	(%)	(%)	(%)	(%)
Deposits of cash and cheques	93	93	91	94	89
Overdrafts and short-term finance	77	85	85	79	80
BACS credits and debits	73	75	75	76	76
Term loans exceeding three months	52	57	57	57	46
Deposit and short-term investment accounts	42	44	22	65	34
CHAPS payments	30	29	29	34	44
Payroll	25	29	18	31	26
Electronic and PC banking	25	23	22	28	48
International payments	22	27	8	12	33
Foreign exchange	19	23	14	17	33
Treasury services	15	18	12	17	17
Asset finance and leasing	15	38	18	13	13
Currency accounts	14	16	5	12	44
Telephone banking	7	4	6	8	4
Euro accounts	5	9	4	4	7
Investment banking services	5	6	6	6	3
Factoring/invoice discounting	3	5	3	2	1
Vehicle management services	1	1	1	2	2

Step nine: prioritization of needs

There are many ways of understanding needs and priorities, including relatively sophisticated trade-off techniques, such as Conjoint analysis. In this
simple case, we can use factor variables to prioritize needs. Building on
our earlier observations, we can see that two factors indeed emerge (see
Table 9.18).

The factors embody the full set of 'strategy' variables. So (and this is also
a relatively typical exercise for Conjoint analysis), for each respondent we
can identify which is the most important driver: inward control, or outward
entrepreneur. In this instance, the prioritization shows that the sample is split
almost evenly between those for whom Factor 1 is most important, and those
where Factor 2 is the focus. As we might expect from an inspection of the visual
map, this is related to business turnover (Table 9.19).

Table 9.11 – Measures of location

		TOTAL
Base		1,100
Q: *How important are each of these to your business strategy?*		(%)
A: Grow the business amongst existing customers	Very important	32
	Quite important	36
	Not particularly important	24
	Not at all important	8
	Mean	2.9
	Mode	3
	Median	3
B: Check that your customers are satisfied	Very important	30
	Quite important	64
	Not particularly important	4
	Not at all important	2
	Mean	3.2
	Mode	3
	Median	3
C: Focus on international markets	Very important	37
	Quite important	13
	Not particularly important	15
	Not at all important	35
	Mean	2.5
	Mode	4
	Median	2.5

Mean: sum of observed values divided by the number of observations; Mode: most frequently occurring value in a set of observations; Median: the value that divides the total frequency into equal halves.

Table 9.12 – Measures of variation

	Standard Deviation	Variance
A: Check customers are satisfied	0.54	0.42
B: Grow amongst existing customers	0.96	0.82
C: Focus on international markets	1.28	1.17

Step ten: segmentation

We can now apply the segmentation technique. Here the goal is identify discreet groups that share particular attitudes, characteristics and behaviour. In this case, we are identifying three clusters, based on business priorities, to assist our understanding of the market.

We now overlay the segment positions onto the visual map (Table 9.20). There are clearly three significantly different territories defined by the cluster summaries (Figure 9.4).

Table 9.13 – Towards measuring significance

	Total	Business sector			
		Manufacturing	Retail	Service	Wholesale/dist
Base	1,100	250	300	250	300
Banking services used	(%)	(%)	(%)	(%)	(%)
Deposits of cash and cheques	93	93	91	94	89
Overdrafts and short-term finance	77	85	85	79	80
BACS credits and debits	73	75	75	76	76
Term loans exceeding three months	52	57	57	57	46
Deposit and short-term investment accounts	42	44	22	65	34
CHAPS payments	30	29	29	34	44
Payroll	25	29	18	31	26
Electronic and PC banking	25	23	22	28	48
International payments	22	27	8	12	33
Foreign exchange	19	23	14	17	33
Treasury services	15	18	12	17	17
Asset finance and leasing	15	38	18	13	13
Currency accounts	14	16	5	12	44
Telephone banking	7	4	6	8	4
Euro accounts	5	9	4	4	7
Investment banking services	5	6	6	6	3
Factoring/invoice discounting	3	5	3	2	1
Vehicle management services	1	1	1	2	2

We can immediately generate a series of hypotheses about the nature of each cluster from the visual map. In line with the Hermeneutic Circle principle, though, we now need to return to the earlier stages in the analytical process and profile the segments against the raw data. Thus, we find the profiles as shown in Table 9.21. In examining the attitudinal data, we arrive at the pattern shown in Table 9.22. Thus, we confirm the solution is of interest because, rather than merely dividing the sample into 'Inward/Outward' clusters (largely corresponding to Cluster 2 vs. Cluster 3), a third cluster emerges (Cluster 1) that is driven almost entirely by 'Risk Aversion'.

Key principles when analysing quantitative data

We now provide seven general principles that highlight the holistic approach to the analysis of quantitative data:

Table 9.14 – Significance of sector difference

	Total	Business sector			
		Manufacturing	Retail	Service	Wholesale/dist
Base	1,100	250	300	250	300
Banking services used: significance of sector differences	(%)	(%)	(%)	(%)	(%)
Deposits of cash and cheques	93	No	No	No	No
Overdrafts and short-term finance	77	No	No	No	No
BACS credits and debits	73	No	No	No	No
Term loans exceeding three months	52	Vs. W	Vs. W	Vs. W	Vs. M, R, S
Deposit and short-term investment accounts	42	Vs. R, S	Vs. M, S, W	Vs. M, R, W	Vs. R, S
CHAPS payments	30	Vs. W	Vs. W	Vs. W	Vs. M, R, S
Payroll	25	Vs. R	Vs. M, S, W	Vs. R	Vs. R
Electronic and PC banking	25	Vs. W	Vs. W	Vs. W	Vs. M, R, S
International payments	22	Vs. R, S	Vs. M, W	Vs. M, W	Vs. R, S
Foreign exchange	19	Vs. W	Vs. W	Vs. W	Vs. M, R, S
Treasury services	15	No	No	No	No
Asset finance and leasing	15	Vs. R, S, W	Vs. M	Vs. M	Vs. M
Currency accounts	14	Vs. R, W	Vs. M, W	Vs. W	Vs. M, R, S
Telephone banking	7	No	No	No	No
Euro accounts	5	No	No	No	No
Investment banking services	5	No	No	No	No
Factoring/invoice discounting	3	No	No	No	No
Vehicle management services	1	No	No	No	No

Example of key: Vs. R, S means that this statistic is significant (at the 95% level of confidence) versus Retail (R) and Service (S).

Table 9.15 – Correlations

	Total	Turnover (£)						
Banking services used		Less than 0.5 m	0.5–1 m	1–2 m	2–5 m	5–10 m	10–50 m	50 m+
Average total services used	5.23	4.28	5.35	6.14	6.52	7.67	8.19	10.4

- *Apply common sense and 'believability' checks*: it is helpful to subject the data being advanced to a basic believability check. (Remember the well-established law: any figure that looks particularly interesting is probably wrong! So all data needs to be initially scrutinized for potential error.)
- *Always be working towards reducing down the data*: the analysis process is characterized by a relentless attempt to reduce the amount of data in front of the end decision-maker. This may be achieved by: simple data reduction techniques; cutting out irrelevant data; and finding elegant ways to summarize data.
- *Apply the principle of the Hermeneutic Circle*: the holistic analyst will tirelessly adhere to the principle of relating what they are learning from the 'big picture' that is being constructed, to the detail they are continually unearthing, while also being flexible enough to allow this analysis of the small detail to modify their initial big picture take on events.

Table 9.16 – Correlations

Correlations		A	B	C	D	E	F	G	H
A	Diversify into new sectors/markets	**1.00**							
B	Grow the business amongst existing customers	0.28	**1.00**						
C	Check that your customers are satisfied	0.19	0.31	**1.00**					
D	Improve internal cost efficiencies	0.22	0.33	0.49	**1.00**				
E	Invest in marketing and promoting the business	0.40	0.08	0.25	−0.24	**1.00**			
F	Avoid risk	−0.18	0.14	0.22	0.34	0.10	**1.00**		
G	Use the latest technology	0.20	0.14	0.15	0.17	0.24	0.13	**1.00**	
H	Focus on international markets	0.52	−0.27	0.05	−0.30	0.41	−0.22	0.26	**1.00**

Table 9.17 – Correlations

Correlations		C	F	B	D	G	A	H	E
C	Check that your customers are satisfied	**1.00**							
F	Avoid risk	0.22	**1.00**						
B	Grow the business amongst existing customers	0.31	0.14	**1.00**					
D	Improve internal cost efficiencies	0.49	0.34	0.33	**1.00**				
G	Use the latest technology	0.15	0.13	0.14	0.17	**1.00**			
A	Diversify into new sectors/markets	0.19	−0.18	0.28	0.22	0.20	**1.00**		
H	Focus on international markets	0.05	−0.22	−0.27	−0.30	0.26	0.52	**1.00**	
E	Invest in marketing and promoting the business	0.25	0.10	0.08	−0.24	0.24	0.40	0.41	**1.00**

- *Having the confidence to put yourself into the analysis and accommodate prior knowledge*: the holistic analyst knows that the *starting* point for making sense of the world is often their own 'working prejudice'. This then needs to be inspected against management prior knowledge and the hard consumer evidence. So, holistic analysis is a continual process of reappraising the data in relation to incoming prior knowledge, and what we know about the problem under investigation.
- *Think in broad, simple, not confusing, little strokes*: the holistic analyst will be aware of general over-arching principles, such as most sub-group analysis simply 'refining' the total storyline, rather than 'suppressing' what *may* be numerous sub-plots. Thus, working with these general principles, the holistic analyst will always be seeking to add simplicity and clarity in quickly searching

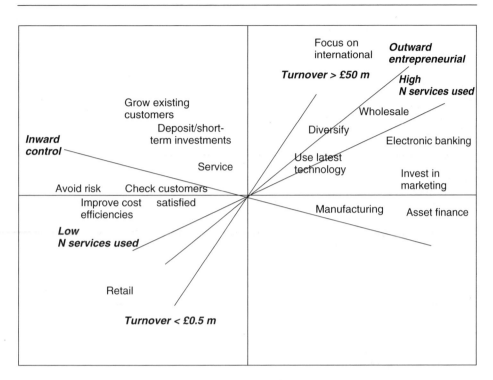

Figure 9.3 – Visual map.

Table 9.18 – Factor analysis

Factor Component Matrix	Factor 1 Outward focus	Factor 2 Inward focus
Focus on international markets	0.75	
Diversify into new sectors/markets	0.68	
Invest in marketing and promoting the business	0.60	−0.30
Use the latest technology	0.57	
Improve internal cost efficiencies		0.72
Check that your customers are satisfied		0.72
Avoid risk	−0.32	0.61
Grow the business amongst existing customers	0.25	0.54

out the central storyline, rather than teasing out confusing minutiae likely to throw the decision-maker off the scent.

- *Think in both holistic and orthodox data analysis modes*: the holistic data analyst will blend together orthodox statistical-based ways of making sense of, for example, the meaning between two different statistics, whilst at the same time being alert to the central tenets and principles of holistic analysis.

Table 9.19 – Factor by turnover

Needs priority	Total (%)	Turnover (£)						
		Less than 0.5 m (%)	0.5–1 m (%)	1–2 m (%)	2–5 m (%)	5–10 m (%)	10–50 m (%)	50 m + (%)
Inward Control	57	66	58	47	39	36	35	28
Outward Entrepreneurial	43	34	42	53	61	64	65	72

Table 9.20 – Segmentation

Cluster analysis results	Factor 1 Outward focus	Factor 2 Inward focus	% of sample
Cluster 1	0.45	1.75	24
Cluster 2	0.98	−1.32	40
Cluster 3	−1.25	0.56	36

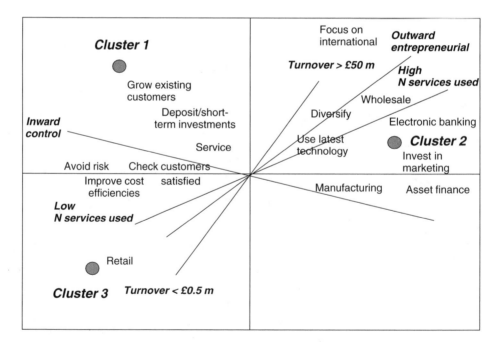

Figure 9.4 – Clusters.

Table 9.21 – Cluster by turnover

Banking services used	Total (%)	Turnover (£)						
		Less than 0.5 m (%)	0.5–1 m (%)	1–2 m (%)	2–5 m (%)	5–10 m (%)	10–50 m (%)	50 m + (%)
Cluster 1	24	19	20	24	26	25	26	25
Cluster 2	40	12	18	28	35	44	48	55
Cluster 3	36	69	62	48	39	31	26	20

Table 9.22 – Attitudes by cluster

		Total %	Clust. 1 %	Clust. 2 %	Clust. 3 %
Diversify into new sectors/markets	Very important	23	8	11	**42**
	Quite important	33	21	26	**44**
	Not particularly important	24	33	32	12
	Not at all important	19	34	28	3
Grow amongst existing customers	Very important	32	11	**54**	64
	Quite important	36	49	**35**	32
	Not particularly important	24	23	7	4
	Not at all important	8	17	3	
Improve internal cost efficiencies	Very important	36	12	**75**	44
	Quite important	27	49	**23**	40
	Not particularly important	20	25	1	16
	Not at all important	17	11	0	
Avoid risk	Very important	46	**60**	21	26
	Quite important	36	**32**	41	39
	Not particularly important	15	8	17	32
	Not at all important	3	1	15	2
Focus on international markets	Very important	37	3	1	**63**
	Quite important	13	9	4	**32**
	Not particularly important	15	22	17	5
	Not at all important	35	63	75	0

Table excludes 'don't knows'.

- *Do not let the process kill the big idea – continually re-inspect the data against the end business objectives*: the holistic data analyst will always be thinking about the end game. They will know what piece of evidence is most pertinent in supporting or rejecting a putative decision. Their analysis will always be formed by continually revisiting the research brief/proposal, to ensure that every ounce of energy they spend on the data is focused towards facilitating informed evidence-based judgements. They will not be sucked into a time-consuming process that loses sight of the whole reason for conducting the research in the first place.

In the last two chapters, we have provided an outline of the way in which the holistic analyst will organize qualitative and quantitative data, prior to getting down to the detail of identifying the significance and meaning behind the data. In the next chapter we address the process of starting to interpret a piece of evidence: the issue of within what range the survey's key statistics should be interpreted. This takes us to looking at establishing the 'interpretation boundary'.

10 Establishing the interpretation boundary

Summary

- We now look at the way the holistic data analyst, when inspecting a data set, will seek to establish the overall boundary within which to interpret the data.
- This is achieved by first establishing the 'constraints' that are imposed on the data. This is the science: it is based on what we know about how sampling theory will help us calculate 'sampling error', and also based on our empirical knowledge of 'sample bias'.
- Then, holistic data analysts will see how far they can legitimately 'stretch' this initial, more statistically driven boundary to take into account what we know about the topic based on existing prior knowledge. We describe this stretching process as the art of applying the 'enabling factors'.
- In advancing the idea of the 'constraints & enablers' technique, we are mindful of the importance of achieving this through a set of user-friendly general principles that convey the 'spirit' of Bayesian thinking, without placing in front of busy commercial practitioners the task of grappling with, what can be quite complex, Bayesian calculations.

Constraining and enabling factors

The next stage of our holistic interpretation framework focuses on establishing the broad parameters within which we can now begin to interpret the data in front of us. This is a process of establishing the overall boundary within which we can safely operate.

This part of our integrated holistic data analysis framework introduces two concepts: the 'constraining factors' and 'enabling devices'. These concepts are helpful in explaining how holistic market researchers, when they first look at statistical data, try to establish the overall 'interpretation boundary'. It is a process of first establishing the broad, more statistically derived 'constraints' within which we all must work, and then applying what we have labelled the 'enablers', to see how far it is legitimate to 'stretch' this initial, more statistically driven, assessment to include what else we know about the problem under investigation.

The science of applying constraining factors

Constraining factors set the initial parameters as to the interpretation we can legitimately place on the data. These include applying familiar concepts from orthodox statistics, such as statistical tests on quantitative data. These constraining factors exert a discipline on our interpretation of data, anchoring it in the most exacting precautionary standards we have available to us.

In considering the constraining factors, let us start by quickly reminding ourselves about the bedrock of the statistical analysis of survey data: the notion of the 'theoretical sampling distribution'. Thus, most market researchers, whether they are from the orthodox or holistic data analysis schools, when interpreting a statistic generated from a sample survey, will – albeit for some, often loosely and impressionistically – locate their survey statistic in an interpretive boundary based on what they know about basic sampling theory.

An overview of the theory of probability sampling

At the heart of sampling theory is the observation that we can prove, mathematically, that the means of all possible samples in a population will equal the population mean. So if, for example, we were to draw all possible samples of men from the UK population and plot the average height that each of our samples revealed, we would find that the distribution of all our survey plottings of these height means followed the bell-curve shape of the normal distribution.

This is a critically important observation, because we know that the normal distribution has certain properties. We know that if we took just one of our surveys of the average male height in the UK, and wanted to use this as an estimate of the true height of the male population in the UK, then we could make certain statements about the accuracy of our single survey. Specifically, we know that there is a 68% chance that our estimate of height of the UK male population from our *single* survey will fall within plus or minus one standard error of the mean. The standard error is a way of measuring the variability in the population. If every man was the same height, clearly, there would be no risk of an error.

Then, by applying a simple formula, we can say that we are confident that, 68 times out of 100, our single survey estimate will be accurate to within a particular margin. If we wish to increase the confidence with which we make our statement, we will need to broaden the error margin (standard errors) within which we are operating. The convention in commercial survey research is to present the statistics at the 95% level of confidence. This allows us to state how confident we are of the survey height of our sample of men falling within plus or minus two standard errors of the mean.

This body of sampling knowledge is important because it not only allows us to make an estimate of the likelihood of our own sample of the height of men being close to the true population height, but it tells us that, as the size of the sample *increases*, the error margin, within which we interpret our survey statistic, will *decrease*. Conversely, as we reduce the size of the sample survey, so the error margin, within which we interpret our survey statistic, will increase.

So, without drawing the reader into the details of exactly how these calculations work, the central point to make is that 'classic' statistical theory provides us with a way of interpreting different survey statistics, drawn from varying sizes of sample, within the appropriate range of error, and at a level of confidence (usually the 95% level). In the Notes section we provide a source for checking within what range to interpret statistics drawn from different sample sizes.

Conducting probability sampling in practice

Understanding the 'constraints' imposed by what sampling theory tells us is an important start point for the holistic data analyst in looking at sample survey data. The holistic analyst will then take the parameters, prescribed by sampling theory, one stage further. The holistic data analyst will now take into account a range of practical and pragmatic considerations about the realities of drawing a commercial sample in real life.

For instance, we know that the theoretical calculation of the estimate of the true statistic for the wider universe under investigation provides a flattering estimate of the range of error within which the statistic should be interpreted. Thus, if, for example, a survey of 1000 London car commuters showed that 30% were resistant to the idea of congestion charging, we will find that the simple statistical formula for pure random sampling will tell us that, with this size of sample, a survey statistic of 30% needs to be interpreted within a range of plus or minus approximately 3% (at the 95% level of confidence). That is to say, with this size of sample, we are confident, 95 times out of 100, that a true survey statistic will fall in the range of 27% to 33%.

The experienced data analyst, however, will realize that the above estimate is based on various, difficult to achieve in practice, assumptions about the way the sample was drawn and, as such, means that, in most cases, we cannot simply apply 'pure' (simple) sampling theory. This is because our theoretical-based estimate fails to take into account many of the vagaries of real life (sub-optimum) commercial research sampling practice. So, the practice of locating a statistic within a theoretically derived boundary is a helpful start, but we then need to be aware of the way various practicalities will affect the 'purist' estimate. These are reviewed below.

The design factor

The design factor is the concept that helps us to place some parameters on the way the sampling practicalities have affected our 'purist' estimates of the accuracy of our survey statistic. Specifically, it helps us to measure the impact that various practical adaptations and modifications to the pure, simple random probability sampling method have had on our estimate of the accuracy of our survey statistic. These modifications include the following.

Stratification

One common modification to pure random sampling is stratification. This works to the advantage of the researcher, by helping to reduce the sampling error. This means that it is good practice, when structuring a sample, to organize (or stratify) the sampling frame (that is, the list of potential respondents for our survey) in a way that will guarantee that the sample will represent the key segments of the overall population.

For example, if we know the proportion of people who live in the North West, as opposed to the South West, of England, then it is sensible to organize our sample into strata (all of the individuals living in the North West and South West and so on), and then select our sample by applying the sample interval *within* each of these strata. By following this process for all of the relevant strata, we are effectively building in a guarantee that our sample will be accurate. This is because we know, in advance, that we will have the appropriate proportions of all the relevant constituent elements. In sum, this process of stratification helps to reduce the size of the sampling error, because it reduces the chances of drawing a 'fluke' sample by chance.

Clustering

Stratification's positive impact on the sampling process could be countered by the fact that, in most commercial samples, there will also be some 'clustering' of interviews, and this will increase the sampling error. Clustering reflects the fact that it will not be practicable to interview people spread across the UK. So, virtually all commercial survey samples will introduce a process of clustering – or grouping – interviews into convenient to access groups. (Although this, of course, is much less of an issue with telephone and Internet surveys.)

This process of moving from a totally unclustered sample to a more practical clustered interviewing design is a major departure from the assumptions underpinning pure, simple random sampling. Clustering will markedly increase the sampling error. Intuitively, we can see why: clearly, there is a risk associated with asking a (small) clustered group of individuals to represent the wider, more scattered, universe. It is like asking just those who live in one block of flats to represent the views of the wider community.

Calculating the 'design factor'

So, to summarize, commercial survey designers will stratify their samples, while also attempting – for face-to-face surveys – to strike a balance between introducing clustering in order to save interviewers' travelling costs, but not dramatically

increasing the sampling error. It is the impact of these practical modifications – stratification and clustering – on the 'classic' sampling error, that are
collectively referred to as the 'design factor'.

Doing the exact calculation of the design factor is complex, so some guidelines
are helpful. First, it is worth noting that, even with some of the most prestigious
UK surveys, where *probability*-based sampling and the minimum of clustering
are employed, the design factor is still in the region of 1.5. (The analyst takes
the sampling error calculated, based on the assumption of pure simple random
sampling, and then multiplies this estimate by the design factor figure of 1.5 to
arrive at a 'realistic' estimate of sampling error.) So, given that few commercial
surveys aspire to the standard of well-funded prestigious surveys, then a typical
probability-based sample survey will often carry a design factor of 2.0. (This
is before we arrive at the issue of less rigorous – non-probability – sampling
methods, which we discuss below.)

Sample bias

Understanding the extent of the sampling *error* for a statistic generated from a
probability sample still only tells us part of the story. We also need to understand
the concept of sampling *bias*. This, the reader will recall, involves understanding:
(a) the extent to which people who should have been included in the sample
were, in fact, included, and (b) the extent to which people who were invited to
take part in the study, did so. Here, empirical experience tells us that meeting
the conditions for true probability sampling – ensuring that each individual in
the sampling universe has an equal (or, to be precise, known) chance of
inclusion – is, in practice, demanding. Below, we look at why it is so difficult to
stay close to the requirements demanded by probability sampling:

- The researcher must locate an appropriate sample frame, one that lists *all* of
  the people in the population under investigation. (This sampling frame must
  be up-to-date, have no omissions, and be free from duplication.)
- From this (best possible) sampling frame, the next task is to select, in a
  completely random way, the individuals to be included in the sample, and
  then *only* to interview these selected individuals. That is, no substitutes can
  be taken. (If the sampling interval falls on the Archbishop of Canterbury, it is
  this person who must be interviewed. It is unacceptable to choose another
  senior cleric, even if he is the Pope!)
- If an individual cannot be interviewed, this needs to be recorded, and declared
  as part of the survey's non-response. As indicated earlier, the target is to obtain
  interviews with 65% of the population under investigation. (Only at this point
  can we safely say that the attitudes and behaviour of those taking part in our
  study are broadly similar to those who do *not* take part in the study.)

Achieving the above conditions for true probability sampling are extremely
demanding and costly. So, as we have already explained, most commercial

market research takes the form of non-probability sampling, most notably *quota* sampling.

Non-probability (quota) sampling

Quota sampling involves a researcher first obtaining up-to-date information about the population under investigation. 'Quotas' to reflect the characteristics of this target universe are then set. These quotas determine the type of individuals that interviewers will be asked to interview. The usual practice is to set 'interlocked' quotas, such that interviewers will be asked to find, for example, males who are aged 34 to 45, and who are in the, for instance, C1/C2 socio-economic group, and also live in North London.

This interlocking practice is a way of helping ensure that interviewers contact interviewees in a *de facto* 'random' way, rather than being able to pick – in a predetermined way – particular individuals who they know meet their quota requirements. Thus, quota sampling is predicated on the idea that the *haphazard* way in which interviewers initially contact people to fill their (interlocked) quotas, will approximate the true random probability procedures outlined above.

Quota sampling is 'validated' by virtue of the fact that methodological research tells us that, in the majority of cases, it leads the commercial researcher to the same result as probability sampling. Methodological research conducted by commercial market researchers – whereby issues are investigated using both probability and non-probability (quota sampling) methods – indicate that the less rigorous quota methodology will be an appropriate fitness-to-purpose design for many market research studies. (Although, clearly, for certain assignments requiring precise measurement, more rigorous probability methods will be required.)

Knowing how to interpret quota sample generated statistics

Misunderstanding abounds when it comes to interpreting statistics drawn from *quota* sampling methods. What many analysts do is simply take what we know about 'classic' sampling theory, outlined above, and make the naïve assumption that this body of knowledge applies to quota sampling as it stands. This is acceptable, insofar as it provides a start point for interpreting a particular survey statistic. However, it is prudent for the analyst to interpret the resulting estimate of the error margin in a less literal, and more realistic way – one that reflects the 'compromises' inherent in the quota sampling process.

Thus, we have already established that, even for 'high specification' *probability* samples, there is a 'design factor' of between 1.5 and 2.0. (That is, we should multiply the simple error margin by this figure, to arrive at a realistic estimate of the true statistic.) Given this, it is perhaps a useful rule of thumb to take any survey statistic generated from a *quota* sample, and to assume that the error margins generated by the simple random sampling formula, should, as an *absolute minimum*, always be 'doubled'.

Of course, sampling error still only tells us part of the story. As we have already stressed, the bigger issue to take into account, when assessing the representativeness of a sample, is not just the concept of sampling *error*, but that of sampling *bias*: the extent to which we have excluded people from our study. This is discussed below.

Understanding the true extent of 'sampling bias'

We have already indicated that, strictly speaking, with a *probability* sample, a minimum of 65% of respondents should have taken part in the survey if we are to feel comfortable about the survey findings reflecting the views of the entire universe: those who did and did not reply to the survey. However, this raises the question of how do you arrive at an estimate of the response rate from a process that followed not probability, but quota, sampling principles.

This is an area of much confusion, even among market research practitioners. So let us explore this issue further and pinpoint some of the misunderstandings that surround market research suppliers' use of the term 'survey response rate'.

The concept of the response rate

Strictly speaking, the term 'response rate' should *only* be used for *probability-based* samples, given that this is the only sampling method that starts life with a list of the respondents (or organizations) to be interviewed. In Table 10.1 we provide a description of the way in which the response rate on such a *probability*-based sample should be presented.

Table 10.1 – Defining a 'true' survey response rate (from a probability-based sample)

• **Number issued for interview:**	**1000**	
• Number deemed as ineligible (e.g. no longer at address):	100	
• Effective sample issued:	900	= 100%
	(No.)	900
		%
• Number who were not contactable:	120	13
• Number who refused:	230	26
• Number who were successfully interviewed:	550	61
• **Response rate (i.e. achieved interviews as % of effective issued sample with full profile of non-response)**		**61%**

As explained, we know, from a body of empirical evidence – methodological research conducted on this topic – that with probability samples, response rates of 65% or more mean that the attitudes and behaviour of those taking part in a survey will broadly reflect the attitudes and behaviour of those who did not. Another way of putting this is to say that, once a response rate of 65% (or over) has been achieved, fairly random factors – that are unrelated to the topic under investigation – tend to explain cooperation and non-cooperation in surveys. However, as the response rate drifts down below 65%, there is the chance that those who have taken part in the survey could be different from those who have not taken part. Or, put another way, it means that factors relating to the very issue one is trying to measure could begin to explain non-cooperation in the survey. For example, if *only* people who have managed to get a job after leaving a training scheme took part in a survey on what they thought about the course, then the survey would, of course, provide a flattering (self-selecting) account of the effectiveness of the training programme.

The concept of the 'strike rate'

The above account of response rates, as they relate to *probability* samples, is comparatively straightforward. The problem starts when market research field-work companies – that most of the time will have employed *quota* sampling methods – decide to describe the 'success' they have had with their interview-ing – their 'strike rate' – by (mistakenly) referring to this as a 'response rate', and compounding this error by missing out important information for the data analyst in interpreting this strike rate.

To unpack this issue, let us start by listing out what information should *ideally* be provided when citing a strike rate, drawn from a quota sample. This is outlined in Table 10.2.

Table 10.2 – The strike rate from a non-probability (quota) sample

• **Total interviews required**	**400**
• Total contacts made by interviewers	1000
• Ineligible contacts (e.g. work in market research or media, etc.)	100
• Contacts made that were (a) immediately refused and (b) 'outside the quota'	300
• Contacts made 'in quota', but refused (ideally giving reasons, e.g. too busy, etc.)	200
• Contacts that become successful interviews	400
Strike rate, i.e. successful interviews as a % of total contacts (but without full information being recorded of the allocation of the non-contacts into each of the three categories shown in above dashed box)	**40%**

With a full breakdown of the strike rate on a quota survey sample, the analyst can make important judgements about the extent to which the sample may be biased towards a particular group, or not. The analyst can look at information about who was contacted 'outside' and 'within' quota: and also examine the refusal rate, and so on. In many cases, a strike rate (in addition to being wrongly presented as a response rate), will simply take the form of citing the total number of interviews obtained from the total number of contacts made, i.e. 400 interviews were obtained from 1000 contacts. This is where problems of interpretation can arise.

For example, in a study about the email behaviour of business executives, it is important to know that the survey fieldwork organization was having difficulty with high levels of refusal because business executives were too busy to take part in interviews. It tells us that there is a risk that we have conducted our survey with the 'easy to interview' part of the business population. We have researched those who are less busy and more minded to take part in a survey, but who perhaps use the email in a totally different way to their colleagues from the more representative universe. So the fieldwork organization – by issuing more and more sample – will have achieved their goal of reaching the target number of interviews, but at the cost of representativeness. By failing to provide the data analyst with the contact information they require, they will have substantially lowered the analyst's ability to adjust for this shortfall at the interpretation stage.

So there is a lesson here for users of market research. They should be demanding and seek clarification from their fieldwork organization on, first, whether they are really referring to a response rate or a strike rate, and secondly, if it is a strike rate, ensuring that there is full information provided about what happened in terms of people's cooperation with the quota survey.

Further sampling bias issues

Let us now look at a few other scenarios where understanding the concept of sampling bias is particularly critical to the data analyst about to place an interpretation on a piece of evidence.

Telephone interviewing

It is worth stressing that market researchers have, through the use of 'random digit dialling', made progress in overcoming the potential bias in telephone interviewing caused by individuals being 'ex-directory', i.e. not listed in telephone directories. Yet the new issue facing market researchers wishing to use the telephone is the growing proportion of individuals who *only* have a mobile phone, i.e. do not have a landline at their home address. The particular difficulty here is obtaining an appropriate listing of mobile phone numbers. So there are questions here for the data analyst to ask, about how effective a telephone survey has been in covering the target universe.

Internet surveys

Attention should also be drawn to the way in which 'contact rates' on Internet surveys are presented. There are two distinct scenarios:

- **When the Internet survey is being presented as a proxy for the total population:** care needs to be taken with Internet surveys that are designed to assess the attitudes of the entire population. Currently, in the UK, only around 52% of UK households are online. So, clearly, asking Internet users to 'represent' the attitudes of behaviour of non-Internet users contains an element of risk.

  It is, of course, possible to re-weight any Internet sample by gender, age, socio-economic group, and other key characteristics, to bring the Internet sample into line with the profile of the total population. Yet this weighting will not 'automatically' adjust for the key *attitudinal* differences that *could* exist between current Internet users and non-users.

  However, market researchers are rapidly making progress in *adjusting* Internet surveys to be representative of the total population. This is referred to as 'propensity weighting', and, in essence, involves building up an empirical understanding of how, across a range of attitudinal and behavioural measures, online and non-online samples view the world, and making appropriate adjustments.

- **Where the focus is on Internet users:** in the scenario where the focus is on Internet users, we could, for instance, be talking about studies aimed at assessing the attitudes of Internet users to different e-commerce offers, such as Lastminute.com, Amazon, Yahoo!, and so on. Here, of course, none of the concerns of equating the Internet survey sample to the general population apply. However, there are still several *sampling bias* issues surfacing that the analyst must take into account. These include:
  - The response rate may be just too low to accept without 'compensatory' interpretation. So it has to be remembered that the general rules we have discussed about response rates still apply to Internet surveys.
  - There are also a potential range of biases associated with the way in which email address databases are created, and Internet surveys operate:
    * Some individuals will simply fail to give the *exact* (and correct) details of their email address.
    * People will also change email addresses (e.g. because they move job), which will then 'bounce back' to the survey researcher.
    * Some people use 'false' email addresses, when registering for certain things, to avoid receiving junk mail. So again, the 'bounce back' from this activity will need to be monitored by the survey researcher.
    * In certain workplace environments, an employee may find that legitimate incoming surveys that use certain types of words (that may be confused with inappropriate material) will be barred at source, thereby introducing further sample bias.

* There are also certain types of hardware and software difficulties that make receiving and transmitting Internet surveys difficult, thereby creating further potential sample bias.
- The general rules we have explained about response rates still apply to Internet surveys (namely that we cannot be certain that a survey represents the attitudes and behaviour of non-respondents if the response rate is not in excess of 65%). So beware of, for example, enthusiastic but naïve researchers who proudly claim that 500 respondents were secured from 3000 contacts. Here, the base number for the analysis seems 'chunky', but this still only represents a 17% response rate, which *could* introduce biases for which we will need to compensate.

Rules for interpreting statistics based on quota sampling

So to sum up, when interpreting statistics from a quota sample, there are three key questions the holistic data analyst should ask:

- *How close to pure probability 'randomness' was the 'haphazard' quota sample?* It is important for the analyst to ask the fieldwork providers exactly what procedures they followed to ensure that the quota sample was as close as possible to pure probability sampling: just what interlocking quotas were employed? This will form the basis for working out the implications of any shortfalls, and compensating for this at the analysis stage.
- *What was the extent of the sample bias?* Were there key sections of the target audience that were excluded from the research study, and were there also individuals who were originally included in the study, but who refused to take part, or who could not be contacted? So, ask the fieldwork company to provide as much information as possible about: (a) who was, and who was not, included in the sample; (b) who was contacted; (c) who was interviewed; and (d) who refused. This is critical to making informed judgements about how to compensate for any groups that have not been appropriately represented.
- *The interpretation boundary.* We know that the 'classic' sampling error formula (designed on the assumption of pure probability sampling) will need adjusting for everyday commercial quota sampling practice. Here, a good rule of thumb is to always *at least* double the sampling error that the (classic) textbook sampling error formula gives us.

Having examined the 'science' of establishing the constraints, let us now turn to the 'art' of applying the 'enablers' to our task of drawing up the interpretation boundary.

The art of applying the enabling devices

The 'enablers' help us stretch the above constraints-driven interpretation boundary. It helps us, on the one hand, to stay close to the data, but it also maximizes our chances of seeking out new insights and obtaining a deeper understanding of what is happening, by going beyond orthodox statistical analysis. Specifically, the aim now is to examine how far it is legitimate to *stretch* the above constraints by applying our enablers.

Thus, the enabling devices are techniques or methods, that represent a set of opposing principles to the above constraining factors, and enable us to move beyond these constraints under specific conditions. They do *not* override the constraining parameters in all circumstances. However, they could do, under a specified set of conditions in which the constraining factors provide only a partial, or incomplete, view of what it is valid to infer from data.

This concept of applying the enablers is a very powerful weapon in the holistic analyst's tool bag. It is particularly necessary when analysing today's market research data, not least because market researchers are invariably analysing (often imperfect) multiple data sets. These days, market researchers are often in a situation where their data – when set in the context of our existing prior knowledge – starts to tell a compelling and powerful story. This can take the data beyond where a conventional statistical analysis of the validity of the data would take us. Such a departure from the discipline of the orthodox constraints, reviewed above, still requires a rigorous analytical framework.

Formalizing the notion of 'directional indicators'

One particular value of the enabler concept is that it formalizes a practice common among commercial market researchers. This is the process of identifying the 'directional indicators' in data. This practice is widespread among market researchers, but, as yet, there is no *theoretical* support for this popular commercial practice. So, this leaves market researchers with no universally accepted framework for communicating to clients (or new graduate researchers) why it is 'valid' to sometimes let this so-called directional indicators approach override the constraints laid down by 'proper' statistical theory. This is the value of our notion of enablers. It allows us to move beyond the constraining factors, and embrace the directional indicator concept, but in a measured and controlled way that can be easily explained to our clients in simple conceptual terms.

So, in developing our new integrated data analysis framework, we are making a case for a revival of some of the principles behind Bayesian statistics – but in a more accessible form. The reader will recall our discussion of Bayesian statistics in Chapter 2: the notion of applying 'subjective' probabilities to different events. Bayesian concepts are currently being applied by market researchers working on certain specialist trade-off (conjoint) analysis models, but they are not regularly used for mainstream data analysis. This seriously weakens our analytical armoury because the principles behind Bayesian statistics are so very powerful. They enable us to go beyond some of the limitations of classic statistics in interpreting what data is telling us, while, at the same time, providing a rigorous interpretative framework. In particular, the Bayesian approach represents a very promising route for holistic researchers in their task of bringing quantitative and qualitative methodologies closer together.

Enabling factors: taking into account prior knowledge

Applying our enabling factors essentially means finding a way of incorporating prior knowledge and subjective probabilities into our assessment of statistical validity. Here, Bayesian statistics provide a solid foundation upon which to legitimize the process of taking more intuitive-based prior knowledge into account as part of the data analysis process. Specifically, Bayesian thinking licences – insists upon – the use of prior knowledge in interpreting data. It is a framework to discipline researchers in their attempt to develop a coherent story that accounts for the pattern in data. It draws on the analyst's prior knowledge of the market, customer behaviour, general psychology and sociology. Researchers already use this notion on an informal basis, but here, we are suggesting incorporating this process of taking into account our prior knowledge on the problem – factoring in hunch and intuition – into an explicitly stated organized analytical framework. We are suggesting that the analyst is proactive in seeking out management 'insights' and 'biases'. Do not leave these only to surface later as tacit asides. Make them explicit, upfront, and build them into your analysis.

The principle of taking prior knowledge into account as part of the analysis process is, of course, something that qualitative researchers have always done. However, we are now advocating extending this to everyday quantitative market research practice. Thus, qualitative researchers will typically assess what grounded theory tells them about the constraints of their evidence. They will then 'stretch' this boundary to make maximum use of their prior knowledge on the topic.

The holistic position: combining prior knowledge with the data

There is probably an element of an 'orthodoxian' and an element of the 'holistic' researcher in all market researchers. Most researchers will have felt the tension between these two positions at some point in their career. This will be particularly true of those who wish to provide their clients with clear objective guidance on the meaning of data, and the implications for their business. At the same time, they may feel trapped by having to stay true to orthodox statistics, and sense that they could go further by drawing on their own experience of how market research 'works', and on management prior knowledge on the subject.

An analogous problem is sometimes encountered in qualitative research. For example, it sometimes happens that, in a group discussion, a minority view that contradicts – or sits at right angles to – the majority opinion, is actually the one that the moderator favours as a true account of the attitudes of all customers. This conviction can be quite strong and often a highly interpretative qualitative researcher will take minority views as key insights into the real workings of the customer mind. Yet this flies in the face of the more conventional view, namely that the most significant issues are those that are mentioned by the most respondents.

So, in sum, many analysts often feel that they are at an impasse: they feel that some data warrants a fairly insightful interpretation, and yet the only formal methodology we have rules out anything other than a fairly straight, yet pedestrian, account of the evidence. It is here where Bayesian thinking can be liberating for holistic data analysts keen to closely relate their data to the decision-making process. At the heart of this issue is the role permitted to *prior knowledge* within orthodox approaches to market research.

The limitations of the Bayesian approach

In singing the praises of Bayesian statistics, it is important to make a number of prefacing comments:

- It must be acknowledged that this is certainly not a new idea. The notion of applying subjective probabilities to the analysis of data has a long tradition, dating back to when the concept was first advanced by Reverend Bayes.
- We are aware that many experienced orthodox statisticians – who are fully aware of the Bayesian approach – tend to shrink away from applying these techniques to *commercial research*, on the grounds that they are too complex and inaccessible for end decision-makers to grasp.
- We also know that, in the hands of the 'glorious amateur', Bayesian principles could perhaps be seen as a licence to play around in a loose way with what the hard data is telling them, rather than being a flexible way of adding prior knowledge into the analysis within a rigid, controlled framework.

Notwithstanding the above caveats, we believe it is important that any theoretical framework to advance the cause of holistic data analysis must – as a minimum – embrace Bayesian *thinking*. This is vital in helping to promote the power of incorporating prior management knowledge into the analysis of market research data. Thus, we have not shrunk from introducing the idea of the Bayesian approach in this book. However, we would qualify our enthusiasm by saying to the reader that, depending on their confidence and familiarity in this area, they can go down one of two roads. They could either attempt to formally work with Bayesian statistical analysis, *or* simply understand the principles that underpin Bayesian *thinking*, and to use these insights as the basis for incorporating prior knowledge into the data analysis process, in a disciplined way.

Making Bayesian statistics accessible

So, let us tackle this issue of bringing Bayesian thinking *alive* for the everyday market research practitioner, by first providing an example of how a traditional statistician, and then, let us call them, statisticians 'informed by Bayesian thinking', might tackle the same data. The purpose of this exercise is to work towards explaining the way in which the holistic analyst will establish a broad interpretative boundary by mapping the statistically driven constraints, and then go beyond this constraint-driven boundary to stretch the interpretation by applying the enablers.

How a 'traditional' and a 'Bayesian informed' statistician might examine the same data

Let us compare the traditional and Bayesian approaches by looking at a simple example which allows us to quickly draw out the key points of difference between the two schools of analysis. Figure 10.1 shows a very simple example of the type of data over which the orthodox and holistic schools would probably part company. It shows data from a quantitative study into a new technology targeted at a consumer market. It shows data for a sub-sample of respondents to whom, for a variety of non-technology-related reasons, the new technology is appropriate, and it also shows this sample analysed by the age categories.

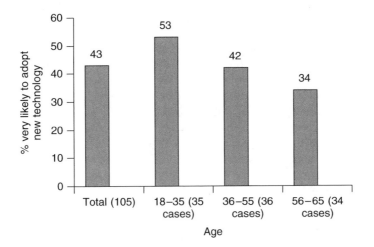

Figure 10.1 – Likelihood of adopting new technology by age.

The data in Figure 10.1 would elicit rather different responses to the data from the following different parties:

- *The intelligent non-researcher (a group which includes most of our end clients for research)*: to this group, these data seem to indicate that older people are less likely to adopt the new technology. Everything we know about age and technology tells us that we can have confidence in the particular shape and pattern in this data. Notwithstanding the trend for lifelong learning, and the presence of older 'silver surfers', it remains the case that, on balance, older people tend to be less able to acquire new skills and – as they are more likely to be established in their chosen careers – are less likely to move to acquire new skills.

- *The researcher trained in orthodox statistics*: these specialists, however, would point out that the base sizes involved mean that the differences are not statistically significant at the 95% level of confidence. For example, to be significant, the difference between the figure for the 56–65-year-old age group and that for the 18–35-year-old age group would have to be about 23%, but it is only 19%.

- *The holistic analyst*: these researchers would want to draw the same conclusion as the intelligent end client (and, left to their own devices, they probably would, in practice). However, confronted by the orthodox researcher's objections to this, they would be unsure how to defend their position, except to say that the conclusion seems 'intuitive', or is what you would 'expect to see'. Neither of these forms of defence seems to adequately address the orthodox researcher's objections. So what do we do? Do we accept the strictly statistical interpretation, or go with our prior knowledge, after taking into account whether there are any special, or unusual, conditions prevailing that could make older people opt for this particular piece of new technology?

In sum, the reason why we feel so confident in concluding from the data in Figure 10.1 that older people will, indeed, be less likely to adopt the new technology, is that we have a great deal of prior knowledge relating to the attitudes of older people, in general, to new technology. We tend (quite correctly) to view older people as being generally, 'late adopters' of technology and 'technophobes'. Thus, to help us out of this impasse, we can apply some of the principles of Bayesian statistical thinking to our analysis of the data. In some cases, this may take the form of a loose application of the notion of prior knowledge, in other cases, it may require the more detailed application of Bayesian generated statistical techniques.

Taking the enabler concept forward

We would argue that we urgently need a new conceptualization of how market research data is interpreted. We believe that to continue with the view that we can simply apply 'classic' statistics to our data flies in the face of the way the market research industry is heading. This would deny the growing trend towards using imperfect evidence drawn from multiple sources. It would also deny the growing client interest in incorporating prior management knowledge and 'grounded' intuition into the data analysis process. In sum, it seems that, over the next decade, the demand for more clinically correct, methodologically pure, orthodox statistical interpretations will decline. Surely, in the future, the demand will be for researchers who can weave the rigour of what we know about statistics together with what other data sources and management prior knowledge are telling us. So we think the Bayesian approach is incredibly powerful, and offers commercial researchers enormous potential.

It provides a methodology for adding rigour and transparency to the process of analysing market research data. It provides a clear-cut set of theory, practice and principles, which allows us to formalize the relationship between what the survey says, and what we would expect to see. Yet it seems unrealistic to expect, after all these years, that commercial researchers will suddenly embrace Bayesian statistics for the everyday interpretation of statistics. Certainly, soundings taken among experienced statisticians in the market research industry show that it is unlikely that pure Bayesian statistics will achieve the status that orthodox statistics has achieved in the world of evidence-based decision-making.

So what seems most likely, is that the (Bayesian) thinking behind the notion of embracing 'subjective' prior probability into everyday market research analysis, will gradually gain more credibility. It seems reasonable to see a day when decision-makers will begin to see the value in a new approach that makes current everyday working practices explicit and transparent.

Therefore, it seems realistic to start promoting frameworks that turn common sense into consistently applied industry-wide common practice. This would create a situation where both the client and the researcher see the benefit of jointly exploring interpretations of the data, bringing their combined knowledge to the market, thereby adding power to the market research findings. However, we accept that this will only be achieved by developing useful heuristics – general principles – rather than taking the Bayesian concept forward in its fullest statistical form.

A simple practical analysis tool

Below, we provide an example of a Bayesian-based model developed for dealing with statistics derived from smaller base sizes. This provides market researchers with a practical tool that enables them to estimate Bayesian prior probabilities without having to make complicated calculations. It is a simple tool – applied in small sample situations – aimed at 'domesticating' the Bayesian approach. Our thinking here is to match one of the great advantages of classic statistical confidence tests, namely their simplicity, which can be readily applied to any sample of more than 30 respondents and are comparatively easy to understand. By contrast, Bayesian tests are very difficult to apply.

So our approach is to employ orthodox significance tests as our guide where we have a large sample, together with what we know about sub-group sample sizes, but to employ simple *Bayesian* tests as our second line of justification when looking at smaller base sizes (of say between 25 and 75). This helps us identify patterns in data which are not sufficiently pronounced to cross the 'finishing line' of orthodox tests.

Our pragmatic solution is of value because it integrates classic and Bayesian tests to achieve the simplicity of confidence interval tests, whilst enabling the analyst to factor prior knowledge into the assessment, thereby ensuring we arrive at a true picture of the way things are. We have embedded this thinking into a simple spreadsheet, which enables researchers to integrate prior knowledge – in the form of prior probabilities – into the confidence limit tests of orthodox statistics. This gives us something analogous – in Bayesian terms – to the standard error calculations for the sample sizes that are now used.

The method simply inverts the usual confidence interval test to yield a single probability measure that an observed difference is, in fact, significant. Thus, instead of setting an arbitrary 'finishing post' of 95% or 99% and a required spread between two figures for a difference to be considered significant, the inverted methodology produces a single measure of probability that an observed difference between two figures is, in fact, significant. Thus, it may give the answer that a difference of 7% between two sub-samples of a particular size is 78% likely to be significant, rather than simply saying that the difference is not significant at the 95% confidence level and leaving it at that. Getting this single figure enables us to take the analysis a step further, and integrate our relevant prior knowledge about the situation to which the figures refer in a formal way.

Let us say that we are about 75% certain, based on what else we know, that a figure does indeed reflect a genuine difference. We can then use a very simple version of Bayes' formula to integrate the 78% likelihood from the inverted classical confidence test into our 75% prior knowledge. If we do this, we get a posterior probability of 91%. Thus, our overall confidence in the data has risen to 91%. Many readers may be surprised that the probability has gone up, expecting the combination of two probabilities to result in a lower probability. The fact that our intuitive response to the idea of combining probabilities tends to lead us astray demonstrates the importance of disciplining such influences with a simple formal tool such as this.

In the related training module to support this book – available on the Wiley website – readers will find details of how to obtain access to the model. In Figure 10.2 we provide a conceptual overview of how the model works.

We conclude this chapter with an example of how the 'constraints & enablers' can work together in establishing the overall interpretation boundary for a multiple data set. Here, we return to our example of assessing the attitudes of small and medium sized UK businesses (SMEs) towards joining the Single European Currency (Table 10.3).

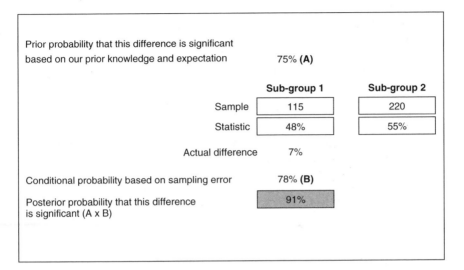

Figure 10.2 – Overview of a Bayesian directional estimator for two sub-samples.

Table 10.3 – An illustrative example of 'constraints & enablers' – Single European Currency example

- *The evidence*: let us say we have: secondary data; 30 depth interviews with SME businesses; 10 interviews with industry experts from the SME sector; 6 focus groups conducted among small businesses; a telephone quota sample survey of 400 UK SMEs; and an Internet survey of 1000 small businesses. How would the holistic data analysts make sense of this multiple data?
- *Step one – applying the theoretical constraints to the qualitative evidence*: what we know about grounded theory allows us to 'formally' evaluate the SMEs and expert depth interviews and focus groups. Here, we could inspect all of the issues that surface from the different types of qualitative research against what we already know. This allows us to distinguish consistently raised concepts from what appear to be outlier observations, not resonant with existing prior knowledge.
- *Step two – applying the theoretically driven constraints to the quantitative data*: we know from the theory of the theoretical sampling distribution that a statistic of 50% drawn from a sample of 400 SMEs will be accurate to plus or minus 5%, at the 95% level of confidence (assuming the conditions of simple random sampling). We could also apply this body of theory to calculate the sampling error for our Internet survey of 1000 businesses, and also conduct various tests to establish whether there is a (statistically significant) difference between different percentages.
- *Step three – applying constraints driven by empirical 'theory'*: there is also the body of empirical evidence that allows us to interpret the implications of the 'response/strike rate' achieved on the telephone quota and Internet sample surveys. Here we know that ideally the response rate should be 65% (or more), if we are to assume that respondents are similar in their attitudes to non-respondents. If it is less than this we will have to factor this 'sample bias' into our interpretation of the evidence.

(continued overleaf)

Table 10.3 – (*continued*)

- *Step four – utilizing the compensation principle*: earlier we introduced the 'compensation principle'. So now, we could, for example, by referring to our desk research and secondary evidence begin to 'compensate' for any limitations in our evidence. For instance, the Internet survey *may* over-represent the more technologically minded. So we would need to 'adjust' for this potential bias by setting it in the context of 'triangulating' our survey data with other available evidence.
- *Step five – applying the 'enablers' to the qualitative and quantitative evidence*: we can now, in the spirit of holistic data analysis, begin to 'stretch' the above boundary – the constraints – laid down by the above theoretical and empirical principles. This could be conducted at two levels:
  - *Level one – applying the 'directional indicators' principle*: we could look at how the evidence from our different sources is coming together to create a general 'shape or pattern', that begins to tell the SME 'story'. In an informal way, we could examine how our data 'fits' with existing prior knowledge on the subject of SMEs and Europe. This understanding of the fit between the pattern of our data, and the wider shape of the contextualizing evidence, could give us the confidence to embrace evidence that, while not statistically significant, does seem to be important, when set in the context of our prior knowledge. We will attach importance to evidence that is directionally consistent, and squares with our current broader prior knowledge on the topic
  - *Level two – the more formal application of Bayesian thinking*: we could, on occasion, take the above Bayesian thinking to a more formal level. To 'stretch' our data beyond the boundaries driven by orthodox analysis, we could work with some of the statistical concepts and principles outlined at the end of this chapter.
- So, in sum, the holistic data analyst will always use orthodox 'constraints' as the bedrock of their evaluation. Then, to enhance their interpretation and the quality of the end decision-making process, they will see how far this take on the data can then be legitimately stretched by our enablers – factoring in what we already know.

Having introduced the reader to the holistic analysis concepts of using enablers to stretch the initially constrained statistical data, we now turn to the way in which the holistic data analyst will apply a range of 'analytical' or 'knowledge filters' in beginning to make sense of what surveys – respondents – are really telling us.

So in the next chapter, we look at the next stage of our holistic analysis framework: applying the knowledge filters.

11 Applying the knowledge filters

Summary

- Surveys provide vital feedback from consumers, but they can be coarse, imperfect measuring instruments. However, over the years, practitioners have learnt where surveys 'work', and where they may be giving us a slightly flawed reading of events. So, it makes sense for this general knowledge about how surveys work – these knowledge filters – to be applied at the interpretation stage of a project.
- Some of this knowledge relates to the way experienced analysts will understand the overall principles underpinning the way surveys – as *aggregate* measuring instruments – need to be interpreted. So, we start this review of the knowledge filters, by looking at the issue of how to make sense of change reported in surveys, and examine what we know about establishing the relationship between cause and effect, together with looking at the relationship between reported attitudes and subsequent behaviour.
- We then look at the knowledge that survey experts have built up about the way in which respondents broach the task of participating in the market research process. The holistic data analyst acknowledges that not all respondents are created equal in their ability to contribute to the survey research process, and has therefore built up a range of knowledge filters to help us get behind respondents' literal responses, and understand the true meaning of what people are trying to tell us.
- In sum, in this chapter, we look at the way in which the experienced holistic data analyst will apply various knowledge, or analytical, filters to bring their overall deep understanding of the survey process to bear on a specific piece of consumer evidence in front of them.
- We start this chapter by examining the power and the legitimacy of 'overriding' certain face-value responses from survey respondents. We then start explaining the first of our 'knowledge filters': what we know about how to intelligently interpret the different types of relationship between different phenomena that can surface in survey data.

The power of knowledge filters

There was, in the past, a tendency for market researchers to be less than transparent in publicly acknowledging that the survey process contains a number of flaws, and that the literal responses from respondents answering our questionnaires needs extremely careful interpretation. Today, though, the holistic school of the interpretation of market research data is more open in acknowledging the difficulties respondents face when confronted with survey questions aimed at eliciting feedback on their behaviour and attitudes. These days, the skill set of the holistic data analyst extends to a good working knowledge of what we know about the strengths and limitations of the qualitative and quantitative research process, and the ability to apply this knowledge to the subsequent data analysis.

Thus, our holistic data analysis model reflects the fact that respondents differ in their ability to identify, and articulate, the true motivations for their actions and, given this, argues that it is sensible to factor what we know about this into the analysis and interpretation process. Therefore, in this chapter, we review the process of applying various knowledge (or analytical) filters in order to get at the true meaning of respondents' responses.

Making what we know explicit

Researchers, over the years, have, of course, been aware of the limitations of the survey research process. The point we are making here is that we now need to make these observations more explicit and transparent to new entrants into the market research industry, and our end users. We believe market researchers will add considerable power to their reputation by explicitly factoring into their analysis of data an understanding of what we know about the relationship between respondents' answers to formal questioning in surveys and qualitative interviews and their *true* motivations and behaviour.

We now have a considerable body of normative knowledge about the market research process. We have a de facto 'theory' of how market research 'works' based on our understanding of consumer psychology and day-to-day pragmatic experience. Therefore, the concept of applying knowledge filters to make sense of respondents' survey responses is a logical development. The goal is to avoid arriving at naïve and uninformed conclusions from consumer data.

So, what we are doing is drawing on what market researchers know about the research process to identify some generalizable rules that help us get to grips with consumers' true attitudes, motivations and behaviour. In this way, we can pinpoint various 'filters' through which we can pass our data at the analysis stage. This gives us a richer understanding of the relationship between respondents' *true* motivations and behaviour, and their answers to formal questioning in surveys and various qualitative interviews.

Building on a strong qualitative tradition

The coyness and reluctance by market researchers to be more transparent and explicit about the *quantitative* survey process is strange when taken in the context of the way *qualitative* researchers have always operated. With qualitative research – where the data collection and analysis phases of a project are more closely intertwined – there has, of course, always been considerable scope for using knowledge filters to improve the quality of the analysis.

The qualitative researcher has always known the value of making (instant) judgements about the competence of the individual respondents in front of them to provide answers that come close to what they really mean. This has meant that qualitative researchers have various analytical frameworks, principles and models for going beyond the initial superficial responses they have been given.

Thus, the experienced qualitative researcher will usually give additional weight to certain minority views because there is a 'quality' to the way the points were made, or something authoritative about the respondent(s) who made them. The qualitative researcher will – given their past experience – know that a particular (minority) response lies closer to the truth than the response of the majority, which they may suspect of being excessively rationalized, designed to impress, and so on.

So, what we are arguing for here is matching this qualitative approach when it comes to quantitative evidence. We are saying that what qualitative researchers do fairly automatically is what we should be doing with quantitative data. The challenge then, for market research, when it comes to *quantitative* data, is to find accessible, user-friendly frameworks that will allow newcomers to understand the process that experienced market researchers go through – that is, passing the data through various knowledge filters when interpreting quantitative data.

In sum we believe that it makes sense for our holistic data analysis model to reflect the fact that the experienced market researcher, when interpreting customer evidence, will apply a series of knowledge filters – rules of thumb (or heuristics) – for interpreting the generated customer data, based on their understanding of the systematic biases that can creep into people's responses to survey questions.

Developing our knowledge filters framework

Before setting out our recommended knowledge filters, we should provide the reader with a health warning. We have referred to there being in existence 'theories' about how market research 'works'. However, it has to be accepted that there is no universally accepted body of knowledge that everyone will sign up to as being *the* theory of market research. What we know about how people behave in particular scenarios, and how to interpret such evidence, exists in pockets of knowledge drawn across many disciplines, including numerous social science and market research journals. So, doing justice to this in one chapter of a book is a challenge. Thus, given the massive scope of this information, all we can do here is provide a broad overview of some of the key knowledge filters that are likely to apply in lots of general situations. So, what we have sought to do, is to develop an organizing – or learning – framework that will, taken in conjunction with the Notes section, guide the reader through the broad areas we feel they may need to focus upon when engaged in a particular data analysis exercise.

An organizing framework for learning

So, our aim here is to provide an overall organizing framework that will help focus the data analyst's thinking about what consumers are trying to tell us, but which we expect the analyst to take to a more detailed level of final application. Thus, what we provide in this chapter is by no means an exhaustive universal set of all known knowledge filters relating to market research evidence. What we seek to do, is to alert the reader to the importance of delving, to find out from the relevant existing bodies of literature, what knowledge filters *might* enhance their upcoming analysis. Specifically, we would expect any data analyst, shaping up to evaluate a particular piece of data, to – in the context of our organizing framework – comb their own niche pool of specialist knowledge filters.

We start our overview of the key knowledge filters by focusing on some general principles of how market research surveys – as aggregate measuring instruments asking standardized questions – work. We follow this by putting the spotlight on what we know about the varying ways in which individuals shape up to the task of giving responses to our survey questions.

Understanding the nature of relationships in survey data

So let us look at our first knowledge filter: what we know about some of the fundamental relationships within survey data. Without this core understanding of the survey process, there is a danger of the analyst drawing naïve and ill-informed conclusions from their observations. There are two particular issues to be alert to:

- It is clearly essential that the analyst understands the difference between statistical correlation and causation. Readers will be aware of numerous illustrations of curious relationships. For example, the consumption of tinned tuna fish is correlated with a higher incidence of mental illness. Is this something to do with the metal from the tin contaminating the fish? No. It simply reflects the fact that tinned tuna fish is more likely to be consumed in parts of the Western world where there is already a higher level of mental illness. Statistically, at one point, more suicides took place in downtown Los Angeles than in the outlying areas of California. Was this because of the ennui generated by living in a concrete jungle? No. It was because there was a greater availability of cheap anonymous motel rooms for the deed. Thus, it was one thing to first establish a statistical correlation between levels of smoking and lung disease (samples of smokers are significantly more likely to contract a lung-related disease than non-smokers); but it was another issue to pinpoint the exact cause of this statistical relationship (nicotine forms on the lung, thereby generating cancerous cells).

- It is also important to be clear about how to draw accurate conclusions about what is a 'cause' and what is an 'effect'. For example, when analysing data about advertising and sales, it is easy to fall into the trap of thinking that the increase in advertising (the cause) has led to an increase in sales (the effect). Here, it is possible that the organization, when sales go up, feels that it now has the revenue, and confidence, to start advertising its product. So, in the latter situation, the cause was increased sales, which led to the effect (increased advertising).

The relationship between reported attitudes and subsequent behaviour

We know that we cannot necessarily always accurately predict someone's behaviour just because we know what a person thinks and how strongly they hold these opinions on this particular issue. Just because a person claims a belief in a principle or value, it does not necessarily mean that we can identify the predicted behaviour that will flow from this attitude. These days, for example, just because an individual goes to church every Sunday, it does not necessarily mean that they believe in God. Similarly, we cannot assume that an individual who believes in God will regularly go to church. In short, today, market researchers are becoming more confident in challenging the simple relationships that, it was previously thought, existed between beliefs and behaviour.

This raises the question of what general lessons about the interrelationship between attitudes and behaviour the holistic data analyst can draw upon when analysing a particular data set. This is a wide area, and we provide some key references in the Notes section. The central point to make here is that it is important to set the claims being made by respondents in surveys about their likely future behaviour in the context of a wide range of influences that could contribute to making this reported attitude volatile and subject to change. Thus, at its most basic, it is important to first recognize that a person's attitude divides into two parts:

- There is that person's *own set of beliefs* about the issue under investigation.
- We also have to take into account that person's *perceptions of what other people think* on this particular issue.

Here, the relative contribution of each of the above two elements may vary, depending on whether the person has a more 'inner' or 'outer' directed focus to their personality. Thus, in making judgements about what current attitudes mean for likely future behaviour, the holistic analyst will be mindful of concepts, such as Gladwell's notion of the 'tipping point'. This, put simply, means that individuals will often keep a 'watching brief' on a particular scenario, for example, whether or not to use email. Then, based on the various reinforcing (or disturbing) messages they receive back from those around them, the individual will eventually arrive at a point where they – and the majority – will (or will not) 'tip over' into widespread acceptance of this new technology. Thus, in understanding attitudes – in the context of commercial market research – it is particularly important to assess how a respondent's current views may be influenced by changes in what people around that individual think about the topic under investigation.

Local, not universal, theories

In terms of practical advice to the holistic data analyst about what body of literature to read to ensure they understand some of the forces at work in terms of the relationship between reported attitudes and behaviour, we would make the following general observation. This is that, today, it is not fashionable to pursue grand universal models of how attitudes link to behaviour, but, instead, to develop local, 'micro-models' of how behaviour and attitudes seem to work in particular market and customer scenarios. Given this, it is sensible for the analyst to locate their data in the appropriate body of local knowledge, and see what mid-range models they might draw upon to help them with their particular analysis. In the world of public service advertising, for example, one particular 'knowledge filter' that could be applied, would centre on what we know about 'cognitive dissonance'. This theory (or body of psychological thinking) tells us that individuals like to be in 'equilibrium'. So, let us say that we show an individual a TV commercial about what may happen if they flew through a car windscreen (because they were not wearing a seatbelt), or contracted HIV (because they were not using condoms). Here, we know from our understanding of the relationship between attitudes and subsequent behaviour that, in this specific scenario, these impactful messages run the possible risk of *not* changing individuals' behaviour in the direction of wearing a seatbelt, or engaging in safe sex. Instead, shocked by the imagery being presented, individuals may respond by associating the communication with the problem. Then, to return to psychological equilibrium, the easiest solution is to 'switch off' from this advertising, thereby rejecting possible solutions along with the problem, rather than engaging in the desired change in behaviour. So, interpreting data in the context of relevant local 'theories', may add power to your analysis of a piece of evidence.

Understanding the dynamics of survey data

Another key body of knowledge, through which the holistic analyst will pass their data in order to enhance their interpretation, centres on our understanding of the nature of the change being reported in aggregate survey data. Here, the first issue to clarify though, is that our comments refer to *ad hoc*, not longitudinal research. The former involves identifying change by identifying the movement observed when studying *ad hoc* samples (i.e. each containing different respondents) taken at different points in time. The latter – longitudinal (or continuous) research – examines the same panel of respondents, who are interviewed at different points in time. Here, we are *only* focusing on the issue of interpreting *ad hoc* data. This is the entire context to, and exclusive focus for, this book. (Longitudinal research skills are, of course, critically important in building the complete information jigsaw, but it is not practicable to embrace the specialist knowledge needed of continuous research into just one volume. But we have provided a key reference in the Notes section that will introduce the analyst to further reading in this area.) So, against this backdrop, let us now look at the types of change that can occur in *ad hoc* surveys, which it is important to understand, so as to minimize the chances of naïve conclusions being drawn.

Compensatory change

Here, we are referring to a situation where the analyst will know there have been various changes to consumers' attitudes and/or behaviour over the period of, say, two *ad hoc* surveys, but where the surveys do not show any differences in terms of the overall total sample statistics being reported. This situation, of course, reflects the way compensatory movements have been made by respondents *within* each study. Thus, if we were to just believe the total sample statistics, we would see little change over a certain period. What, of course, has happened here, is that a change in one direction (reported by one respondent), will be compensated for by a change in the other direction (reported by another).

Flows and snapshots

Following on from the above, let us give a practical illustration of why understanding the dynamics of survey findings is important. Let us take the example of interpreting unemployment statistics. We could look at two *ad hoc* surveys taken over, for example, a three-year period, and conclude that, because the total sample statistics show the same level of unemployment, then there has been no change in the balance of the employed and unemployed. But, in fact, unemployment is of course a 'flow'. There will be people coming out of employment and going into unemployment and vice versa. This observation is clearly important in reading the 'mood of the nation'. Clearly knowing that, say, 10% of the population are *currently* unemployed is one thing, but that over a period of three years, possibly up to 40% of individuals will have experienced some form of unemployment, adds more power to our understanding. So, in sum, the experienced survey analyst will know that, while the overall shape of a survey distribution may, from one survey to the other, remain similar or the same, there could be substantial change taking place within this sample that will be concealed by the (compensatory) nature of this change.

Actual change based on 'real' events

Over a period of time there could, of course, be true, or actual, change in a person's attitude towards, for example, a hotel that they use regularly. For instance, an individual, based on their experiences, may shift from being 'totally satisfied' to being 'totally dissatisfied'. (Again, the analyst needs to be mindful of the fact that there could be compensatory movements between hotel guests *within* any one sample, such that the survey totals on customer satisfaction remain exactly the same over time.)

Change that is a function of the insensitivity of the measuring instrument

Another scenario is where the survey's measuring instruments are not sufficiently precise to capture what could be comparatively 'fine' differences in the attitude in question. For example, let us say that, in a survey to evaluate the roller coaster of emotions associated with a lifelong commitment to the local football team, one of the authors is presented with only two broad options: are they a 'good' team – or are they a 'bad' team? Given the reduction of the 'beautiful game' to this level of over-simplification, he could be forgiven for fluctuating – depending on whether the boys won or lost last week – across these two categorizations. This volatility largely reflects the coarse measuring instrument, however, rather than any serious attempt to measure an always slightly varying, but essentially core, allegiance to the local team.

Change reflecting our genuine inconsistency and varying 'mood states'

We also have to accept that we, as individuals, are inconsistent in the way we fashion our attitudes and comment on our experiences. Thus, returning to our example of customers' satisfaction with a hotel, here we could find a situation where there has been no substantive change in the standard of service or facilities provided by the hotel, but where, over, for example, two surveys, an individual will elect to dramatically change their satisfaction assessment. This reflects the way in which some individuals, on certain topics, may float around, in terms of deciding – in their own heads – against what criteria they should be judging the hotel. This point links into a wide body of literature on 'reversal theory' that helps us understand the idea of individuals leading their lives in different 'mood states'. Sometimes individuals will be in playful, light-hearted, non-demanding mode, and take bad experiences with a hotel in good part. In other scenarios, the same individual will be in a dutiful and more demanding mood state, whereby any small peccadilloes on the part of the hotel, will be seized upon by the customer as evidence of gross incompetence.

The register in which market research engages

Another key body of knowledge that will inform how the holistic data analyst will make sense of their survey data, centres on what we know about the 'register', in which individuals will engage about brands, advertising, promotions, and the commercial aspect to their lives. In making sense of respondents' attitudes to these issues, we need to acknowledge the fact that we know that some people will sometimes want to downplay the role of what are, by most objective accounts, extremely powerful external influences. Here, accepting respondents' protestations that 'advertising doesn't have any affect on me', of course, flies in the face of what we know about the power of mass communications in forming consumer attitudes, and influencing how these attitudes change over time. Put another way, we have to accept that there are various scenarios where the face value comments of individuals would need to be over-ridden, because there are more deep-seated, socio-economic, sociological, and/or powerful communication factors at play, that, whilst they are the cause of respondents' responses, are only likely to be hinted at in the replies given to us by individuals taking part in surveys.

Thus, experienced holistic market researchers will be aware of the way in which consumer attitudes, in many scenarios, are shaped over time, in a 'low process/low involvement' mode. Here, we are indebted to Robert Heath, for his coherent and articulate account of how certain communications can operate in a very tacit, subtle, low-key way, over time. The customer/respondent may be unaware of these influences, but they are nonetheless still at work. Thus, the holistic analyst will be alert to communications likely to be overtly recalled, and explicitly acknowledged, by respondents, together with communications that work in a more covert way. This, of course, opens up the significant issue of how the assessment of advertising should be conducted. Here, it is sufficient to say that it is clearly inappropriate to focus exclusively on measures, such as the impact and memorability of an advertising campaign, as this *may* understate the value of communications that are working subliminally over time.

In sum, the holistic researcher will be alert to the overall 'engagement register' in which the respondent provided their survey responses. On the one hand, the holistic data analyst will need to be sensitive to respondents' comments about how they feel they may have been influenced by different forms of marketing communications. On the other hand, the analyst will need to contextualize these 'literal' responses in the wider context of what we know about the power of 'low process/low involvement' communications.

The motives of respondents taking part in surveys

In reviewing some general principles about the way surveys 'work', it is important to register a fundamental observation about the nature of the motives of respondents taking part in market research interviews. Some pundits speculate about respondents being some kind of 'trickster', who come to the interview process with complex Machiavellian agendas. It is true that some respondents, on some occasions, will try to exaggerate their position and aggrandize their self-image, be guilty of hyperbole, forget certain key details, fail to concentrate on important detail, and be more or less able to articulate their 'true' views. But importantly, the majority of the respondents *will* try to answer survey questions as truthfully as possible. To suggest that they do not, in most cases, is a crude form of cynicism.

There are, of course, scenarios where various mind games will come into play during the course of the survey process. For example, some respondents may tell opinion pollsters a 'lie' about their likely voting intentions at a General Election because they are caught up in a 'tactical voting' initiative to secure a particular outcome (Tory voters deciding to vote Liberal to oust a Labour supporter, and so on).

In addition, we know that there is a tendency for respondents at certain questions to over-anticipate what the question they are being asked is trying to achieve. For example, it is customary for market researchers to ask individuals about 'the last purchase'. The researcher, in asking such questions, knows that a feature of the sampling process is that 'freak' situations – where an individual's 'last purchase' departed from their usual behaviour – will be 'compensated' for by someone else in the sample, who engages in equally atypical behaviour, but in the exact opposite direction. (Thus, if person A goes into a BP garage for the first time in 20 years, rather than their usual Shell garage, this will be compensated for by a motorist who does the exact opposite.) However, some respondents, in their keenness to 'please' the researcher, will play back in their answer what they perceive the researcher wants, and will not give their 'last', but their 'modal', behaviour. This kind of response will, of course, interfere with obtaining a robust distribution of the true incidence of behaviour on the phenomenon under investigation. Similarly, as we have explained, if, in a survey aimed at assessing priorities for a local authority, we cast our respondent in the role of the Chief Executive Officer, and then switch him back to the role of being an ordinary rate payer, we will not be surprised to find that this 'role switch' may have inflated the respondent's socially-minded responses, and so on. But the point to stress here is that the responses given in these varying scenarios are done out of helpfulness, and not out of any attempt at deceit or mendacity.

People's ability to understand questions and recall their behaviour and attitudes

Individuals vary enormously, of course, in their intellectual ability to absorb complex questions. So, clearly, it is the responsibility of the market researcher to make their interviewing vehicle one that can be understood across the intellectual spectrum. It is critical for the market researcher to ensure that questions that are incomprehensible to a large number of respondents are simply not asked. Clearly, no amount of intelligent interpretation – no amount of the application of our concept of 'compensation' principle and the passing of responses through our knowledge filters – is going to overcome a fundamental flaw in the way that a question was couched. Thus, the researcher needs to be sensitive to the different ways in which individuals receive communications – reflecting, for example, on what we said about neurolinguistic programming modes – and factor this into the market research process.

So, on the assumption that our survey questions have been understood, let us now take into account what we know about an individual's ability to then recall key facts about their past behaviour or experience. The overall point to be made is that memory for events and experiences as a general rule, as we all know, deteriorates over time. Yet, memory for events and experiences seen by the respondent as particularly important will be better than for events that are less important to them. One of the authors can remember how many classic wooden sailing boats he has purchased in his lifetime, but not the number of second-hand hatchbacks. Similarly, we know that respondents are more likely to recall events – and do so in a constructive way – where the respondent has some interest in projecting an image of him or herself through the answers he or she gives. (GCSE Grade A's in romantic subjects, such as English Literature, tend to make their way onto the curriculum vitae, and stay on into old age, whereas failures, all those years ago, in pesky little science subjects are neatly airbrushed out of history.)

In addition, the data analyst, particularly when interpreting reported attitudes in surveys, should be alert to people's tendency to 'infill', or construct, their memories around events that seem consistent with their general understanding of the world. In particular, we know that people's actual recollections of their own personal experience may be distorted by the stereotype of the issue being discussed. Thus, the stereotypes – that accountants are boring, salesmen are pushy, and estate agents are dishonest – might get in the way of our own personal experiences.

Similarly, there are various language and cliché traps that can also distort our memory. For instance, certain phrases can gain such common currency in a culture, thereby making it hard for people to recall their own personal experiences outside of these dominant clichés. One such example is the phrase 'provides value for money'. This is a convenient, off-the-peg way for respondents to summarize particular products and services. These days, when someone sums up their experiences of a product, in this now tired and overworked way, it may not actually be a recollection that describes someone who spends time and effort achieving an optimum balance between price and product benefits. It is simply a clichéd, shorthand way of saying that this product was 'OK', or 'acceptable'.

This body of knowledge on how people recall their experiences has led market researchers to know how best to encourage and prompt accurate recall. For instance, robust recall is best facilitated when the question is located in the context in which the behaviour being asked about took place. For example, 'thinking back to when you were last standing in front of the freezer cabinet at Tesco's, what frozen products did you. . .?'. Similarly, we know that respondents are more likely to recall events on a prompted, rather than unprompted, basis. (Although, of course, the researcher will often want to first record a spontaneous recollection.) In short, analysts should always be alert to the limitations of respondents' memory in their interpretation of the evidence.

Let us now move away from making general observations about how surveys 'work', to focus directly on the sharp variation that exists in people's individual ability to contribute to the research process.

All respondents are not created equal

Market researchers are now becoming more confident in *openly* acknowledging that not all consumers are created equal in their ability to help inform the business decision process. There will be various scenarios where the face value comments of respondents will need to be 'overridden', given what we know about people's psychological tendencies. This includes people's desire to present themselves in a flattering way, and a tendency to exaggerate the rational, at the expense of the emotional reasons for our responses. Of course, none of this is new, but it is an important observation, in the sense that we have now arrived at a more widespread acceptance of the fact that each individual in a survey does not carry an equal weight in the contribution they make to our understanding of the problem under investigation.

In fact, it is strange that a situation should have arisen whereby market researchers have, on the one hand, built up a wealth of understanding about how the survey process 'works', but on the other, seem reluctant to be more open about the need for literal face value consumer responses to be heavily interpreted. There is nothing sinister, or elitist, about our observation that respondents' responses to surveys need to be heavily interpreted. It simply reflects the reality that not all respondents are created equal in their ability to make sense of survey questions. Respondents may genuinely attempt to explain their true attitudes and report their current behaviour in an honest and straightforward way. But for various reasons, what people say they do, and think, *could* be different from what they really believe, and do. So why not set these literal consumer responses in the context of the powerful set of normative rules, principles and precepts, that is *de facto* market research 'theory', and make this accessible to newcomers to market research?

In thinking about the variability in survey respondents, it is helpful to think about where each respondent in our study sits in terms of the following three key criteria.

Respondent's ability to see issues from the third corner: conceptual versus concrete thinking skills

- There is a body of theoretical knowledge that tells us about people who have an ability to think *conceptually*, but who have a more limited appetite for leading their understanding of an issue through mastery of the concrete detail. Conversely, some individuals are more comfortable thinking first in terms of specific examples, and later grappling with the abstractions.
- This notion of there being conceptual and more detailed thinkers has its roots in what psychologists tell us about *passive* (binary) thinkers – who tend to respond to existing constructs – as opposed to more *active* (ternary) thinkers – who will generate their own constructs to look at a problem in a new way. Thus, the binary thinkers will tend to have a fairly narrow perspective in evaluating issues, often tending to look at matters in terms of black versus white and win or lose. Ternary thinkers, though, have the ability to look at issues from the 'third corner', specifically having the ability to identify the key, often higher-order, concepts that relate to the issue under investigation.
- Therefore, putting together the above ideas, we find, from the commercial market researchers' perspective, that it is helpful – when asking questions of individuals, and subsequently interpreting their responses – to establish whether an individual will be most comfortable thinking in an abstract, conceptual way, as opposed to a detailed, concrete way.

Willingness to embrace new ideas and change

- Another dimension of personality that it is helpful for commercial researchers to take into account when talking to respondents centres on where they fit on a scale that runs from a willingness to welcome new ideas, through a reluctance to embrace the new.
- Here, we know, of course, about the 'early innovator'/'late adopter' model, and there is some evidence to suggest that the notion of being an 'early innovator' is related to the idea of inner (as opposed to other or outer) directedness. This tells us that 'inner directed' individuals tend to rely on their own inner values and standards to direct thinking and behaviour, while 'outer directed' personalities rely on the values of those with whom

they interact. In short, inner directed individuals may be more open-minded, whereas the 'outer directed' need more affirmation from those around them before embracing the new.

- The above notion also links to the idea of there being 'reflective' and 'projective' thinkers. Thus, we have individuals who think about information as it is presented in an immediate 'here and now' way. This contrasts to those who are more able to move beyond the immediate, and project their thinking about the incoming information to what might be out there in the future.

Opportunities, willingness and ability to articulate views and opinions

- A further personality dimension, on which commercial researchers will eval-uate respondents, centres on the opportunities, willingness, and ability the individual has to express their views. In part, this could be linked to quite prosaic matters surrounding the length of time made available for an inter-view, for example, in a business-to-business research interview with a board level director. Here, a sheer shortage of time may limit the researcher's ability to do justice to a senior business expert's knowledge.
- However, there could be other dimensions at work. For example, based on what we know about introversion and extroversion, we can speculate that some respondents will be more willing to open up and articulate their views than others. Related to this, we know that some individuals are very task and time orientated (associated with Type A personality types). This group stands in contrast to the Type B personality, who are more likely to be relaxed (even playful) in their approach to issues, such as taking part in research interviews.

The three dimensions to an interview

So, in summary, respondents are not equally placed to contribute to the survey process. In Figure 11.1 we represent the above conceptualization of the kinds of people taking part in surveys. This highlights the fact that the experienced data analyst will not fall into the trap of thinking that *all* respondents in the survey are: comfortable understanding the higher-order concepts we are presenting; willing to project forward and embrace new ideas; and have the mental space and time to take part in survey research. In short, respondents will be distributed around the three-dimensional space, shown in the figure. The experienced analyst will not suspend disbelief and make the assumption that everyone will be sitting in the top right-hand corner of the matrix. Instead, they will understand how their sample distributes around our three dimensions.

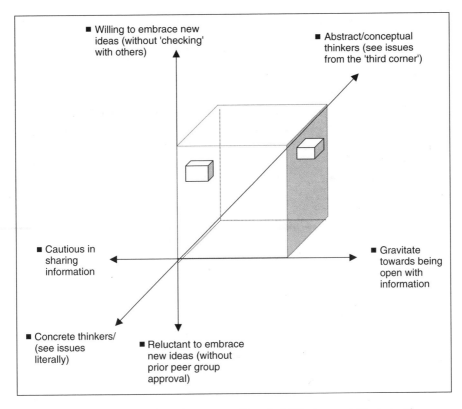

Willing to embrace new ideas (without 'checking' with others)

Abstract/conceptual thinkers (see issues from the 'third corner')

Cautious in sharing information

Gravitate towards being open with information

Concrete thinkers/ (see issues literally)

Reluctant to embrace new ideas (without prior peer group approval)

Figure 11.1 – Variations in respondents' ability to contribute to the survey process.

Interpreting respondents' accounts of their actions

So far in this chapter, we have established that people – who will vary in the way that they 'receive' what we are asking them to do in surveys – on balance, are keen to provide honest responses to the surveys. Yet we also know that there are a range of factors that influence their accounts of their actions. We know that people tend to:

- Project a positive image of themselves.
- Flatter their position.
- Lean on contexts that privilege the kind of person they believe themselves to be.
- Build their own self-esteem.
- Rationalize their actions.
- Express themselves in easy to reel off, generalized 'platitudes', rather than articulating, with precision, their true attitudes.

So, at the heart of the intelligent analysis of survey evidence, will be a grasp of the way these various contextual influences work on individual responses. So, below, we outline what we know about this issue.

Conversational accounting

Rom Harre argues that one of the dominant preoccupations of individuals is to defend their 'self-image' (who it is they think they are) in the face of others. From this basic premise, Harre goes on to argue that many individuals do not so much have 'conversations', but instead spend an inordinate amount of time providing (conversational) 'accounts' of themselves, and their behaviour, in support of the self-image they have constructed. We have all heard, and perhaps been guilty ourselves of having, these 'conversations'. For example, take someone who, for whatever reason, did not go to university, but who obviously wanted to. Rather than acknowledging this fact, they will engage in endless conversational 'accounting'. You know the kind of thing: 'My home correspondence course gave me the discipline and backbone that most university graduates just don't get these days'.

Privileging selective contexts

Another useful analytical concept for interpreting survey feedback is what we now know about how people construct 'frameworks of meaning' to provide consistent representations of themselves. This body of knowledge, building on Harre's point, tells us that people are constantly 'managing' the meanings they give to their actions and their experiences. This is based on the idea that we all like to believe that the meanings we provide for ourselves, and those around us, are reasonably consistent. This notion of an individual managing the contexts in which they live – the idea of people operating with different frameworks of meaning – is a powerful concept because it tells us that people are motivated to promote, or 'privilege', specific contexts that make sense of what they say or do in support of their self-image. For example, a senior business executive who usually flies first or business class – but who will also use low-cost airlines from time to time – may be quick to 'privilege' certain types of contexts (say information in the media) that highlight the way in which low-cost airlines are now being used by seasoned, upmarket, putative first class business travellers.

In sum, the holistic researcher will be constantly alert to respondents' preoccupation with the management of their self-image, and their tendency to provide flattering accounts of their behaviour.

Post-rationalized attitudes

Building on the above points, let us now illustrate, with a very simplistic worked example, a particular manifestation of the tendency for individuals to post-rationalize their attitudes. In Figure 11.2 we show the results of an open-ended, multiple-choice question about reasons for fabric softener selection.

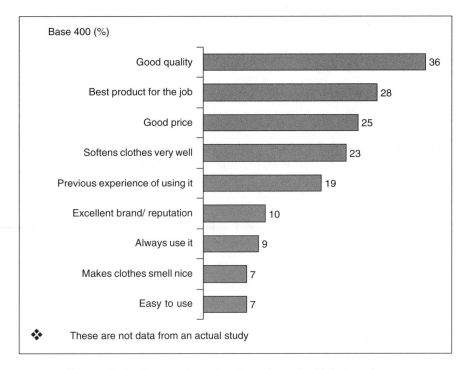

Figure 11.2 – Reason for selecting a brand of fabric softener.

We could interpret the data in a rather two-dimensional way: simply noting the weighting attached to the different responses and presenting this as the customers' priorities for the product. Alternatively, we could take into account that motives for purchase, or action, are often non-rational, based on emotional habit, and take place in a survey interview environment, where an objective assessment is still considered to be the appropriate way of explaining oneself.

Therefore, at the analysis stage, it makes sense to *upgrade* 'non-rational' reasons when we see them in data. So, a more sophisticated interpretation would be to use what we know about how consumers respond to this type of question, to up-weight those responses which we know customers tend to be reluctant or unable to give. These responses include:

- Motives for purchase or action which are non-rational – that is, are based on emotion or habit where objective assessment is considered appropriate. We know from consumer psychology that people tend to decide on largely emotional or impulsive grounds and then justify their decisions afterwards on rational grounds.
- Reasons, other than irrationality, which might be thought to show respondents in a poor light, such as anti-social reasons, which are lacking in virtue.

- Issues that are subtle, or of very low salience. For example, a consumer might, in spite of the risk of appearing to be irrational, be prepared to admit that the eye-catching colour of the packaging was what made them buy a product, but simply be unaware that this was the case.

In the case of the data in Figure 11.2, compared with reasons, such as product quality and price, *'excellent brand/reputation'*, *'previous experience of using it'* and *'I always use it'*, appear to be more non-rational responses. Therefore, we should consider 'up-weighting' these in our interpretation of the data, perhaps to the point where we would conclude that brand choice in this market is likely to be very habitual and that, as long as product quality, price, and so on (which are all clearly important), are maintained, consumers will be loyal to a brand, rather than seeking out new products.

The combination of the slightly more rational *'previous experience'*, and the more bluntly habitual *'I always use it'*, suggests that both proximate mechanisms for rational criteria, as well as pure habit or inertia, are at work. Previous experience is important because this is a category where judgements of quality are virtually impossible to make, prior to consumption or usage. (This is not the case in other categories, such as automotive or 'brown' goods, where reasonably good cues to quality – including very rational ones, such as technical specifications – are available without recourse to full consumption.)

These motivational related knowledge filters could be applied to prompted, pre-coded quantitative questions, as well as open-ended questions. However, we have found that open-ended questioning in quantitative studies represents an important bridge between qualitative and quantitative practice.

In sum, what we are saying here, with this simple illustration, is that a more informed, powerful type of analysis will include a detailed appreciation of what goes on in respondents' heads when they give answers. We want to know when people are providing rationalized accounts of their behaviour. And also establish when they are providing 'platitudes' – easy to reel off, generalized, stereotypical, or clichéd answers – to particular lines of questioning, that seem to broadly 'fit' in with the way they have heard people around them discuss these issues.

Respondents' reporting of usage levels

It is also well documented in the market research literature that individuals' estimates of whether they are high, medium or low users of a particular product or service, can be particularly unreliable. For example, Lee reports that *heavy* users of a service will tend to underestimate their usage, whereas *light* users tend to overestimate their usage, and that light users tend to be less accurate in their reporting than heavy users. So, here is a further example of survey research questioning where the holistic analyst should have the confidence to challenge the 'literal' survey feedback, and to interpret the evidence in light of what we know about this genre of data.

In applying this principle – bringing our knowledge filters into play – we need to be aware that our understanding of the way people respond to the survey process has not yet – and will probably never – have the character of an immutable law of behaviour. So, holistic analysts continually have to make allowances for the difference between the specific market and prevailing research conditions in which a general 'discovery' of a particular knowledge filter was made, and the scenario to which it is being applied. (What is true of a telephone survey conducted on baked beans might not be true of an Internet survey conducted on political voting intentions.)

However, to make matters more straightforward, the 'fundamental' reasoning which underlies the various knowledge filters we outline here, remain fairly robust, subject to adaptation to local conditions. So, when it comes to interpreting the accuracy of the way heavy and light users report behaviour, we know that 'heavy users' will want to play down their consumption of certain goods, such as sugar, which they may feel is currently too high. Similarly, light users of sugar may wish to exaggerate their usage in an interview, perhaps to make themselves appear more important customers, and thereby push up the probability of them getting their point of view across to the interviewer. In sum, what market researchers know about consumption – these analytical filters – provide a useful, general starting point for a critical and interpretative assessment of the usage patterns in a particular market.

The influence of 'technicalities' on survey responses

To complete this review of the knowledge filter principle, we now look at the issue of 'research effects', which bear on our interpretation of the data. Here, there is only space to illustrate a few examples of what we mean, but by following up on the various references referred to in the Notes section the reader will build up a strong picture of what works and does not work in surveys.

- *The halo effect*: this tells us that individuals who hold generally favourable attitudes towards a brand or organization, have a tendency to rate it highly in *every* dimension. Thus, if the 'overall' evaluation is positive, we may not be securing the assessment of individual elements on an 'objective' basis. Given this phenomenon, market researchers will often seek to obtain an overall evaluation *before* dealing with the individual elements, and will sometimes – for comparative purposes – also secure an overall evaluation *after* the ratings of the individual elements.
- *Ordering effects*: we know that if respondents are invited to select responses that are given from a list (either read out or from a 'Showcard'), then the items that appear at the top, and also the bottom of the list, are more likely to be selected than those in the middle. This is why market researchers usually rotate the order of presenting the options.

- *Fatigue effects*: respondent 'fatigue' can set in when the same type of question is asked over and over again, with each question having exactly the same type of response options. (For example, 'I am going to read out 83 statements people have made about petrol-driven lawnmowers, and for each, I want you to tell me whether this applies to you, or does not apply to you?') Respondents will cease to discriminate between the different statements being asked, and opt for the answer that will most speedily get them to the end of this chore.

To conclude this chapter, we should point out that what we have provided by way of knowledge filters is by no means an exhaustive list of what the holistic analyst knows about the survey process. However, it is an indicative guide to the areas in which the reader – making use of the Notes section – should, themselves, follow up on. So, we have reviewed the quality of *respondents'* thinking, and reviewed the way this needs to be taken into account – adjusted for – at the interpretation stage. Let us now move on to techniques that the data analyst has in the tool bag, to improve the quality of their *own* thinking about what the data is telling us. Thus, we now move on to the reframing of data.

Reframing the data

Summary

- We now review various techniques that help the analyst reframe the data, or problem, they are investigating in a novel and innovative way. Just as our knowledge filters help to enhance our understanding of the way that *respondents* behave in survey interviews, our reframing – or interpretative props – help enhance the *researcher's* thinking about the data.

- Specifically, we provide an organizing framework for guiding the reader through four areas, where an understanding of available concepts and principles provides a possible opportunity to reframe their data.

- The first category of reframing options centres on locating the specific survey evidence in the context of various models about the way markets generally operate.

- We then put the spotlight on the way in which locating survey data, in the context of what is contained in the organization's own marketing intelligence or knowledge management system, may add a new perspective to the analyst's understanding.

- In the next category, we look at ways of reframing data by looking at the evidence from the 'third corner'. This includes techniques, such as semiotics (taking an 'outside-in' look at the data).

- In the final category, we look at various novel techniques that could help the analyst obtain a fresh perspective on their data.

Giving the analysis a new perspective

The holistic data analyst is always keen to identify new perspectives, or angles, from which their evidence can be interpreted. So the next stage of our holistic analysis framework looks at ways of adding power to the data analysis by embracing various techniques that allow us to 'reframe' the data, or problem, in an innovative way. We can think of these techniques as 'interpretative props': devices that facilitate insightful interpretation by reframing the data in a novel way.

Our knowledge (or analytical) filters, discussed in the last chapter, involves applying what we know about the psychology of the survey process, to our interpretation of the variable way *respondents* react to the questions we ask them. Our reframing techniques – or interpretative props – again apply our understanding of psychology, but this time to enhance the *researcher's* thinking about the data. These props help to reframe a data set in a way that will help researchers to see the evidence from a fresh angle.

Our taxonomy

There are numerous taxonomies that could be deployed to explain the various reframing options open to analysts. Our approach is made up of the four elements shown below. Again, we have presented our ideas as an outline organizing framework that will allow the reader – referring to our Notes section – to pinpoint the literature that will assist them in learning more about the broad ideas we introduce.

Locating evidence in the context of general marketing models

The explosion of marketing literature in the last 30 years means that we now have, in the public domain, in an explicit and generalizable form, a significant body of learning about how markets (and customers) behave. By locating a particular piece of incoming survey evidence in the context of these generic accounts of how markets typically operate, the analyst *may* identify certain clues that add power to their analysis. The aim is to encourage the analyst to think on a bigger canvas in a more conceptual way, thereby providing fresh ideas on how to slice the data in different ways, and on how to identify any bigger principles or concepts that might lie behind their particular data set.

Space does not permit us to summarize all the different types of business marketing and consumer models that could be helpful to the data analyst. So, below, we have provided an illustrative guide to the different genres of general business models that are available. Then, in the Notes section, we provide details as to where the reader may find the relevant references.

- *Overarching accounts of people's motivation and needs*: in this first category, we find generalized frameworks that seek to explain, at a macro level, what motivates people's actions. One notable example of this genre of model is Maslow's theory that we progress through various need states. We start by satisfying basic physiological needs. We then progress through the need for security; social contact; status and appreciation; before eventually arriving at the highest point – the need for self-actualization.

- *Models that explain the structure and dynamics of markets*: there is a wealth of helpful models that may help the analyst better understand the structure of the market within which their data is located. Here, we would include the Boston Consultancy Group's (BCG's) matrix that examines the relationship between high and low market growth, and relative market share. We would also include McKinsey's development of the original BCG matrix that examines the relationship between market attractiveness and strategic position.
- *Models about competitive analysis*: there are models that seek to explain how competitors might behave in different marketing scenarios. Again, we cannot do justice, in a few lines, to the (potential) power of how these competitor-related conceptualizations, principles, and concepts can help the analyst reframe their data. All we can do is refer the reader to the various models, notably those developed by Michael Porter, a leader in this field, that define the competitive forces which seem to characterize an effective strategy. Other competitive frameworks would include the BCG's notion of examining the competitive position of an organization by identifying the relative size of the advantage it enjoys over the next biggest company in the market place, and then identifying the number of opportunities that the next biggest competitor(s) has for overhauling this leading position.
- *Generic models of how products behave in the market place*: there is a body of literature that tells us about the lifecycle through which products and brands develop. This, of course, includes the notion of the 'product lifecycle', with products being seen to go through the following phases: initial launch; early growth; late growth; maturity; and decline.
- *Customer service models*: one particular model of note here, by way of illustration, is the Nordic School of Service Marketing. This focuses on the idea that the better the perceived quality, then the greater the customers' inclination to buy, which in turn improves the company's profile, and subsequent profitability.

The point we would stress here, in overviewing the various general marketing models, is that, in isolation, some of the principles and concepts may seem rather thin, and indeed obvious. When these concepts are applied to a particular data set, however, then they can have a major innovative impact by helping the analyst lift their data from the pedestrian to a higher level of conceptualization and insight. So, as holistic analysts, we would commend this activity to the reader. In short, contextualizing a particular piece of data, in terms of the concepts and principles handed down to us from general marketing models, generally pays dividends.

Reframing in the context of market knowledge

Another powerful way of obtaining new insights on a data set is to set the evidence in the context of the client organization's own market knowledge.

Meta analysis

It is often possible to obtain a helpful insight by analysing, at a meta level, the tactical points being made in various related market studies. These will have been conducted for a variety of different purposes, but when analysed at a high level of conceptual abstraction, we can often gain an insight that takes the analysis of the data forward.

Let us illustrate this point with an example of a meta analysis conducted for a major telecommunications supplier across a whole range of *tactical* studies. These tactical studies – when analysed collectively at a high (meta) level – led to the identification of the fact that the telecommunications company in question was consistently seen as not being 'genuine' in virtually any marketing or customer-facing promotional or sales activity, in which it was engaged. Here, the important point to stress is that the concept of 'genuineness', although hinted at across these various studies, was never *explicitly* raised by customers. The realization of this fundamental weakness in the company's current market positioning only appeared on the radar by looking across the various tactical levels – at a higher level of abstraction – to identify the underlying attitudinal traits at work. Thus, the crystallization of this issue put the analyst clearly in a better position to look at their data from a fresh perspective.

Understanding cultural trends

Setting data in the context of wider cultural trends is another powerful reframing tool. Let us illustrate the point with an example from the world of home decorating. In Germany, the proportion of people who decorate their homes, who are prepared to mix together different shades of paint to get their desired colour, is far greater than the proportion in the UK. In understanding this market difference, it is helpful to note various cultural differences between the two countries. Germany has a strong chemical engineering tradition, and a high proportion of young Germans go through vocational education and training. So, taking these factors into account, we can possibly see the reasons why there should be such a marked difference between German and British attitudes towards paint mixing.

Identifying mega-trends

Another reframing technique is to identify the mega-trends at work in a market, and then to identify the long-term implications for the specific survey data being analysed. So, for example, in the world of football, we would be able to identify the following pattern: growing disposable income among football fans; increasing willingness to travel throughout Europe to follow sport; growing expectations of sport always being a major international high profile event (with declining interest in many low-key local and regional activities); political moves to integrate more countries into the European Union; and increasing need for football clubs to be as financially secure as businesses, and so on. Taking all this different financial, political, and consumer information together, one can see why it is extremely likely that we are heading towards the creation of a European super football league, whereby the top clubs within each country will be regularly playing each other, with fans travelling between London, Paris, Barcelona, Milan, Madrid, etc.

Predictive models

There are also various models – that are often proprietary to clients or possibly survey organizations – that examine the relationship between past survey predictions and what actually happened in the market place. Setting our data in the context of this normative information can, of course, be an extremely powerful trigger to fresh thinking about our data.

Looking at the data from the third corner

Another powerful reframing technique is to step back and look at the data from a totally different perspective. In particular, it can be helpful to stand outside the immediate issue and understand the wider context – the hinterland – within which a particular piece of survey data was collected.

The outside-in approach

One technique for taking this *outside-in* approach is semiotics. Semiotics asks questions about how concepts, issues, and ideas get into people's heads in the first place. Where do they come from? So, whereas traditional qualitative research tends to take an *inside-out* perspective – that is, delve into psychological phenomenon, such as perspectives, attitudes and beliefs, that exist *within* people's heads to try and understand what makes them tick – semiotics takes its cue from the outside surrounding culture. Semioticians are looking for the 'discourses' that are going on behind the immediate action. The semiotician is looking for clues about the meaning of things; they are trying to pinpoint the unspoken cultural 'rules' or 'codes' that underpin communications.

Imagine a packet of chocolate biscuits with gold packaging. When market researchers ask consumers 'what kind of biscuits are these?', most people perceive the biscuits as a 'luxury'. Here, when lots of people produce the same interpretation, it is reasonable to assume that, in arriving at this same 'luxury' viewpoint, they are drawing on 'shared cultural resource'. In short, we all know gold is a shorthand for 'riches and wealth', so a connection is made between gold and luxury.

The Consignia example

Now a commercial example of the way semiotic thinking can help us understand what is really going on 'behind' symbols and brand labels, and add power to the analysis of customer feedback. Let us illustrate the point with the rebranding of Royal Mail, Parcelforce and Post Office Counters as 'Consignia'. It seems that Consignia was seen as a good choice for the new collective name to describe the three organizations. It is a word that seemed to link together what all of the three organizations did: 'consigning' letters and parcels to different destinations. Therefore developing a single brand name that embraces the idea of consigning (i.e. Consignia) could be seen as a powerful linking theme. It was a name that found resonance in the world of 'consignee notes', and the like.

However, to the semiotician, the word 'consigned' (and hence Consignia) sends out an entirely different signal. Looked at from the outside-in perspective, the word consigned is one that, in everyday language, has very little to do with the technicalities of consigning packages. It is a word that is closely associated with various negative 'discourses'. So here, the semiotician would have unearthed the way that people may talk about 'consigning' someone, or an issue, 'to history'. They would have also detected that people often talk in terms of issues being 'consigned' to the rubbish bin. In short, it is difficult to find any positive discourses going on around the Consignia name. So when Consignia started to flounder as the flagship name around which to rebuild the Royal Mail et al., the media had lots of ready-made jibes with which to bash the Consignia name. Consequently, we understand that the Consignia name has now been dropped as a customer-facing name.

Thinking via analogies

Another technique that can help the analyst look at their data in a fresh perspective is the notion of thinking through analogies. One technique that is often used by qualitative researchers, at the data collection stage, is 'synectics'. Essentially, this is a kind of brainstorming exercise, except that instead of releasing the immediate problem under investigation, only the concepts and issues related to the problem are released, rather than the actual problem itself.

The idea behind this is that, by releasing the specific problem too soon, respondents may prematurely focus on the specifics and minutiae associated with this particular issue. By releasing only related principles and concepts, we can encourage individuals to think across analogous fields that could provide some new insights.

For an illustration, let us go back to the days when the Euro Tunnel was first being marketed, and decisions had to be made about what kinds of service to provide customers. Here, there would be benefit in presenting the problem in the widest possible terms, by asking customers what they are looking for when 'getting to France', rather than focusing on the specifics of a car train going through a tunnel.

This broadening of the problem could open up opportunities for customers to provide their feedback on sea and air, and possibly toll bridge, travel. Thus, Euro Tunnel would then have the benefit of picking from a selection of customer service paradigms in deciding on how best to fashion their own service.

Lateral thinking

Building on the above idea, there is, of course, a wide body of literature on lateral thinking, led notably by Edward de Bono, that could provide clues for the data analyst on how to think about the interpretation of a piece of data in a fresh and innovative way. Let us illustrate the power of lateral thinking with one example. One of many techniques is to continually challenge the underlying assumptions that underpin a particular practice. So, for example, in the past, car designers automatically had to make provision for a spare wheel – everybody expected that their car would have a spare wheel. Yet this only came about because in the very beginning tyres were not very reliable. And there were not many 24-hour repair companies around, and few roadside repair motoring organizations. Moreover, few people had mobile phones to ring for help. In addition, instant repair kits (pumping foam into the tyre) had not been developed, and compact high-pressure pumps were not readily available. Now, all of the above has changed. So the lateral thought here was to challenge all of the assumptions made about why cars always carry a spare wheel. So now some cars do not carry a conventional spare wheel. So in sum, the power of lateral thinking is in turning problems on their head, exploring the wider context, evaluating the underlying assumptions, and looking at the problem afresh.

Further techniques to encourage innovative thinking

There will be various other techniques that, in certain situations, could be helpful to trigger fresh insights and new angles on the data. Below we look at a couple of specific examples.

Telling the story as an individual narrative

Another way of reframing data to provide creative opportunities for the analyst is to present the data for the *entire* survey sample as if it were the data for a *single* respondent. At first glance this seems strange. We all know that surveys work by piecing together a sample of individuals – each with their own partial view of the world – to build up the total picture of the phenomenon under investigation. Here it is helpful to think of a quantitative data sample as having a 'beehive-like' quality. The sample can be seen as a 'collective' with respondents each giving a partial or incomplete account of their attitudes, with these combining to produce the complete sample picture. Yet this conceptualization also allows us to think of individuals within a sample being able to change places – having the potential to respond like each other – but always combining to produce an overall picture which remains the same. This observation opens up the idea of presenting total sample survey statistics as if we were telling the story of just one individual. It is a reframing technique that can sharpen the analyst's thinking on the issues under investigation, and is also one that can engage the audience.

We identify with individual accounts

The idea of the analyst treating survey responses from a large-scale data set as if they were the views of an *individual* respondent reflects recent developments in psychology. This tells us that people have a strong tendency to deal with *all* kinds of problems in the same way that we would deal with *social* problems – that is problems involved with one or a small group of people. Thus, when abstract problems are couched in terms of problems involving small numbers of people, we usually find them far easier to solve. This is why airline stewards and stewardesses, when instructing passengers to comply with the safety rules, do so not around the language of 'would you do this on behalf of British Airways?', but 'would you please turn off your mobile phone *for me*'. The 'for me' is not there by chance, it subtly transfers what could be construed as organizational bureaucracy into an (interpersonal) social relationship.

An example of the narrative as a reframing tool

In Table 12.1 we provide an example of how data from an aggregate survey can be presented as though it represented a *single* consumer's attitude towards, in this case, purchasing a particular product.

Thus, by treating a data set from the total sample as the motivational profile for a *single* respondent (and by introducing prior knowledge) we are able to produce an interpretation which links the data together in a single coherent narrative. If we then wanted to reflect the likelihood of different needs and preferences between different types of customer, we could add a rider that different groups of respondents might place different emphasis on various parts of this account (cross-tabbing the data with other respondent profile categories might help to make this clear). These differences could be expressed as variations on the central story outlined above. The key issue is to link the data in a single, coherent (and therefore memorable) and insightful way. Nuances can then be bolted on to this simple, main dominant structure.

In essence, the point we are making is that, by treating the respondents in the data set as if they reflected the view of one or a few respondents, the researcher will find it easier to get to grips with the true meaning of the data. In sum, presenting research data as a compelling narrative or story about an individual

Table 12.1 – An example of the narrative as a reframing tool

- **The consumer in this market will continue to use a familiar brand. . .** *'Previous experience of using it' (19%)* and *'Always use it' (9%)* both up-weighted to allow for non-rational bias
- **. . . as long as it meets the important quality criteria. . .** *'Softening clothes' (23%) and making clothes 'smell nice' (7%)*
- **. . . is convenient. . .** *'Easy to use' (7%)*
- **. . . and represents value for money.** *'Good price' third most important behind 'Good quality' and 'Best product for the job' - i.e. it is not simply a case of buying the lowest-priced product.*
- **However, the consumer is also concerned to ensure there is nothing better on the market. . .** *'Best product for the job' (28%)*
- **. . . and given that she is aware that her purchase can be rather habitual and unreflective** *('Always use it'),* **she is likely occasionally to try a new brand (or a 'new improved' version of her current brand) if it holds out the possibility of being an improvement on the current brand/product.**
- **If a new product/brand fails to impress on trial, the consumer will revert to her original brand.**
- **Perceptions of positive product benefits and likelihood to try a new product will be reinforced by brand perceptions.** *'Excellent brand/reputation' (10%),* up-weighted for non-rational bias and combined with prior knowledge of the role of brands in product perception.

is a simple and clear way that can help the decision-making audience better understand the data.

Interpreting 'split decisions'

Another reframing technique is to examine respondents' responses around the conceptualization – or context – of each answer being a matter of probability. This requires us to apply some of the Bayesian probability-based thinking that we discussed earlier. This reframing technique can be powerful, even when looking at apparently innocuous data. It helps us address the issue we raised before, about the way that, across the sample as a whole, the proportions of respondents giving a particular answer will remain the same, even though high proportions of respondents will be known to give different responses to exactly the same survey question when asked on separate occasions. (Even when this question relates to some form of behaviour, or the profiling of facts.) As we explained earlier, this phenomenon of respondents switching between categories within the overall total sample proportions can be a source of confusion to the inexperienced analyst.

To get beyond this limitation, it is helpful to take a slight imaginative leap to help us better understand the data. Specifically, it is helpful to treat each respondent's answer on a particular question as a matter of probability, and the overall profile of the sample as the sum of these probabilities. Thus, a split in an overall sample of 70%: 30% on a particular question could be treated, at the level of an individual respondent, as a probability of 0.7 that the respondent would choose one option, and a 0.3 probability that they would choose the other option.

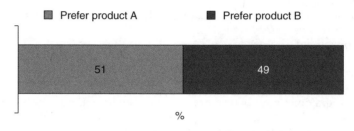

Figure 12.1 – Preferences for product concept (base = 400).

To illustrate this point, consider the very simple data in Figure 12.1. One interpretation of these data could be that one half of all respondents prefer product A and one half prefer product B. However, if we take the probabilistic view of the sample, the data could show that all consumers are in two minds about the product concept – and their opting for one, or the other, is simply a matter of probability. So, if we analysed these responses by socio-demographic categories, or some other form of cross-break, and found that different categories varied in their responses, we would, of course, modify this conclusion, and talk about different levels of preference amongst different types of respondent. However, if there were no major differences in the 50/50 split across *all* the various cross-breaks we analysed, then the conclusion that all consumers were in two minds, could be a reasonable one.

In the next chapter, we look at how to piece together the qualitative and quantitative research evidence and, building on the above ideas, construct a compelling narrative that will engage the decision-making audience and facilitate effective decision-making.

Integrating the evidence and presenting research as a narrative

13

Summary

- We start by looking at an analytical framework for helping the holistic analyst combine evidence drawn from different qualitative and quantitative data sets. This introduces the concepts of the weight, power and direction of multiple data sets.
- The process of drawing together evidence from different sources is a key stepping stone in allowing the holistic analyst to then present their (integrated) evidence in the form of a compelling 'narrative'. This takes the decision-maker through the available evidence in an easy-to-understand, memorable way that also facilitates effective decision-making.
- We see this narrative approach as being, in most scenarios, preferable to the more conventional 'building block' approach, whereby categories of evidence – desk, qualitative, quantitative – would be presented, with only a limited link between the data and the decision that needs to be made. (Although it is acknowledged that, for certain presentations, this 'conventional' approach will still be appropriate.)
- To illustrate this approach, we provide an example of how results on a study about the development of tourism in a seaside town might be most effectively presented, employing the narrative format.

Communicating the whole story

There have been two key themes running through our account of the holistic approach to data analysis. One theme centres on the importance of integrating, and placing in context, different sources of evidence. The second key theme centres on the importance of always attempting to simplify the data, add clarity, reduce it down to its essence, and constantly focus on the end decision-making process.

In this chapter, we continue with these two key themes by first presenting some ideas on frameworks within which to present data drawn from different sources, and then by highlighting the power of always attempting to present market research evidence in the form of a compelling narrative, rather than simply as isolated blocks of evidence. So, let us start by examining the issue of drawing together information from different sources, and presenting this in an integrated way.

Frameworks for combining multiple qualitative and quantitative data sets

We look now at frameworks for drawing together different sets of data, and arriving at an assessment of the overall actionability of the information in relation to the decision. Here, we introduce the concepts of the 'weight', 'power' and 'direction' of evidence. These are ideas that we first floated in our earlier book, *Inside Information: Making Sense of Marketing Data*. We have now developed our thinking about how these concepts might be best applied to holistic data analysis. Let us start by providing a recap on what these three concepts are all about.

Weight of evidence

The concept of the 'weight of the evidence', as shown in Figure 13.1, is measured on two axes:

- *Balance of opinion*: what proportion of the data set are in favour of a particular phenomenon (for example, a product or service)? Here, the balance

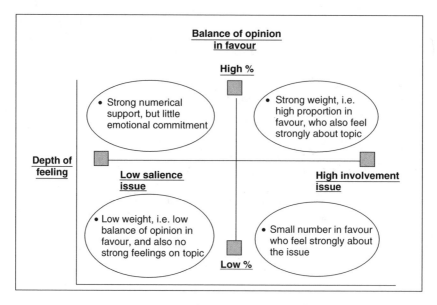

Figure 13.1 – The weight of evidence.

of opinion provides a 'quantitative' assessment of how many individuals favour one option rather than another. (In a quantitative survey, this would be statistically based, and in a qualitative study, it would possibly be based on 'counts' taken as part of the content analysis of transcripts.)

- *Depth of feeling*: this is an insight into the intensity of feeling that people experience on this topic. (This could be based on a qualitative assessment of verbatim comments, and/or based on more structured quantitative attitude questioning.)

Power of evidence

The second concept that forms part of our analytical framework for the holistic analysis of different data sets is the notion of the 'power of evidence'. Here, we are working with the following combination of concepts:

- *Prior knowledge*: here we are taking into account how a specific piece of data fits into the wider context of what we already know from management prior knowledge, or intuitively, about this topic.
- *The status of the data after applying the knowledge filters*: here we are looking at what we know about the nature – the core integrity – of this genre of marketing evidence. What have we learnt about this type of data by passing it through our knowledge filters? Is this 'hard-nosed' data that, in the past, has been a good predictor, or more 'flaky' evidence that needs very careful interpretation? As we can see in Figure 13.2, putting these two

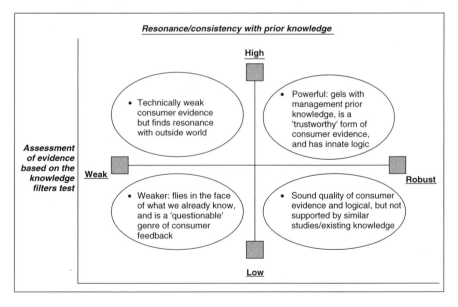

Figure 13.2 – The power of evidence.

concepts together becomes an important part of our analytical framework for integrating different forms of evidence.

Direction of evidence

The third element of our framework for looking at a series of data sets, is the notion of the 'direction of evidence'. Here, we are working with two ideas:

- *Internal consistency of the data*: there is the issue of whether there is high or low internal consistency *within* each data set that compromises the overall evidence on the topic under investigation. Is it a consistently strong, or rather fragmented and patchy, 'storyline'?
- *External consistency across the different data sets*: this focuses on the consistency *across* various multiple data sets being used by the holistic data analyst. Is all of the available evidence pointing in a particular direction, or not? For example, do we have a pattern of results that hold true across the desk, qualitative and quantitative components of the research study, or is the conclusion based on a much more disjointed picture (see Figure 13.3)?

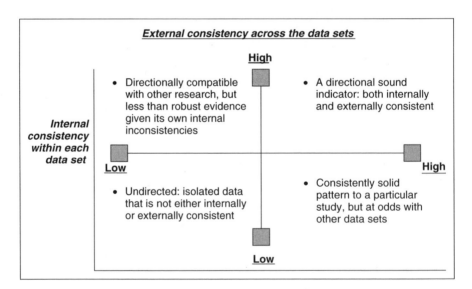

Figure 13.3 – The direction of evidence.

Frameworks for converting evidence into a decision support system

Here, we are indebted to Gerald Michaluk who, in his book *Riding the Storm: Strategic planning in turbulent markets*, applied our concept of evaluating data sets in terms of their 'weight, power and direction of evidence', to show how these could form a 'decision support system' that could help turn data into marketing intelligence. Michaluk, in effect, created a fuzzy logic decision table. It works as follows.

Constructing a fuzzy logic decision table

The concepts of the weight of the evidence (depth of feeling and balance of opinion in favour), power of evidence (resonance with prior knowledge and the strength of the evidence in terms of our knowledge filters), and direction of evidence (internal and external consistency) can be combined and modelled into a fuzzy logic decision table. Fuzzy logic algorithms allow even the most complex decisions to be modelled using only a few rule sets. In this case, there are three matrices, each with two variables. Therefore, there are six variables which, if we use an 'actionability scale' ranging from very high, high, medium, low to very low, we arrive at 7776 possible combinations. However, this can be simplified by a selection from each quadrant on each matrix to create the decision 'rule set' shown in Figure 13.4.

Weight of evidence	Power of evidence	Direction of evidence	Decision actionability
Upper right box	Upper right box	Upper right box	Very high
			High
			Average
			Low
Lower left box	Lower left box	Lower left box	Very low

Figure 13.4 – Illustration of simplified fuzzy logic decision table.

A worked example of the weight, power and direction concepts in practice

In Table 13.1 we provide an example of the application of the weight, power and direction concepts in helping the analyst integrate different data sets as a stepping stone to creating the overall narrative to be presented to the end client. Here, we should point out that we have made the assumption that each individual data set has been subject to the various stages of the analysis process outlined in this book. Thus, the analyst will have dealt with: compensating for shortfalls; applying orthodox tests to establish the constraints; stretching this boundary by applying the enablers and various knowledge filters; and considering ways in which the data might be reframed, and so on.

Table 13.1 – Integrating multiple data sets – applying the weight, power and direction concepts

- **Decision:** should Top Flight Holidays continue, after six years, to sponsor a men's tennis tournament in the UK?
- **Summary of key evidence:**
  - *Desk research*: pundits on sponsorship highlight the growing, then declining 'pay-off' during the 'lifecycle' of a typical sports sponsorship.
  - *Expert opinion with the tennis cognoscenti*: depth interviews with tennis journalists and PR consultants highlight a certain 'fatigue factor' with Top Flight Holidays' continued sponsorship of the tennis tournament.
  - *Qualitative research with visitors to the tournament*: depth interviews and group discussions held with visitors to the last tennis tournament showed declining positive association between the values Top Flight Holidays is trying to promote and the image of this particular tennis tournament.
  - *Visitors' surveys conducted at the tournament*: the event seems to be professionally run, but there is comparatively low level of recall of Top Flight Holidays as the *main* sponsor of the event (secondary sponsors do almost as well).
  - *General household population survey*: reasonable awareness of Top Flight Holidays as an expanding company, and tennis also seen as being broadly compatible with the image of the company. But other sports, notably Formula One Motor Racing and Premiership Football, are seen as being more compatible with Top Flight Holidays' image.
  - *Media audit*: evidence of falling references to Top Flight Holidays in the way the tennis tournament is presented on television and in the print media.
  - *Internal audit of Top Flight Holidays management opinion*: board sharply divided: some feel the need to stay with sponsorship of tennis to get further benefits, but majority feel that tennis has now become a low-key, bland, unexciting sport, that does not square with plans for the next phase of Top Flight's initiative.
  - *A 'cost–benefit' analysis of the sponsorship*: this would involve:
    * Listing the *costs* of the event, from the most directly accountable, such as the actual costs of sponsoring the event and entertainment, etc., to less directly accountable, such as the notional allocation of management time involved in organizing and attending the event.
    * Listing the most directly identifiable *benefits,* ranging from the most accountable, such as column inches achieved in the newspaper (costed out at equivalent advertising rates), through to less identifiable benefits (i.e. goodwill generated among the tennis community towards Top Flight Holidays).
- **Integrating the multiple evidence into an overall analysis**
  - *Weight of evidence*
    * In terms of the *balance of opinion*, the overall numerical support in favour of withdrawing, as opposed to continuing with the sponsorship, would be assessed. (Here, we can see that the depth interviews, group discussions, visitors' survey, and general population survey all paint a fairly unfavourable picture about continuing with the sponsorship.)

Table 13.1 – (*continued*)

* The above 'numbers' would be assessed alongside *depth of feeling* – that is, just how intense do different individuals feel about Top Flight Holidays continuing their involvement with tennis. (This would show quite strong depth of feeling among the Top Flight Holidays' senior management team, ranging from tennis fans – who originally made the decision and are arguing for continuation, through to slightly less influential groups – who feel that tennis is not exciting enough to spearhead the new marketing initiatives.)

— *Power of evidence*

* The extent to which the various *external* evidence (the consumer qualitative research, visitors' survey, and the general population survey), is consistent with the *internal* prior knowledge (such as internal management views, and the views of experts, the media, and public relations specialists). Our analysis shows that there is a high level of consistency between the external consumer evidence and our existing management prior knowledge – tennis seems to be losing its edge in supporting Top Flight Holidays as being an exciting holiday company.

* The other dimension here will take into account what we know about the robustness of different categories of evidence. How well did each piece of evidence do, after we applied the knowledge filters? For example, the analyst would take into account the fact that journalists, who favoured Top Flight Holidays continuing with their sponsorship, have a vested interest. (It is a very pleasant 'jolly' for them, and they want to see continuing money coming into tennis, rather than to other sports.)

* A further illustration would be the observation the analyst would make about the comparative weakness of market research in the field of evaluating sponsorship. This centres on the difficulties of 'calculating' the cumulative way in which a sponsorship builds, and how it 'embeds positive values' throughout a broad network of stakeholders. In addition, it is difficult for research to disentangle the specific impact of the tennis sponsorship from other concurrent marketing communications with which Top Flight Holidays is involved, including its involvement as a minor sponsor of various snowboarding and windsurfing events.

— *Direction of evidence*

* The holistic analyst would establish what variation in opinion existed *within* each of the different pieces of consumer evidence (the qualitative research, visitors' survey, the general population survey, and so on). Were there wild variations by different age, gender, and regional subgroups within each survey? Here, let us assume a strong central storyline, with the dominant 'refining', rather than exceptional 'suppressor', pattern being in evidence on each survey.

* How consistent, *across* the different visitors, general population, and expert samples, was the evidence? Here, we have different intensities of views, but we do not seem to have wildly different views about the way tennis is losing some of its appeal, and Top Flight Holidays seems to be moving into a new register, requiring a new exciting sponsorship companion.

(*continued overleaf*)

Table 13.1 – (*continued*)

- **The final evaluation**

  In our brief evaluation here, we can see that there is quite a solid body of evidence that, if we were to apply our decision logic table, would fall into the 'upper right' boxes of our weight, power and direction matrices. That is to say, there is substantial evidence that is of a strong weight. For example:

  — Numerically strong evidence: supported by intense commitment to a point of view.

  — Powerful evidence: that has taken into account the limitations of consumer evidence in commenting on sponsorship issues, but noted the strong resonance between what external and internal experts, and the consumer evidence, are saying.

  — Consistency: we have a series of data sets that seem to be internally consistent, with no wild variations by subgroup, and also a central storyline that seems, with certain exceptions, consistent across the different data sets.

  Given this, there would seem to be a strong case to seriously consider withdrawing Top Flight Holidays' sponsorship of the UK tennis tournament, and to begin putting energy behind a new, more exciting sponsorship opportunity.

Communicating the research findings as a narrative

We have explained the way in which the holistic data analyst, in making sense of data, throughout the process, will seek to develop a coherent and plausible 'story' that accounts for the patterns in the data. Put simply, the narrative approach is one that identifies the key issues or factors that relate to the problem under investigation, and then, in an 'attacking' way, focuses directly on these issues, drawing in appropriate supporting evidence as the story unfolds. This is in sharp contrast to the traditional building block approach, where the evidence is listed, but in a way that leaves the reader to identify what this evidence is saying about the specific critical issues under investigation.

Clearly, we need checks and balances in place to ensure we fully scrutinize the emerging story: throughout this book we have stressed the dangers of market researchers presenting plausible, but essentially untrue, stories. In setting market researchers the objective of producing compelling true stories, we need to be aware of the psychological tendency we have to produce, and believe, over-elaborate explanations of data. So the task of drawing together the available evidence, and making this accessible to the decision-maker in the form of a compelling powerful narrative, needs to be rigorously monitored. We look at ways of achieving this shortly, after reviewing the growing popularity of business presentations taking the form of a narrative.

The power of corporate story-telling

The idea of communicating business issues in story form is a powerful one. Importantly, the story-telling technique is particularly helpful to market researchers who, over the years, have often been criticized for providing incoherent, disjointed summaries of individual isolated blocks of evidence that do not explain what the combined evidence – taken in conjunction with existing management prior knowledge – is saying.

Of course, a distinction must be drawn between fictional story-telling and the adaptation of this technique for the purposes of better communication in business. However, the idea of presenting market research studies as a compelling narrative, is certainly gaining popularity. Specifically, it offers a number of key benefits. For example, it can:

- *Help communicate the complex whole*: narratives are particularly effective where they provide a vivid picture, linking together key relationships and sequences in a way that allows individual elements, that may otherwise have been lost, to be remembered as a complex whole.
- *Aid comprehension*: putting data in the form of a coherent narrative means that it is more likely to be understood, absorbed and recalled by clients, and therefore more likely to be successfully used as part of the decision-making process.
- *Enrich and involve*: stories are particularly powerful when they are colourful, and use symbols and metaphors that enrich the listeners' feelings, and therefore enhances their chances of getting involved in key issues.
- *Be inspirational*: visionary stories can inspire and educate the audience, and lead to an effective thinking process that helps the audience resolve particular dilemmas.
- *An opportunity to entertain*: it is an approach that is especially powerful when facts are combined with an interest and entertainment factor.
- *Enhance actionability*: tackling complexity in organizations by telling memorable narratives is a way of reducing barriers to change, bringing plans and potential actions to life, and also a way of vividly communicating corporate values.
- *Help gain buy-in*: if the 'stories' are seen as relevant and timely, they are more likely to be disseminated within the organization, and gain currency.

The limitations of the 'old' market research building block approach

In the past, many market research presentations would have involved no more than assembling, and then presenting, different 'blocks' of evidence. So, a presentation might typically look as follows:

- A review of the desk research.
- A summary of the qualitative research findings.
- A listing of the survey results.
- Then there would be quite a big 'leap' to the conclusions to the study.

The attraction of this approach was that it stayed true to the traditional market research 'paradigm', by presenting the evidence in an objective, detached format. It kept the evidence free from any confusion between the data itself and the interpretation that had been placed on it. In fairness, in situations where the decision-making audience has a considerable amount of knowledge and experience of how market research works, presenting market research evidence in this building block format can still be extremely valuable. So it has to be acknowledged that, for certain market research studies, this 'building block' approach is exactly what the audience will still require.

On the downside, there are two distinct concerns with the building block approach:

- *Wisdom lost in too much information*: the research itself may have been professionally conducted, but a rather laborious reportage of the findings of the different building blocks of evidence is unlikely to engage the audience, and ensure that the key messages are being successfully communicated.
- *It does not impact on the decision*: the building block approach often presents the decision-taker with a big gap between the data that has just been presented, and the decision they have to make. The big leap that is often required between the end point of the reportage of findings, and what decisions need to be made, has been a long-standing criticism of many market research studies.

The power of the narrative market research presentation

We have already identified the general reasons why story-telling is growing in popularity as an influential business communications concept, and we now build on this by reviewing the specific reasons why presenting market research evidence as a narrative is so powerful. Specifically, we highlight three attractions to applying the story-telling concept to market research presentations.

- *It is the way decision-makers think*: the narrative approach reflects the fact that decision-makers are now busy and time-urgent, and do not want to see any 'joins' in the evidence with which they are being presented. They do not want ponderous, disjointed presentations of various unrelated pieces of evidence. They are looking for an overall presentation that provides a clear explanation of what the collective evidence is telling them.

    In fact, research now available tells us that many 'high achiever' personality types will, during the market research presentation, be making certain judgements and decisions 'there and then', 'on the run', in 'real time'. These are people who want the main story upfront. These are not personality types prepared to go through the classic, linear building block decision-making process. They do *not* want to first listen patiently to the person presenting different elements of the argument, and then, at the end of the presentation – after reflecting on the evidence – eventually arrive at their decision.

In today's pressured work environment, these individuals will be *instantly* making judgements and decisions based on what incoming information is telling them. This explains the restlessness of many individuals in 'classic' linear, building block type (market research) presentations. So it is important to present the evidence as a narrative that takes the presentation audience through the decisions that need to be made, allowing them to evaluate the robustness of the arguments and evidence 'on the run', so that they can make decisions on an ongoing basis, thereby minimizing the leap between the data and the evidence.

- *The big picture/zoom-in option*: the narrative approach also allows the presenter to make decisions, during the course of a presentation, about whether to stay with the main narrative, or whether, at certain points, to dip into, in more depth, particular building blocks of detailed evidence. In short, it gives the final presentation style the 'zoom' dimension: the presenter can alternate between explaining the key big picture points, while at the same time, as appropriate, drilling down to deal with certain specific issues at a greater level of detail. (Put another way, the narrative style can accommodate the building block approach as a subset, but this does not work the other way round. If the lead style is the building block approach, it becomes difficult for the decision-maker to see the story.)
- *It symbolizes the holistic data analysis method*: the narrative method also serves as a *symbol* for the way the entire holistic analysis process has been conducted. By presenting the research evidence in story form, the research team can convey how they have worked in an eclectic way, drawing together different sources of information to arrive at their interpretation.

As we keep stressing, telling the market research story as a narrative that is true, requires rigorous methods. The stories need to be rich, coherent, narrative accounts of consumers' behaviour, attitudes and motivations, but ones that are firmly based on a tight evaluation of the incoming new data. They must also be consistent with our prior knowledge and experience of the topic, and subject to close analytical examination and numerous reality checks. With this in mind, let us look at an example of how this narrative approach to presenting market research evidence works in practice, highlighting as we do so, the various checks and balances that are built into the process, to ensure vigorous scrutiny of the data.

The building block and narrative approaches to presenting market research data

Below, we start by outlining a particular data analysis assignment. We follow this by explaining how the data might be presented in a building block format, and then following this, we highlight the advantages of presenting the data in the narrative format.

The task

To develop a strategy for the development of tourism in Brightbourne, a mythical town on the South Coast of England. This strategy needs to strike an appropriate balance in meeting the needs and requirements of the following 'stakeholders':

- Permanent residents in employment
- The retired (including those who have recently retired from elsewhere to the town)
- Weekend residents
- Local employers
- Year-round local employees
- Part-time seasonal workers
- 'Day-tripper' visitors
- Visitors staying for longer periods of time
- Day delegates at conferences
- Non-profit organizations, such as the National Trust and other heritage groups with sites in the town.

The building block presentation

Typically, the approach to presenting research studies conducted to assess the views of the above stakeholder groups would have the following character.

- *The desk research evidence*: this would review what existing information is available for each of the above categories of respondent.
- *The qualitative evidence*: this might include a review of what depth interviews and focus groups, conducted with each of the stakeholder categories, was telling us about the frustrations, aspirations and expectations of each type of stakeholder in Brightbourne.
- *The survey evidence*: the presentation would then move on to review various quantitative surveys conducted amongst various stakeholder groups.
- *The conclusions*: the survey would conclude with a professional and comprehensive summary of the different opinions and expectations of the various stakeholder groups.
- *The leap between the data and decision*: the limitation of the above approach is that it will have successfully summarized the needs and requirements for key stakeholder groups, but will have *failed* in the following respects:
  — it would not have made maximum use of existing prior knowledge on what we know about Brightbourne;
  — it will have not integrated the research evidence in a way that is compatible with the way decision-makers think about this type of problem;

— it would have not have focused the evidence on the precise decisions that need to be made, e.g. how, strategically, the town can strike the optimum balance between the tensions that exist between the needs and requirements of the different stakeholder groups (older residents, who want a peaceful, affluent infrastructure, and day-trippers, who want recreational activities for children during the day, and nightclubs for teenagers in the evening, and so on).

The narrative style presentation

The narrative style of presenting the above body of evidence would help close the gap between the data and the decisions that need to be made. The narrative form better engages the audience, and thereby facilitates a more effective decision-making process. Below, we outline how the evidence collected about the different tensions within Brightbourne might be presented in a narrative form. This presentation format facilitates sound decision-making on the development of an appropriate tourist strategy for the town.

- *What we already know about the town and what is best for its future*: the presentation could start by reviewing what the decision-making group currently believe to be the facts about the opportunities for building appropriate tourism in the town. This review, building on the problem-definition stage of our ten-stage analysis model, would look at what is already known. This review would begin the process of introducing the power of prior knowledge, and start signalling how this, throughout the presentation, will be integrated with the consumer evidence.

- *An overview pen-portrait of how the town is currently perceived by stakeholders*: the presentation would then – drawing on all the different types of desk, qualitative, and quantitative evidence conducted among the different stakeholder groups, ranging from residents to tourists – compare and contrast the differing views among the different stakeholder groups. This integration of all the evidence to present the topline picture would have taken the holistic data analyst through our process of: 'compensating' for any shortfalls in the data; applying the 'constraints' in order to establish the statistical robustness of data; applying the 'enablers' to look at how this might be stretched, based on prior knowledge; and, throughout, benefited from all of the tips and techniques that we have outlined about organizing data and reducing it to its essence. Thus, at this point in the story, the decision-making audience will know the topline story.

- *A review of attitudes towards different tourism initiatives*: the presentation would then address how the different stakeholder groups reacted to various questions aimed at establishing what tourism strategy the town should adopt. Should this centre around maintaining the status quo; adopting a slightly more progressive approach, upgrading the town in certain areas, but essentially maintaining its character; or go for a more radical approach that would introduce a whole raft of new entertainment and cultural attractions that may change the character of the town? In presenting this type of evidence, the holistic analyst would demonstrate their mastery of the knowledge filters, for example, communicating to the audience the limitations of asking respondents certain types of hypothetical questions about the future. Here, the analyst would also be able to explain the way some of the data could be reframed to add some fresh perspectives in generating new ideas for developing the town.

- *The common ground*: the presentation would then focus on where there is general agreement about initiatives that would benefit the town. In the spirit of holistic analysis, this would continue to blend the prior knowledge of key local authority decision-makers with that of the consumer evidence. Specifically, at this point the presentation would:
    - Map out where there is broad agreement across the stakeholder groups, about strengths, delights, and 'positives' of the town – things that *everyone* is keen to preserve.
    - Identify where there is general agreement among stakeholders about the frustrations and limitations of living in the town – the areas everyone thinks should be improved.

    This style of drawing together the 'quick win' decision areas early on in the narrative, is one that is generally appreciated by decision-makers, who can then concentrate their decision-making efforts on more problematic decision-making areas.
- *The tension points in developing a tourism strategy*: the presentation could then itemize the biggest tensions between the stakeholder groups, i.e. where quite opposing requirements have been expressed by the different stakeholder groups. For example, this might be day-trippers wanting more late-night clubs, with nearby residents wanting more serenity and peace, and a curfew on late-night activities.
- *Striking the right strategic compromises*: at this point in the narrative, the analyst can start drawing together the evidence to present the critical trade-off decisions that will need to be made in striking a balance between the conflicting needs of different stakeholder groups.
- *Decision-facilitation*: here there is the option of drawing the evidence together into some kind of 'decision balance sheet'. A framework that helps the decision-making audience see the key decision trade-offs in clear, straightforward terms. Thus, our narrative on Brightbourne could conclude by showing the 'upside' and the 'downside' for different stakeholder groups when making different kinds of decisions.

Presenting the Brightbourne story in an impactful way

A further point to make about the narrative style is that today, market researchers have the technical capability to create charts (supported by embedded video clips and other devices) that tell the narrative in a visually powerful way. In

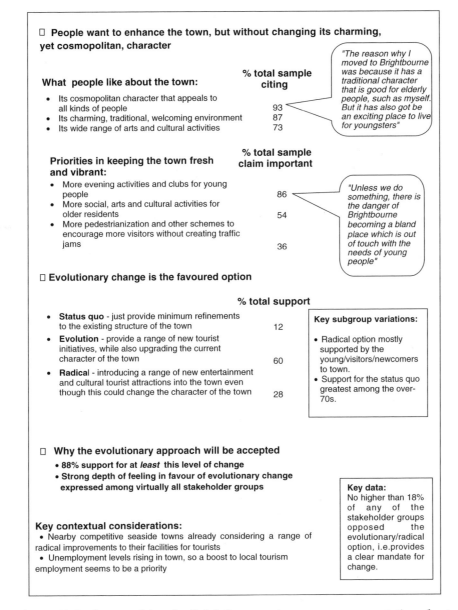

Figure 13.5 – Summarizing the Brightbourne story on one presentation chart.

Figure 13.5 we give an illustration of how the 'Brightbourne story' may be visually summarized on just one chart.

In the next chapter, we look at the final destination of holistic data analysis: helping decision-makers make informed judgements.

Facilitating informed decision-making

Summary

- The holistic analyst will be willing to go beyond the data and take a broader role to ensure that informed decision-making flows from the market research process.
- We now provide a guide on ways in which market researchers might extend their understanding of the decision-making process, to better apply their evidence.
- We start this task by reviewing how people, when faced with making a decision, are prone to default to flaws, sub-optimum behaviour and sloppy thinking. Understanding this provides a helpful context to data analysts charged with the task of advising on evidence-based decisions.
- We then review some techniques to help the market researcher better facilitate informed decision-making and stay in control to ensure the appropriate implementation of the decision.
- Specifically, we put the spotlight on making sure that the decisions driven by consumer evidence are 'safe', that is, follow from an intelligent and objective interpretation of the data, while still being flexible, and factoring prior knowledge and intuition into the process in a controlled way.

Bridging the data–decision gap

In the past, market researchers perhaps felt that their role, as the collectors and interpreters of evidence, did not extend to offering precise recommendations about exactly what this meant for the decisions being made by their end clients. Yet this is not true of the holistic data analyst who will analyse and intelligently interpret the evidence, and take a role in 'facilitating' an effective final decision.

The holistic data analyst will be prepared to go beyond simply providing an interpretation of the market research findings. They will be willing to help the decision-maker test the safety of putative decisions that may be made based on the data. Given this, it is important for the holistic market researcher to develop their decision-facilitation skills to help them ensure that their market research evidence is being actioned and implemented appropriately.

Making informed judgements

Progress made by market researchers in straddling the gap between the data they provide and the decisions that need to be made, has been slow. Theoretical decision-making frameworks have always been in abundance, but there have been comparatively few practical applied frameworks that help market researchers, on a day-to-day basis, reduce the gap that often exists between the evidence they are presenting and the decisions to be based on this data. So the emphasis in this chapter is on practical suggestions to help market researchers ensure that the way their evidence is being applied is sensible.

Before reviewing some of these practical suggestions, it is helpful to review what constitutes the 'ideal decision process'. It could be argued that the ideal decision process should involve the following stages:

- Make sure that you always work on the right problem.
- Precisely define the real problem.
- Be clear about the difference between the *symptoms* and the *causes* of the problem.
- Clarify all of the uncertainties associated with the problem, clearly specify the decision-making objectives, and tightly identify the criteria upon which the decision will be based.
- Weight (or prioritize) each of the above decision criteria on which the decision will be made.
- Review all of the alternative courses of action open to the decision-maker in a flexible, imaginative and innovative way.
- Itemize all the consequences of following each of the different possible decision outcomes.
- Then evaluate each alternative possible course of action against the above (weighted) criteria. (This could involve going through the formal process of rating each of the options against the prioritized criteria and then going with the decision with the highest sum rating).

It could be argued that, if decision-makers followed the above, they would have arrived at the *optimum* decision. Of course, in practice, rarely will it be possible to stay even remotely close to this 'ideal' decision-making process. However, the above framework is helpful because it provides a starting point for evaluating just how far – given the rough-and-tumble and imperfection of commercial decision-making – we have been cajoled and nudged away from the counsel of perfection.

How we broach decision-making

We now move on to understanding the flaws and shortfalls in how we make decisions. This is another important building block, prior to arriving at practical frameworks to help market researchers facilitate business decision-making.

Flawed self-knowledge and confused motives

One difficulty we face in making 'informed judgements' when solving a problem, is that we can easily be thrown off course by flawed self-perceptions of our own capabilities, and by a general confusion about our core goals and motives. Below we briefly review some of the issues:

- Individuals usually lack some of the critically important information on various aspects of the ideal decision process, outlined above, to make the 'optimum' decision. This is often referred to as the concept of 'bounded rationality'. That is, we are invariably making decisions that are based on less than perfect information.
- There is also the considerable body of evidence that tells us that, as individuals, we tend to cultivate positive illusions about ourselves in order to enhance and protect our self-esteem, increase our personal contentment, and help us through difficult situations. This leads us to believe that we have more control over events than we really do. Thus, we often believe that we can contribute to successful outcomes, but fail to look at the hard reality of our chances of contributing to failure.
- It is also well documented that we make unrealistically positive self-evaluations across a vast range of social contexts. For instance, most of us perceive ourselves as being superior to others in traits such as honestly, cooperativeness, rationality, level of health, intelligence and driving skills. (Amazingly 97% of British motorists consider that they are above-average drivers!)
- Added to this is our tendency to deceive ourselves about what we actually do, and what we think we should do. It seems that, within each of us, there are two selves: our 'of the moment' and our 'long-term benefit' persona. Thus, people often want to engage in decisions that will fulfil their immediate desires. At the same time, though, they believe that they should act differently to maximize their long-term goals. We are all aware of being subject to a series of pushes and pulls and inconsistencies in deciding whether to opt for short-term gratification or longer-term benefits. This is sometimes referred to as 'bounded willpower', whereby, on balance, we will give greater weight to present rather than future concerns.
- In addition, we are often inconsistent in terms of when we operate in our own self-interest and when in the interest of others. There will be many scenarios

where we care about the outcomes for others, but in other situations, we will be driven by self-interest.

Given the above observations, it is often the case that, from the outset, we, as individuals, will not be seeking to achieve the 'optimum' decision. Many decision-makers will forego the best solution in favour of one that is acceptable or reasonable. Here, the term 'satisficing' is often used to describe the way many individuals search out a solution that meets the minimum acceptable, but certainly not optimum, outcome. In short, if self-knowledge, awareness, and clarity of thinking in knowing our true goals and beliefs is the highest mental state, then we, as individuals, have a long way to go to achieve this as our start point for informed decision-making.

Lack of technical knowledge can undermine sound decision-making

There are also situations where, notwithstanding our best endeavours to arrive at an informed judgement, our lack of critically important knowledge can impair our ability to make sound observations.

- When children are asked what is happening when an ice cube is placed into a glass of hot water, most children – in the absence of knowledge about thermodynamic equilibrium theory – will *intuitively* (and sensibly) argue that the cold ice cube is cooling down the hot water. What is happening here though – in terms of the energy at work in the glass as it seeks equilibrium – is much more complex, including the fact that the hot water is also heating up the ice cube. So, in these situations, brave intuition is no substitute for attending physics lessons!
- Building on the above, there is also Piaget's famous experiment involving young children being shown that two differently sized jugs each contain exactly the same amount of liquid. The child is then asked which of the two jugs, the taller or the wider, contains the most liquid. Piaget showed that children up to the age of about eight will always claim that it is the taller jug that contains the most water, not the wider jug. This reflects the fact that children, up to the age of eight, are only able to concentrate on either the height of the jug, or the width of the jug, but not both. This limited way of reasoning does not disappear until the child is able to compensate for the effects of one feature, with reference to the other.
- Extending this point to the market research arena, there are many decision-making areas where our limitations in, for example, understanding probability theory, will badly distort our intuitive attempts at sorting out issues of chance. Thus, we know that there is often confusion about the notion of statistically 'significant', as opposed to statistically 'important', data. We also know that

some individuals will be confused with the difference between a statistical relationship between two events and a proven, causal relationship. Thus, inspired, but uninformed, intuition, is no substitute for understanding the basic laws of statistics.

- Building on the above point, there is also often misunderstanding about how research can be a powerful way of reflecting *relative* change, while being less robust in terms of measuring the *absolute* position. Thus, a market research study, in arguing that seven out of ten visitors to a hotel were 'dissatisfied', may – given all of the 'errors' inherent in the survey research process – provide only a fairly impressionistic guide to how well the hotel is really doing. If, one year later, using exactly the same methodology (and questionnaire), we find that levels of satisfaction with the hotel have plummeted to only two out ten, then irrespective of the accuracy of the 'absolute' measure, here we have powerful 'relative' evidence to suggest that some kind of intervention is needed to investigate what is happening at the hotel. In short, a technical appreciation of how market research works is needed to make sense of certain data.

- Another specific and critical issue relating to market research evidence is ensuring that decisions are based on information that is representative, as opposed to information that just happens to be 'available'. Thus, we may receive a piece of information that says that four out of five dentists have recommended sugarless chewing gum, but unless we were aware of the size and structure of the sample, we should not make appropriate judgements as to the robustness of this claim. (This, as we have discovered, would include also knowing about the percentage 'response' or 'strike' rate for the study.)

Simplistic, lazy, clichéd or stereotypic thinking

We are often guilty of resorting to over-simplistic devices to make sense of the complexity all around us. These may have an 'intuitive appeal' – particularly in the 'macho' business world – but they do not ultimately help our cause of achieving sound, informed decision-making.

- One tendency that can lead to flawed decision-making is our predilection, when there is a complex array of choices, to reduce these down to a straight choice between two alternatives. Thus, the issue of the UK joining the Single European Currency becomes a two-way conflict, between 'surrendering our sovereignty' versus 'seizing our only opportunity for international expansion'. Setting up such false dichotomies is a common tactic in business, and is very dangerous, because it glosses over some of the more subtle solutions open to us in solving a problem.

- Another one of our fundamental problems, when facing up to making decisions, is the mistaken belief that, if the decision was delayed, then some of the current risk and uncertainty will later be reduced. There is a view that contextual events could change to our advantage and/or that the subsequent provision of further information will be to our benefit. We are all aware of 'enquiries' being set up to delay the point at which a decision will be made. Frequently this is a mistaken assumption. The delay adds nothing to the quality of our decision-making. Often all that individuals are doing is anchoring in their own safe 'comfort zone', rather than seriously confronting the decision at hand.

- Market research evidence will also often be presented based on a critical, false underlying assumption. For example, financial regulatory authorities in the UK deal with the notion of 'financial detriment', in evaluating the issue of individuals 'cashing in' endowment insurance policies before they have run their full term. That is, the assumption is made that the termination of a policy before the end of its term is sub-optimum, in the sense that the individual will 'lose money'. This seems reasonable enough. Consumers, although in part evaluating their position by applying the concept of financial detriment, in many cases will also address this issue with a different psychological mindset. For many, the premature cashing in of an endowment policy is a positive action. Many see it as a form of 'psychological deck clearing' that can generate cash for fresh, exciting, new initiatives (although, technically, they will have lost money).

- When evaluating a particular scenario, we know that we have a tendency to focus on the successful situation in front of us, rather than logically evaluating every scenario, from both the positive and negative angle. Thus, for example, in evaluating a TV commercial that features a well-liked and famous footballer, strictly speaking, to bring objectivity to this situation, we should analyse the issue as follows: commercials with footballers that have been successful; commercials with footballers that have not been successful; commercials without footballers that have been successful; and commercials without footballers that have not been successful. Yet invariably, the apparently successful commercial in front of us – with a famous footballer – is the one that will dominate our evaluation of this mode of promotion. So we come to the conclusion that footballers' endorsements in commercials are a good idea.

- We also often operate with tired, or stereotypic, thinking in making sense of evidence. For instance, with regard to drug usage, we could, by reflex, draw on our loose impressionistic understanding of this issue, based on the associations that already exist in our heads. We 'presume' that drug taking is 'what difficult youngsters do'. This stereotypic instant reaction will often precede a tighter analysis of the actual relationships between drug taking and different age bands throughout the general population. In sum, our instant 'intuitive' associations, and thought processes, can often take us too quickly, and wrongly, to the wrong conclusion.

- Similarly, some events, because they evoke such powerful images in our heads, can set up faulty reasoning patterns in our minds. For example, each year we celebrate the bravery of all involved with the evacuation from Dunkirk, in 1940, of the British Expeditionary Force. This has built in our minds pictures of 'little boats rescuing soldiers from the beach'. It is true that the little boats played a vitally important role, but of all the men rescued, only around 10% were actually transported by small boats. The bulk of the evacuation, given the sheer scale of the operation, had to be conducted by transferring men, via pontoons, on to Royal Navy destroyers and minesweepers. Thus, putative field marshals and future admirals, contemplating a beach rescue, if ever the situation should arise again, would do well not to be overpowered by the powerful imagery of the little boats, but instead should look dispassionately at the hard logistical facts of how such a large number of men were actually successfully rescued.

Responding to uncertainty with superficial thinking

People tend to become anxious when they sense uncertainty and may infill this vacuum with flawed thinking. In short, uncertainty is an environment in which we are prone to let loose our intuitive 'reasoning' in a way that may take us badly off course. Some examples of this are discussed below:

- When faced with uncertainty, we will often, too readily, automatically accept facts that are untrue as generally 'received wisdom' without challenging them. This leads to building our analysis on feet of clay. (This is sometimes called the 'Pennsylvania Dutch' effect. This is because the original founders of Pennsylvania were from Germany (i.e. the Deutsch), but subsequent American pronunciations of this transformed it into 'Dutch', with the result that is now generally accepted wisdom that the founders of Pennsylvania were from Holland, rather than Germany!)
- Similarly, we often settle for a partial or superficial understanding that helps us through our uncertainty. This is sometimes called the 'Piccadilly effect'. (Piccadilly Circus is so called because a shirt-maker once produced special collars, called 'piccadills', at this site. But this only gets us so far because nobody knows why the collars were so called.)

Over-influenced by accessible and easy to understand evidence

Marketing evidence that is easily available to us can be disproportionately over-represented in our thinking when making decisions. Thus, we know that the sheer immediacy, and availability of a solitary piece of information, can dominate and cloud our clear thinking on an issue:

- We know that our decision-making is often influenced by the *first* piece of information with which we are provided. This can then often become the benchmark, or anchor, against which we then tend to evaluate all subsequent evidence. So, for example, we may find initial 'guestimates' of market share – which are no more than optimistic guesses – becoming enshrined in current thinking, such that all subsequent estimates are somehow linked, or related, to this initial arbitrary anchor. In short, people start making assessments by beginning from an initial value, and adjusting this to yield a final decision. However, this initial anchor may be little more than a random starting point.

- We must also be alert to the dangers of decision-makers (intuitively) basing their decisions on the most impactful information, rather than on all of the evidence. In the US, a long-running, largely unsuccessful, campaign to communicate the dangers of HIV was transformed when one woman, in an emotional outburst on national television, said that she was deliberately trying to spread the disease out of revenge. Everybody remembered this incident.

- Another problem for the market researcher is the fact that the originator of the research brief may not make explicit critical pieces of information, on the grounds that it is so well known to them, that it surely must be known by everybody. This false belief explains why manuals on how to pre-record a programme on a video recorder, and the like, are often incomprehensible. What is totally implicit and clear to the designer of a piece of equipment is anything but obvious to the person who must use it. So market researchers need to work hard to draw out those implicit assumptions, to make sure that the start point for understanding a problem, and subsequently making effective decisions, is as comprehensive as possible.

- In particular, it is important to put checks and balances in place that allow us to keep under control our tendency to over-interpret qualitative market research evidence. For example, a solitary, but powerful and emotional, account by a woman motorist stranded late at night at the side of the road – in a focus group viewed by clients – about the poor service she had received at the hands of a roadside assistance organization could be acted upon, but conceal the fact that this was the only incident of its type in ten years.

Methodological expertise and weaknesses can distort our thinking

Sometimes our decision-making, and judgements, will be driven by our methodological prowess, rather than by a more balanced approach to evidence:

- Some people who are 'figure phobic' will totally ignore sound numerical arguments, tending to supplant this with easier-to-understand, but what could be flawed, qualitative arguments.

- Some people will operate the other way round, attaching too much importance to statistical data (which they understand), rather than powerful qualitative evidence about people's feelings (which they feel uncomfortable about taking into account).

Psychological mind games and applying arbitrary criteria

We will also often play psychological mind games and apply arbitrary criteria when it comes to handling decision scenarios.

- Let us illustrate the point with the experiment involving the following two scenarios. In scenario one, people were asked what they would do if they inadvertently lost a £10 theatre ticket. Assuming they could buy another ticket on the door that night, would they still go to the theatre, or not? People in the other sample in the experiment were asked what they would do if they were going to the theatre that night to buy a ticket at the door (for £10), but lost a £10 note on the way. In this example, the £10 note and the £10 ticket are exactly the same unit of transaction. So the question asked of each group should produce exactly the same answer. But the experiment showed that individuals who lose an actual theatre ticket report that it would be 'extravagant to dip yet again into their (psychological) entertainment budget' and are therefore less likely to say they will buy another ticket at the theatre. Whereas the individuals who lost an actual £10 note are more likely to report that losing the £10 note was 'bad luck', and that they would still go ahead and buy a ticket at the door. So it is all in the head.
- Similarly, we often seek out benchmarks for our decision-making in a rather idiosyncratic way, using arbitrary criteria that defy pure logic and rationality. For example, we know, logically speaking, that the Olympic gold medallist in a particular sport must have performed 'better' than the silver medal winner, who, in turn, must have been 'better' than the bronze medallist. Yet in a study conducted amongst Olympic silver and bronze medallists, it was shown that Olympic bronze medal winners tend to be more satisfied with the outcome of their endeavours than silver medal holders. This is because the silver medal winners tend to anchor their achievement against the benchmark of having failed to attain the gold medal, thereby concluding that they have lost in some way. In contrast, bronze medallists tend to anchor their medal winning performance against the possibility of having come all the way to the Olympics, and having not won a medal at all. It is all mind games, we know, but it all makes for a messy picture when it comes to understanding the decision-making process.
- Resorting to arbitrary touchstones is another laziness that bedevils sound decision-making. Readers will be familiar with the idea of managers making salary decisions by adjusting an employee's current salary, which is a long way from evaluating the worth of that individual relative to other employees

and the market place. This also explains why individuals will often tend to evaluate the fairness of the price being asked for a car, against the original *list* price, rather than against the current supply and demand determined price. Ultimatums are another variant of the notion of 'false anchoring'. In the event of a dispute, it is often argued that a fair solution would be a '50/50 split'. Of course, such a 50/50 split could be quite arbitrary: the facts of the situation could suggest that the *start point* for the next phase of negotiation should be a 70/30 split.

- In the world of business decision-making, it is important to know that a large number of individuals will change from 'risk-averse' to 'risk-seeking' behaviour, purely as a result of whether the problem has been positively or negatively framed, even though the two outcomes being explained are objectively the same. This is a critically important observation that is based on an authoritative body of knowledge about decision-making, called 'Prospect Theory'. (In the Notes section to the book, we provide the reader with some detailed references on the important observation we are making here about decision-making depending on the way in which the different decision propositions are initially framed.)

The competition factor

It has to be remembered that market research conclusions are usually based on the 'ceteris paribus' condition. That is, they assume – during the duration of the research process – that everything else will be held constant (will remain equal). Of course, we know that this condition will rarely hold true, and therefore we need to be mindful of the implications of this in the way we apply evidence to business decision-making.

- Following on from what we have said above about applying knowledge filters, we need to accept that consumers' responses take place within the narrow canvas of the interview, and as such, do not reflect some of the 'market noise' that will explain how individuals, in real life, will play out their survey preferences. Thus, in good faith, a customer will say that they will 'definitely' buy product X, but we know from our knowledge filters (empirical market research evidence) that typically only one-third of individuals opting for the top scale position of a 'likely to buy' scale will actually convert this preference into an actual purchase.
- Of course, a feature of the competitive environment is that if a company changes the price of a brand, for example, then there is a reasonable chance that it will set off a chain of reactive events that will disrupt the very market that informed the basis of the original market research study. (In the Notes section, we provide key references on the subject of 'game theory': making an assessment of the likely competitive response to a market intervention.)

Taking appropriate action

People often forget that making a decision is not just about having the 'thought', but about actually taking action in relation to this conclusion. This opens up another range of sub-optimum behaviours that explain why much business decision-making is subject to flaws, poor thinking, and so-called 'intuitive' contributions that should have been more thoroughly 'validated'.

- One scenario centres on how we make decisions about actually acting on our observations in a group setting. It is known, for example, that there is a tendency among certain individuals, in a group setting, to suppress any doubts they may have about a decision, in order to conform with the prevailing group view on that particular issue. This is sometimes known as the 'bystander effect' or the 'group think' problem. That is, people tend to refrain from acting in a situation where others are present. Individuals seem to perceive themselves as not being subject to being proven wrong if they do *not* take a position.
- The reluctance of individuals to stand up and be counted in a group setting is dangerous, particularly in the context of organizational group decision-making. It is well documented that some of the (dysfunctional) characteristics of group organizational behaviour include: an illusion of invulnerability; a tendency to discount early warnings; extreme over-optimism; the suppression of doubts; putting pressure on dissidents; and an unquestionable belief in the morality of the dominant group. Thus, if each individual in a group fails to stand up and be counted, then we can see how group-based organizational decisions can gradually drift out of control. (It was Jack Kennedy who said that 'courageous' decisions are ones where all objective, rational reasoning suggests it will be to the advantage of a particular group, but where the group in question, in the short-term, cannot see the advantages, and are critical of the decision.)
- In addition, our society has managed to persuade itself that making a U-turn – going back on an original decision – is generally considered to be a bad thing, or a sign of weakness. This phenomenon explains why, for instance, there is a lot of poor decision-making near the summit of Everest. A lot of deaths are the result of climbers who, having invested so much energy in getting so close to the top of the world, then refuse to accept the professional advice that they should now turn back, because to stay a few more hours, in the worsening weather conditions, would be fatal.
- There is also the problem we face of not wanting to let go of past decisions (even if they are flawed). This is sometimes called the problem of 'sunk costs' or the 'endowment' effect. (The latter is a reference to the fact that the value a seller may place on a commodity, not only includes its intrinsic worth, but the value the owner places on his or her emotional attachment to that item.) Transferring this observation to a business example, we might find the originator of an excellent dot.com idea to which she is emotionally attached,

clinging on to this intrinsically good idea in the face of mounting evidence that tells her that this is not a scheme that will generate the expected revenue.

- It is also important to ensure – when a decision has been made – that the market researcher is alert to how the market research evidence is subsequently being actioned. The literature abounds with examples of market research *allegedly* failing to successfully predict what might happen. Often what has happened is that, in certain scenarios, the feedback from the research has been basically correct, but has been misinterpreted. This is a particular problem in what we would label as the 'amber light' scenario. These are situations where market research is not providing a definite no-go 'red' signal, but neither is it providing a clear-cut, go, 'green' signal. It is providing an 'amber light' message. It is saying that there is sufficient evidence to proceed with the initiative, providing care is taken in precisely executing some of the qualifying conditions associated with the provisional support for the idea. It is in this 'amber light' situation that a failure, on the part of both market researchers and the decision-maker, to carefully implement the research findings can lead to difficulties.

- Looking in the other direction, we can identify (already) numerous cases of an inappropriate imperative in favour of (wrongly) 'acting', rather than 'not acting', following an evaluation of the options, leading to ruin. In many organizational scenarios, as we have indicated, 'macho-thinking' can prevail – an environment where there is a strong presumption that action must be preferred to inaction. For example, at the end of a management consultancy's evaluation of a company, where large fees have changed hands, there is usually an expectation that action must follow. In certain situations, though, it might be entirely logical to conclude that no action is required. This phenomenon partly explains why, following an explosion of a chemical plant several years ago, there was an immediate closure by this organization of all its plants, even though the other plants had much better safety records than the plant that was subject to the accident.

Facilitating sound evidence-based decision-making

The above review highlights the importance of developing analytical frameworks that maintain orthodox rigorous traditional thinking associated with sound professional market research, while also still helping the data analyst stretch their understanding to embrace what we might label 'informed intuition'. This is intuition based on creative, innovative (right brain) thinking, but in a way that minimizes some of the flaws outlined above. We need to embrace the power of this lateral, less formal and 'rational', thinking, into market research analysis. Equally, we must be alert to the dangers and difficulties of just going with the natural flow of our intuitive thought.

So, in the rest of this chapter, we look at some techniques that market researchers can draw on to test the 'safety' of different evidence-based decisions:

how far can we trust the evidence supporting a putative decision. We look at three different decision-facilitation skill sets. First, helping decision-makers think clearly, logically, and deeply about the evidence. Secondly, helping decision-makers *stretch* their thinking, to think big and imaginatively about what the data might mean. Thirdly, ensuring that the decision brings the above two perspectives together, and is grounded in reality.

Clear, accurate and deep logical thinking about the evidence

One option is for market researchers, where decision-takers are faced with two or more competing outcomes, to offer various decision-facilitation services – possibly in the form of a 'workshop' that follows the market research presentation. At these sessions, a useful start point are various techniques that ensure everybody involved in the decision has a clear, accurate and deep-seated grasp about the accuracy, reliability and robustness of the evidence. The following checklist provides food for thought on the kinds of techniques that will pay dividends.

- *Logic and reasoning*: we have listed above some of the flaws that characterize the way people go about applying information to decision-making. So the first question to ask is: 'have all these lessons been applied to the data set?'
- *The compensation process*: list all the possible sources of error that could have crept into the research process. Inspect the way these have been 'compensated' for. Then decide whether the compensation has been sound, or has taken the data a 'bridge too far'.
- *Ambiguity checks*: remember our earlier reference to a survey showing that 'British tourists preferred Sydney to New York'. But, was this a survey of tourists who had visited *both* locations, or was it based on two monadic surveys (with a higher percentage of tourists to Sydney than New York rating the city more favourably)?
- *Timeliness*: if you are looking at data on airline security, as we discussed, the issue of whether this study was conducted pre or post September 11th will, of course, be an issue.
- *Omissions*: you may, for various reasons, end up missing information on issues that prove to be critical, so make a wish list of the 'ideal' information you would have liked at the outset of the project. Then, compare this with the information you have at your disposal, and decide on the criticalness of the 'missing information'.
- *Sensitivity checks*: if the marketing recommendation hinges on the delivery of a specific level of service, then go back and assess what may happen if it proves impossible to deliver the *precise* specifics of what customers want.
- *Spin and soundbites*: the evidence you are looking at may have been dumbed down into soundbite form, thereby losing some of its critical contextual

meaning. In addition, some of the arguments may have been spun to advance a particular agenda. So, pass all the evidence through this media filter.

Thinking bigger: stretching the decision-makers' horizons

We now look at some decision-facilitation techniques designed to encourage decision-takers to go beyond the orthodox interpretation of the evidence, and to think in a more innovative way about what the data could be trying to tell us:

- *Depersonalizing*: some managers may feel constrained by offering more 'creative' interpretations of evidence in a public setting. So perhaps comments could be sought on an anonymous basis.
- *Make it personal*: as a counterpoint to the above, ask managers whether they would make the same decision if they were using their *own* money.
- *Get in touch with true feelings*: tell managers that if a coin comes down heads it is a 'go' decision, and if it comes down tails, it is a 'no' decision. As the coin comes down, everyone must immediately give their spontaneous reaction on what has happened.
- *Think bigger picture*: how do people feel about the micro decision once we have been through the process of seeing how the ripples from this decision affect increasingly bigger meso to macro contexts.
- *Level of abstraction*: getting people to ladder up to deal with higher-order constructs in looking at the problem can also help broaden our horizons. So is a holiday company ultimately in the business of providing periods of calm, reflective quality time?
- *Go beyond the default position*: most organizations have a 'default position' when they are in trouble. Banks will go from espousing the value of understanding customers' longer-term needs, to short-term, accountancy-driven, cost-saving initiatives. So, be honest about your own organization's default position, and ask yourself whether the decision you are making will truly break the mould, or is just playing safe.
- *Visualization*: ask people to 'visualize' what they think the world will be like in five years' time, and then come back to what this means for the decision they are making now.

Bringing it all together: creative yet disciplined, evidence-based decision-making

The ultimate measure of the success of holistic data analysis is its ability to stretch the decision-makers' imagination and to do justice to brilliant, intuitive thinking, while ensuring that these creative insights are grounded in reality. This requires the application of various checks and balances. Some suggestions for prudent decision-facilitation to achieve this goal are itemized below.

- *Is this strategic vision or tactical excellence?*: business success is ultimately explained through brilliant strategic vision, not through tactical excellence. So ask, is this a decision that hinges primarily on day-to-day, tactical survival, rather than informed, strategic thinking? If so, perhaps we need to think again.
- *Working through the 'what if' scenarios*: list out all of the uncontrollables that impinge on the decision, and see what difference this might make to your decision.
- *Seek concrete examples*: try to turn extravagant, abstract, outrageous or woolly claims, being made to advance an argument, into concrete examples of the key decision points being made.
- *Confirmation tests*: take some of the putative decisions to third parties and see what they think – possibly suppliers of the data on which you are basing your decision.
- *Role-play the idea from the perspective of the customer from hell*: work through all aspects of the proposed product offering and see how well it performs in this 'nightmare scenario'.
- *Look at the decision from the third corner*: what does this decision look like from the perspective, not only of customers, but also employees, shareholders, key industry opinion formers, industry journalists and other groups?
- *Do the 'game theory'*: what are your competitors likely to do in the face of a particular decision? Have you been honest about the quality of your competitors? How will your decision fare against the world's most formidable competitor? When you have done this, see how your idea will play against a more realistic 'best in class' competitor in your field.

In the next chapter, we identify where we need to hone our holistic data analysis skills, so this growing competence can be applied to future analysis projects.

15 Developing holistic data analysis

Summary

- Ongoing development and new thinking is critical to building market researchers' holistic analysis skills. So, it is helpful to pinpoint where the cultivation of particular holistic analysis skills is likely to pay dividends.
- Here, the first distinguishing feature of the holistic approach is the emphasis it places on: intelligently integrating qualitative and quantitative evidence drawn from across multiple data sets; knowing how to 'compensate' for shortfalls in the data; and being able to position each individual piece of evidence in the wider context of other available relevant data. So, we review the lessons that are being learnt, and look at how this can be used to enhance the holistic analysis 'craft'.
- The second feature of the holistic approach to data analysis is the importance it places on developing 'knowledge filters' and 'reframing techniques'. This adds power to the analysis process, giving the analyst the *option* of setting literal survey responses in the wider context of what we know about how well respondents 'perform' in the survey process, while enhancing the quality of the analysts' 'take' on the consumer data. So, conceptualizing and disseminating this body of knowledge will enhance the quality of further holistic data analysis.
- The third differentiating characteristic of the holistic approach is the emphasis it puts on 'engaging' the decision-maker with an impactful narrative. The researcher should not be detached and remote from the decision-making process. Drawing together industry experiences on the success (or not) of evidence-based decision-making will be invaluable in building the holistic analysis discipline.

Progressing holistic analysis

If the holistic approach to the analysis of market research data is to gain currency, and become an accepted skill set that the market research industry fosters in order to meet its clients' needs, then the techniques outlined in this book will need to be developed. This brings us to the last part of our ten-stage framework: identifying some of the key skills and competencies that will need to be developed, so that this can be fed back to enhance the quality of future data analysis assignments.

A summary of the holistic data analysis process

Before reviewing the skill set and capabilities required of the new holistic data analyst, it will be helpful to briefly summarize the key concepts and principles underpinning the ten-stage holistic analysis process outlined in this book. So, in Figure 15.1 we provide a summary of the holistic analysis approach, together with an itemization of some of the key principles that underpin this way of analysing market research data. This overview provides a backdrop for looking at areas where we need to enhance our skills and/or work harder to communicate these new concepts to newcomers to new market research.

So, let us now look at the key areas where we believe the skills of holistic data analysts can be sharpened by a sharing of experiences, and the dissemination of good practice throughout the industry, thereby improving the quality of future holistic data analysis assignments.

Contextualizing, compensating for, and integrating multiple imperfect evidence

The start point for making sense of data is clearly the orthodox methodological principles we have available, including establishing the validity and reliability of the data, and establishing what sampling theory, and other statistical knowledge, tells us about the data. The holistic data analyst will then build on this by contextualizing their data in terms of the wider marketing information picture, and establishing how far they can compensate for shortfalls in their (imperfect) data.

The holistic analyst will also use a range of concepts – including the weight, power and direction evidence – to help integrate different types of data, while at the same time, as appropriate, factoring management prior knowledge into the analysis equation. So, learning how to develop frameworks that, on the one hand, respect orthodox methodological ways of evaluating data, but at the same time, know how to stretch out to embrace ideas, such as working with the notion of 'constraints/enablers', is a challenge for the development of the holistic data analysis movement. The theoretical underpinning for this idea – given the rich tradition of Bayesian statistics – is well established. Thus, the continuing challenge is pulling down the somewhat complex Bayesian ideas and making them accessible and practicable for practising commercial market researchers.

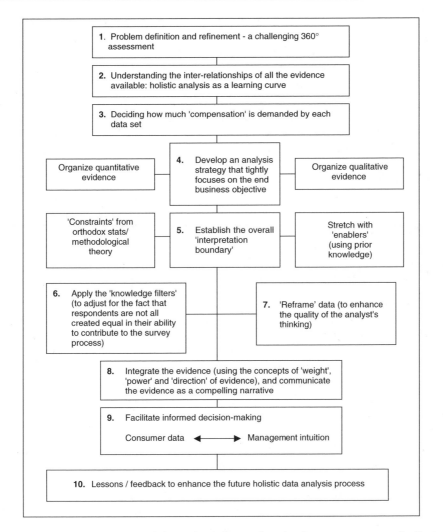

Figure 15.1 – A summary of the principles underpinning our ten-stage holistic data analysis framework.

Developing the knowledge filters and reframing techniques to add continuing power to our analysis

Another distinctive feature of the holistic data analysis approach centres on developing a range of knowledge filters (about how the research process 'works'), to add power to the analysis and interpretation of what respondents are trying to tell us in surveys. We also need to cultivate various data reframing techniques to broaden the horizons of the analysts' thinking at the interpretation stage.

Here, we should point out that the future does not lie in building grand theories about how market research works. Clearly, there are dangers to seeking the holy grail of some kind of universal truth. However, the future does lie in developing an understanding of how knowledge filters can be applied in certain circumstances, given the fact that all respondents are not created equal in their ability to participate in the survey process. Similarly, in cultivating various reframing techniques that add innovation, and depth of understanding, to our interpretation of data, we probably need to think on a smaller, rather than grand, canvas. We need to explain how these techniques will work for particular groups of customers and/or in specific markets. So, another challenge for holistic analysts, is to collate together – at an appropriate level of abstraction and conceptualization – explicit guidance for newcomers to market research as to which knowledge filters and reframing techniques to apply in different circumstances, to various kinds of data.

Engaging the end decision-making audience

A further distinctive feature of the holistic data analysis approach is its commitment to presenting evidence in a way that will constructively impact on the decision-making process. This is why we have strongly commended the idea of presenting research evidence in the form of a compelling narrative. Not only is this approach known to keep the decision-making audiences' attention, but it is one that facilitates the integration of more intuitive-based observations, that can then be evaluated alongside the evidence. It is also an approach that segues into the ultimate purpose of conducting market research in the first place, namely to improve the quality of information-based judgements and decision-making.

So, looking to the future, there is the challenge for the holistic data analyst to develop techniques that will help with the process of 'testing the safety' of evidence-based decisions. This is a stepping stone towards eventually being able to closely link how different combinations of research evidence have led to different types of successful – and less successful – decisions. In turn, these could be linked to the different business outcomes that were eventually achieved through this decision.

A win–win development

We believe that the cultivation of the holistic data analysis approach advocated in this book is a 'win/win'. It is clearly a win for market researchers who wish to add an extra dimension to their armoury, thereby allowing them to engage more successfully with end decision-makers, who now seem to be looking for a more integrated approach that impacts directly on decisions. Importantly, though, it is also a win for market researchers who wish to focus on more orthodox methodological and statistical-based approaches. Clearly, these orthodox skills remain critical in interpreting the marketing information jigsaw. The arrival of the holistic approach to data analysis, for certain assignments, should not represent any threat to those who wish to continue working in the core of the market research industry. In sum, the holistic approach simply represents a *possible* option for extending the role of the market researcher.

So, in summary, in writing this guide to holistic analysis, we believe we have provided – albeit only at a meta level – a framework that will help newcomers to new market research organize their thinking and learning about the art and science of data analysis. We feel it will be helpful for newcomers to study the way holistic analysts move up the analytical learning curve, starting with intensive efforts to define the problem, working through orthodox and less conventional methods to understand the data, eventually arriving at helping with decision-facilitation.

One concern about the stretching of market researchers' (original) remit is that it will stretch our methodological understanding too thinly. There will be concerns about the holistic approach representing an 'haute vulgarization' of the discipline. On this point though, we would argue that, in putting together our overall organizing framework for thinking about problems in an holistic way we are improving the probability of the next generation of market researchers meeting the expectations of business decision-makers. We would argue that psychologists, sociologists, orthodox survey methodologists, statisticians and anthropologists, who may be frowning at the way we have dipped into, in such a cavalier way, many of their concepts and principles to harness them to our holistic philosophy, have nothing to fear from the holistic approach. Their specialist work clearly must continue, leaving the holistic market researcher to link together these ideas, and make them accessible to commercial market researchers.

So, all we can do here is call for generosity of spirit from these experts. In weaving together and summarizing the first-class contributions made by various specialists, our goal has been to provide a practical, accessible guide for everyday market researchers. It has not been to undercut the importance of continuing specialist excellence in these areas.

Our goal has been to stimulate some curiosity in new ways of thinking about business problems and evidence, with the aim of enhancing the quality of evidence-based decision-making. Thus, our book is no more than a modest start at developing an organizing framework for thinking about how market researchers might become more effective, and respond to their clients' increasing expectations of what market research must now deliver. The authors believe that the ideas and frameworks in this book are a platform upon which to build. We believe that what is now needed is continued innovation and creativity to develop the holistic approach to analysis and business problem-solving. We need people who are prepared to continue to think big, and stretch the existing canvas, so as to make 'new market research' even more effective.

Guide to the supporting training module

16

Summary

- We now explain how we have structured the training module to support this book – available via the Wiley website (http://www.wiley.europe.com/go/smith).
- The training module, which has been structured into ten units, mirrors the ten stages of the holistic data analysis model outlined in this book.
- The modules are in the form of Microsoft PowerPoint charts. Here, we simply provide an overview of what the reader might expect to find in each of the units.

Unit one: The theoretical principles underpinning 'new' holistic data analysis

In this opening module, we review the reasons behind the emergence of 'new' market research, and the key principles underpinning this approach to data analysis. This unit draws on Chapters 1, 2 and 3 of this book.

Unit two: Problem definition and refinement

This unit draws mainly from the material in Chapter 4, and provides a guide – using a range of case study examples – of how to identify the 'true' problem, rather than being deflected with various related symptoms.

Unit three: Understanding how information works together to solve problems

This unit of the course – drawing primarily on the material from Chapter 5 of this book – explains how the holistic analyst, when addressing particular marketing problems, will be skilled in piecing together different types of evidence drawn from different sources.

Unit four: How to compensate for today's imperfect data

In this unit – based mainly on Chapter 6 – we look at the more traditional methods for assessing the robustness of data, and then move on to look at the way in which, today, analysts, working within certain guidelines, will seek to 'compensate' for the imperfection of certain data. In short, this unit tells the analyst how far they can go with different types of imperfect evidence.

Unit five: The key principles of the holistic approach to data analysis

In this unit – which is based on Chapter 7 of the book – we provide, again using various illustrations and case studies, guidance on how to fashion an analysis strategy that will answer the end decision-makers' expectations in terms of the judgements and decisions to be made.

Unit six: Organizing the qualitative data

Drawing on Chapter 8 of this book, we put the spotlight on the ways in which qualitative researchers work – using tapes, transcripts and notes, to arrive at an informed overall interpretation. We provide worked examples that show how different types of qualitative analysis can be used on varying types of evidence.

Unit seven: Organizing the quantitative data

In this unit we provide a detailed account of how to reduce unmanageable data down to an accessible form that aids the interpretation process. We use various illustrations, building on those already provided in Chapters 9 and 10 of the book.

Unit eight: Setting survey evidence in the context of what we know about the survey process

In this unit we build on Chapter 11 of the book – applying the knowledge filters – by giving various worked examples of the power of locating survey evidence in the wider normative context of what we know about the limitations of the survey process.

Unit nine: Ensuring the interpretation of data is fresh and innovative

In this unit, we look at the way in which the holistic data analyst will reframe data. We build on the illustrative examples outlined in Chapter 12 of this book, to highlight the opportunities for thinking about data in a novel and innovative way to tease out fresh insights.

Unit ten: Presenting research evidence and bridging the data–decision gap

In the final unit, we provide illustrations – drawing on Chapter 13 of the book – of ways of integrating evidence and telling the research evidence as a powerful, compelling story. We also – building on the material in Chapter 14 – look at how the market researcher can take their presentation one step further and help with the facilitation of business decisions. Again, we provide, in this unit, numerous examples of these techniques in practice.

Notes

We have kept the number of references provided to support the ideas presented in each chapter to a minimum. Our goal for each of the topics we investigate has been to select essentially introductory accounts. We believe that our choice of supporting references provides a sufficiently rigorous underpinning for the key concepts presented in this book, while at the same time not setting our target audience – newcomers to market research – an unrealistic task with their supplementary reading.

We have, though, also included *some* more specialist references. This will help readers who are keen to take their exploration of holistic data analysis a stage further. In addition, we shall be providing another layer of detailed references to deal with various specialist topics as a support to the supplementary training model that accompanies this book.

Chapter 1: 'New' market research

- For a review of the issues associated with emergence of a new 'paradigm' for market research, Spackman, Barker and Nancarrow (2000) provide a review of the emergence of the era of 'informed eclecticism'.
- Valentine and Gordon (2000) provide a review of the way in which the business culture, and ways of thinking about consumers, are changing as we progress into the 21st Century.
- Smith and Fletcher (2000), in their earlier book, outline their initial thinking on the emergence of the 'holistic' school of market research.

Chapter 2: Not a science, but a scientific approach

- For a review of the key issues associated with sound social scientific enquiry, Ziman (1991) discusses the key issues.
- For an examination of the role of survey evidence in social and commercial investigation, see Marsh (1982).
- A useful overview of what constitutes robust research evidence is provided by Salmon (2003).

- For an authoritative review of Bayesian statistics and its relevance to probability-based judgement, see Baron (1997).
- For a full account of grounded theory readers are referred to the pioneering work by Glaser & Strauss (1967).
- For further information on the healthy and sickly cells experiment to which we refer, see Watzlawick (1976).
- Two articles that readers may wish to follow up concerning hypothesis testing are Alt & Brighton (1981), with a rejoinder by Lawrence (1982).
- Readers particularly interested in the contribution of different branches of statistics will find the review of the philosophy of statistics by Lindley (2000) helpful.

Chapter 3: Data-rich intuitive analysis

- For a practical view of the way in which businesses broach the task of making decisions, see Dearlove (1998).
- Claxton (1997) provides an excellent review of intuitive thinking, which can be supplemented by referring to Goleman (1997) on the subject of 'emotional intelligence', while Wiseman (2003) looks at the so-called 'luck factor' in business.
- Further insights on the idea of factoring management prior knowledge into the decision process is provided by Baumard (1999).

Chapter 4: Analysing the right problem

- Barabba & Zaltman (1991) review the creative use of marketing information to fully understand the market place prior to solving business problems.
- For a review of the preparatory work undertaken by market researchers, prior to designing a research study, Smith (1998) examines many of the issues.
- Leonard & Straus (1999) provide a useful review of the benefits of putting the company's 'whole brain' to work when solving organizational problems.
- For a discussion of the challenge of teasing out implicit knowledge when solving problems, see Reber (1993).
- The notion of 'mapping an individual's world' is a powerful paradigm underpinning much market research, and readers may wish to refer to the original work of Kelly (1955).

Chapter 5: Understanding the big information picture

- Ward (1998) provides an informative introduction to different types of quantitative research, as does Goodyear (1998) on qualitative research.

- Smith & Dexter (1994) review the challenge for market researchers in combining qualitative understanding and quantitative measurement, including an illustrative example.
- For further reading on the way in which market research evidence works together to solve business problems, the reader should refer to various case study examples of good practice in market research. A useful start point here is the 'Research Works' series published by the British Market Research Association. The latest volume (no. 4) was published in 2002.

Chapter 6: Compensating for imperfect data

- It is important to have a sound grasp of sampling theory, including a clear understanding of concepts of sampling error and sampling bias. Here, the lucid account by Collins (1998) will be invaluable.
- Collins (1997) is also an important reference for understanding the issues associated with interviewer variability.
- For a review of some of the psychological issues associated with conducting Internet surveys, see Dexter, Smith & Brown (2000) and Dexter & Brown (2001).
- For a review of observation effects in qualitative research, see Robson & Wardle (1988).
- For a useful review of different approaches to interviewing groups and individuals in qualitative research, see Chrzanowska (2002).
- Miller & Read (1998) provide a comprehensive review of the issues associated with professional questionnaire design.
- For a comprehensive, up-to-date review of professional survey fieldwork practice, the best sources exist in the form of proprietary material confidential to different agencies. However, the account of the survey process edited by Hoinville & Jowell, written in 1988, lays down some timeless parameters for good practice.

Chapter 7: Developing the analysis strategy

- Ereaut (2002) provides a comprehensive review of the qualitative approach to analysis, which, read in conjunction with Miles & Huberman (1984), will provide some background to the 'Hermeneutic Circle' process discussed in this chapter.
- The Dolan & Ayland (2001) experiment on the effectiveness of different qualitative analysis techniques, provides useful insights into choosing the most appropriate analysis strategy.
- Callingham (2000) outlines the power of combining qualitative evidence and intuitive insights, with rigorous quantitative analysis in an excellent paper that can be obtained via the British Market Research Association.

- For a guide to interpreting survey statistics drawn from different samples, the reader is referred to the supporting training unit number seven.

Chapter 8: Organizing the qualitative data

- Robson & Hedges (1993) provide a comprehensive review of the analysis of qualitative data.
- Gordon (1999) (particularly the chapters on models of thinking, fuzzy thinking, and breaking the mould) provides an informed account of the qualitative research craft, as do Imms & Ereaut (2002) in their introduction to qualitative market research.

Chapter 9: Organizing the quantitative data

- Ehrenberg (1974) and (1994) leads the way with illustrating the importance, and skill, of data reduction. This is *must* reading for the holistic (quantitative) analyst.
- Harris (1998) provides a clear account of the role of statistical and significant testing, and Baker (1998) clearly explains the role of multivariate analysis.

Chapter 10: Establishing the interpretation boundary

- The underpinning for the idea of establishing the 'constraints' when establishing the interpretation boundary could be pursued by reading the Collins (1998) reference cited for Chapter 6 above.
- With regard to the thinking underpinning the notion of applying the 'enablers', here the most important reference is Baron (1997), cited in Chapter 2.
- The Bayesian model developed by the authors is further explained in the supplementary training module that accompanies the book.
- The supporting training unit number seven, referred to in Chapter 7 above, includes a useful guide to interpreting the significance of different survey statistics.

Chapter 11: Applying the knowledge filters

- The series of readings in Fishbein (1967) serve as a useful introduction to the different issues associated with attitude measurement.
- Franzen & Bouwman (2001) provide an informed account of how the brain 'works' in relation to brands.
- Heath (2001) coherently and authoritatively sets out a detailed review of the 'register' in which communications (and market research) 'engages'.

- For a review of issues associated with 'reversal theory' psychology see Apter (2001).
- Readers may wish to further explore the idea of 'conversational accounting' by referring to Harre (1979).
- Pearce & Cronen (1980) is the core reference in further understanding the notion of 'privileging selective contexts'. The more recent account, West & Turner (2000), shows how thinking has developed.
- Festinger & Carlsmith (1959), with their theory of cognitive dissonance, based on experimental evidence, show how people adapt their beliefs and attitudes to fit the way they behave in such a way as to maintain an image of themselves as a rational agent.
- Gazzaniga (1978) demonstrated a neural basis of the above psychological mechanism in his experiments with split-brain patients.
- For further information about the reporting of behavioural information in surveys being distorted, see Lee, Hu & Toh (2000)
- Delmus & Levy (1998) review the role of consumer panels.

Chapter 12: Reframing the data

- For a useful overview of general marketing and business models, see Karlöf (1993). The reader should also look at general marketing textbooks, such as Kotler (2002), which will provide explanations of a number of useful frameworks.
- Ries & Trout (1994) review of the basic 'laws of marketing' is also a useful source of 'reframing' ideas.
- Some may wish to explore the issue of locating business problems in the most relevant analytical framework by referring to Jackson (2001), who reviews various management consultancy approaches.
- Work by Porter (1998) on competitive intelligence is a minimum *must* read in understanding the key issues in this field.
- An authoritative review of semiotics is provided by Valentine & Evans (1993).
- For a review of lateral thinking that could lead to ideas for reframing your data set, de Bono (1990 and 2000) are helpful sources.

Chapter 13: Integrating the evidence and presenting research as a narrative

- For an illustration of the way in which the concepts of 'weight', 'power' and 'direction' can be applied to 'fuzzy' decision-making, see Michaluk (2002).
- The credentials of the storytelling approach to business communications are outlined by Breuer (1998) and Kaye & Jacobson (1999).
- And for inspirational ideas on the impactful visual presentation of data see Tufte (1990 and 1992).

Chapter 14: Facilitating informed decision-making

- Bazerman (2002) provides an authoritative review of the challenge of making sound management judgements and decisions.
- Nutt (1997) explains the results of his large research project conducted in the USA on the way managers make decisions.
- For the views of an experienced market research practitioner on the skill of applying research to successful decision-making, see Mahmoud (2002).
- To follow up on 'Prospect Theory', Kahneman & Tversky (1979) is the key source, and it is also an access point to further more detailed reading.
- The review by Harries & Hardman (2002) of judgement in decision-making is also informative.
- For an authoritative examination of the value of applying game theory to improve the quality of evidence-based decisions, see Dexter & Fletcher (2000).

Chapter 15: Developing holistic data analysis

- Valentine (2002) takes the discussion about the introduction of 'new' market research forward by discussing the way the 'new' market research industry should now be positioned.
- Smith & Dexter (2001) review the changing nature of the market research industry and the need for a new approach to meeting clients' needs.

References

Alt, M. & Brighton, M. (1981) Analysing data or telling stories. *Journal of the Market Research Society*, Vol. 23, No. 4.

Apter, M.J. (2001) *An Introduction to Reversal Theory*. Washington, DC: American Psychological Society.

Baker, K. (1998) Multivariate analysis of survey data. In *ESOMAR Handbook of Market and Opinion Research (4th edition)*, edited by McDonald and Vangelder. Amsterdam: ESOMAR.

Barabba, V.P. & Zaltman, G. (1991) *Hearing the Voice of the Market: Competitive Advantage through Creative Use of Market Information*. Boston: Harvard Business School Press.

Baron, J. (1997) *Thinking and Deciding*. Cambridge University Press.

BMRA *Research Works* (2002) Vol. 4. *Papers from the BMRA Research Effectiveness Awards*.

Baumard, P. (1999) *Tacit Knowledge in Organizations*. London: Sage.

Bazerman, M. (2002) *Judgement in Managerial Decision Making (5th edition)*. New York: Wiley.

Breuer, N.L. (1998) *The Power of Storytelling*. Workforce (December).

Callingham, M. (2000) Beyond the horizon: how market research will develop. Paper presented at a *British Market Research Association Seminar*.

Chrzanowska, J. (2002) *Interviewing Groups and Individuals in Qualitative Market Research*. Vol. 2 of the Qualitative Market Research series. London: Sage.

Claxton, G.L. (1997) *Hare Brain, Tortoise Mind: Why Intelligence Increases When You Think Less*. London: Fourth Estate.

Collins, M. (1997) Interviewer variability: a review of the problem. *Journal of the Market Research Society*, Vol. 39, No. 1.

Collins, M. (1998) Sampling. In *ESOMAR Handbook of Market and Opinion Research (4th edition)*, edited by McDonald and Vangelder. Amsterdam: ESOMAR.

Dearlove, D. (1998) *Key Management Decisions: Tools and Techniques of the Executive Decision-Maker*. London: Financial Times, Pitman Publishing.

de Bono, E. (1990) *Lateral Thinking: A Textbook of Creativity*. London: Penguin.

de Bono, E. (2000) *New Thinking for the New Millennium*. London: Penguin.

Delmas, D. & Levy, D. (1998) Consumer Panels. In *ESOMAR Handbook of Market and Opinion Research (4th edition)*, edited by McDonald and Vangelder. Amsterdam: ESOMAR.

Dexter, A., Smith, D. & Brown, J. (2000) No matches found: the hidden personality of the internet user. *Proceedings of the ESOMAR Congress*, Vienna. Amsterdam: ESOMAR.

Dexter, A. & Fletcher, J. (2000) A calculated risk: applying game theory to strategic multi-country research. *Excellence in International Research*. Amsterdam: ESOMAR.

Dexter, A. & Brown, J. (2001) Hypercontext: same as it never was. *The Proceedings of the ESOMAR Congress.*

Dolan, A. & Ayland, C. (2001) Analysis on trial. *International Journal of Market Research*, Vol. 43, No. 4.

Drever, J. (1965) *A Dictionary of Psychology*. London: Penguin.

Ehrenberg, A.S.C. (1974) *Data Reduction: Analysing and Interpreting Statistical Data.* London: Wiley.

Ehrenberg, A.S.C. (1994) *A Primer in Data Reduction: An Introductory Statistics Textbook.* Chichester: Wiley.

Ereaut, G. (2002) *Analysis and Interpretation in Qualitative Market Research.* Vol. 4 of the Qualitative Market Research series. London: Sage.

Festinger, L. & Carlsmith, J.M. (1959). Cognitive consequences of forced compliance. *Journal of Abnormal and Social Psychology*, Vol. 58.

Fishbein, M. (Ed.) (1967) *Readings in Attitude Theory and Measurement*. New York: Wiley.

Franzen, G. & Bouwman, M. (2001) *The Mental World of Brands*. Henley-on-Thames: WARC.

Gazzaniga, M. (1978) *The Integrated Mind*. New York: Plenum Press.

Glaser, B.G. & Strauss, A.L. (1967) *The Discovery of Grounded Theory: Strategies for Qualitative Research*. Chicago: Aldine.

Goleman, D. (1997) *Emotional Intelligence: Why It Can Matter More Than IQ*. New York: Bantam Books.

Goodyear, M. (1998) Qualitative research. In *Handbook of Market and Opinion Research* (*4th edition*), edited by McDonald and Vangelder. Amsterdam: ESOMAR.

Gordon, W. (1999) *Goodthinking: A Guide to Qualitative Research*. London: ADMAP.

Harre, R. (1979) *Social Being*. Oxford: Blackwell.

Harries, C. & Hardman, D. (2002) Decisions, decisions. *The Psychologist*, Vol. 15, No. 2.

Harris, P. (1998) Statistics and significance testing. In *ESOMAR Handbook of Market and Opinion Research* (*4th edition*), edited by McDonald and Vangelder. Amsterdam: ESOMAR.

Heath, R. (2001) *The Hidden Power of Advertising*. London: ADMAP Publications.

Hoinville, G. & Jowell, R. (Eds.) (1988) *Survey Research Practice*. London: Heinemann.

Imms, M. & Ereaut, G. (2002) *An Introduction to Qualitative Market Research.* Vol. 1 of The Qualitative Market Research Series. London: Sage.

Jackson, B. (2001) *Management Gurus and Management Fashions*. London: Routledge.

Kahneman, D. & Tversky, A. (1979) Prospect theory: an analysis of decision under risk. *Econometrica*, Vol. 47.

Karlöf, B. (translated by Gilderson, A.J.) (1993) *Key Business Concepts: A Concise Guide*. London: Routledge.

Kaye, B. & Jacobson, B. (1999) True tales and tall tales: the power of organisational storytelling. *Training & Development* (March).

Kelly, G. (1955) *Psychology of Personal Constructs*, Vols. 1 & 2. New York: Norton.

Kotler, P. (2002) *Marketing Management: Analysis Planning Implementation and Control* (*11th edition*). London: Prentice-Hall International

Lawrence, R.J. (1982) To hypothesise or not to hypothesise? The correct approach to survey research. *Journal of the Market Research Society*, Vol. 24, No. 4.

Lee, E., Hu, M.Y. & Toh, R.S. (2000) Are consumer survey results distorted? Systematic impact of behavioural frequency and duration on survey responses. *Journal of Market Research Society*, Vol. 37, No. 1.

Leonard, D. & Straus, S. (1999) Putting your company's whole brain to work. *Harvard Business Review: Breakthrough Thinking*. Harvard Business School Press.

Lindley, D.V. (2000) The philosophy of statistics. *The Statistician*, Vol. 49 (Part 3).

Mahmoud, O. (2002) The operation was successful but the patient died: why research on innovation is successful yet innovations fail. *Proceedings of the ESOMAR Congress*.

Marsh, C. (1982) *The Survey Method: The Contribution of Surveys to Sociological Explanation*. London: George Allen & Unwin.

Michaluk, G. (2002) *Riding the Storm: Strategic Planning in Turbulent Markets*. London: McGraw-Hill.

Miles, M.B. & Huberman, A.M. (1984) *Qualitative Data Analysis: A Sourcebook of New Methods*. London: Sage.

Miller, S. & Read, G. (1998) Questionnaire design. In *ESOMAR Handbook of Market and Opinion Research (4th edition)*, edited by McDonald and Vangelder. Amsterdam: ESOMAR.

Nutt, P. (1997) Better decision-making: a field study. *Business Strategy Review*, Vol. 8, Issue 4.

Pearce, W.B. & Cronen, V. (1980) *Communication, Action and Meaning: The Creation of Social Realities*. New York: Praeger.

Porter, M.E. (1998) *Competitive Strategy: Techniques for Analysing Industries and Competitors*. New York: Free Press.

Reber, A.S. (1993) *Implicit Learning and Tacit Knowledge: An Essay in the Cognitive Unconscious*. New York: Oxford University Press.

Ries, A. & Trout, J. (1994) *The 22 Immutable Laws of Marketing: Violate Them at Your Own Risk*. London: Harper Business.

Robson, S. & Wardle, J. (1988) Who's watching whom: a study of the effects of observers on group discussions. *Journal of the Market Research Society*, Vol. 30, No. 3.

Robson, S. & Hedges, A. (1993) Analysis and interpretation of qualitative findings. *Journal of the Market Research Society*, Vol. 35, No. 1.

Salmon, P. (2003) How we recognise good research? *The Psychologist*, Vol. 16, No. 1.

Smith, D.V.L. & Dexter, A. (1994) Quality in market research: hard frameworks for soft problems. *Journal of the Market Research Society*, Vol. 36, No. 2.

Smith, D.V.L. (1998) Designing market research studies. In *ESOMAR Handbook of Market and Opinion Research (4th edition)*, edited by McDonald and Vangelder. Amsterdam: ESOMAR.

Smith, D.V.L. & Fletcher, J.H. (2000) *Inside Information: Making Sense of Marketing Data*. Chichester: Wiley.

Smith, D.V.L. & Dexter, A. (2001) Whenever I hear the word 'paradigm' I reach for my gun: how to stop talking and start walking. *Proceedings of the Market Research Society Conference*.

Spackman, N., Barker, A. & Nancarrow, C. (2000) Happy new millennium: a research paradigm for the 21st century. *Proceedings of the Market Research Society Conference*.

Tufte, E.R. (1990) *Envisioning Information*. Connecticut: Graphics Press

Tufte, E.R. (1992) *The Visual Display of Quantitative Information*. Connecticut: Graphics Press

Valentine, V. & Evans, M. (1993) The dark side of the onion: rethinking the meanings of 'rational' and 'emotional' responses. *Journal of the Market Research Society*, Vol. 35 No. 2.

Valentine, V. & Gordon, W. (2000) The 21st century consumer – a new model of thinking. *Proceedings of the Market Research Society Conference.*

Valentine, V. (2002) Repositioning research: a new MR language model. *Journal of Market Research Society* Vol. 44, No. 2.

Ward, D. (1998) Quantitative research. In *ESOMAR Handbook of Market and Opinion Research (4th edition)*, edited by McDonald and Vangelder. Amsterdam: ESOMAR.

Watzlawick, P. (1976) *How Real is Real? Confusion, Disinformation, Communication.* New York: Vintage Books, Random House.

West, R. & Turner, L.H. (2000) *Introducing Communication Theory: Analysis and Application.* California: Mountain View.

Wiseman, R. (2003) *The Luck Factor.* London: Century.

Ziman, J. (1991) *Reliable Knowledge. An Exploration of the Grounds for Belief in Science.* Cambridge University Press.

Glossary of holistic analysis terms

This glossary explains some of the key terms we have used to help explain the 'holistic' data analysis principles we are advancing.

Holistic: we have used this term to refer to the school of analysis that (a) attempts to integrate qualitative and quantitative research evidence, (b) makes explicit management prior knowledge and intuition, and attempts to factor this into the interpretation process, (c) works with a range of analytical concepts that reflect the imperfection of many of the (multiple) information sources market researchers now use, and (d) helps users of the data make more informed, evidence-based decisions.

Bayesian thinking: we use this term to acknowledge the power of applying to the interpretation of consumer data the principles and concepts behind Bayesian statistics (while not necessarily applying the formal statistical calculations). In short, we use this term to highlight the power of formally inspecting incoming survey data in the context of existing prior knowledge.

The compensation principle: this acknowledges the fact that today's market researcher needs to know when it is legitimate to 'compensate' for shortfalls in their data, and still use the data as part of their analysis, in conjunction with other evidence, as opposed to rejecting the data completely.

The Hermeneutic Circle: this highlights the way the holistic analyst will first focus on understanding the overall 'big picture' storyline that is emerging from the data set, but may then revise this initial overall interpretation after rigorously inspecting the detailed evidence. This process continues with this revised appreciation of the overall storyline then prompting a refinement to the way the detailed evidence has been interpreted.

The constraints: we have used this term to illustrate the way in which the holistic data analyst, in the first instance, will apply orthodox, statistical theories (related to sampling error and so on) in order to arrive at the initial 'boundary' within which data should be interpreted.

The enablers: we have used this term to indicate how the holistic analyst will (having established the constraints) stretch the above, 'orthodox' driven boundary, by factoring in to their analysis existing prior knowledge.

The knowledge filters: this term has been used to refer to the analytical process of passing consumer's face-value responses through the body of knowledge that we might call *de facto* market research 'theory'. This process *may* lead to refinements and adjustments being made to the literal consumer data in order to reflect what we know about the effectiveness of survey questioning in eliciting accurate accounts of people's attitudes and behaviour.

Reframing: we have used this term to refer to the range of techniques that an analyst may wish to apply in order to stretch their own analytical thinking about what a particular piece of data might mean when it is set in a wider context, or examined from a deeper angle or fresh perspective.

Weight, power and direction of evidence: these are concepts we commend to help the analyst integrate multiple information sources (desk research, qualitative and quantitative data sets) into a coordinated analysis. These concepts take into account: balance of opinion; depth of feeling; what we already know from prior knowledge; our assessment of the strength of this type of evidence; the internal consistency within any one data set; and the consistency of the findings across different data sets.

The research narrative: here we refer to the power of presenting research evidence not as a series of isolated building blocks of evidence, but as a coordinated 'story' that links together all of the desk, qualitative and quantitative evidence into a storyline that will help answer the end decision-makers' business objectives.

Decision facilitation: we use this term to refer to a set of skills that market researchers might elect to offer on certain projects after the presentation of the main market research findings. The aim of decision facilitation is to test the 'safety' of using various types of consumer evidence to support a particular decision.

Index